Testimonials

Praise for *Jim's Flight: One Soul's Perspective from Heaven*
By Christine Frank Petosa and Elizabeth Williams

"*Jim's Flight* takes us on a flight from the heart to the sky and up to the heavens. Jim's messages remind us that we are here to continue our soul's development and that we are all connected through our hearts. The hidden pearl of wisdom is the realization that there is no need to worry—ever, for we are love and loved, and only love is real and everlasting. This book will help many on their journey to the heavens."

— JOAN CERIO, Author of *Hardwired to Heaven: Download Your Divinity Through Your Heart and Create Your Deepest Desires*

"This book offers encouragement for anyone who has ever loved and lost, struggled through a heartbreaking illness, or pondered the idea of something beyond ordinary existence. It is the story of a love that escapes the bounds of time and space and endures beyond the limits of both. Assisted by Elizabeth Williams, Chris and Jim Petosa explore what it means to love completely, to transcend overwhelming odds, and to explore the larger questions of life and death. Their fascinating story is a vision of hope for us all."

— SUSAN HYNDS, PHD

"This book is an inspiration for all of humanity who have lived, loved and lost a loved one. It certainly is a real privilege and blessing for us in the human plane to be allowed a glimpse into the spiritual realm which our souls seek agelessly! There definitely is "more than meets the eye."

— MARGARET S. CHAO, MD

"Jim's final days and the courage, understanding and ultimate acceptance that he and Chris experienced is in itself a compelling story. Chris and Elizabeth have now taken this to another level. After reading the initial draft of their work I am truly amazed at the insight and clarity that defines their spiritual discoveries and beliefs. I feel as illuminat   ter-
est in the afterlife while reading about 7   ce
as a teenager. If the purpose of our life's j   es-
tions of "who are we; why are we here; a   ?,"
then this book may provide that insigh   eth

D1114033

could potentially be one of the premier books of that genre. It is an absolute must for anyone on that spiritual quest."

— RICK DEPALMA, Retired Pilot

"This book is aviator Jim Petosa's love story of life on earth and his soul's ultimate take off to the Heavens. Jim has a copilot in the inspiration of his beloved wife Christine, as well as the extraordinary abilities of Elizabeth Williams at ground control—a gifted communicator with the spiritual and divine beyond this world. Together they take us aboard a flight of angels where we soar with them to the realms of the sacred and celestial. This account is pure testimony to the truth and beauty of life after life. And the authors' message is as clear as the brightest star in the sky. Physical death does not end life. There is no ending. Life is one gloriously luminous continuation."

— MARIA DITULLIO, EDD, Associate Professor, Department of Psychology,

Le Moyne College, Syracuse, New York

"For those who believe in life after life, this book will solidify your faith. If you are guarded as you consider the destiny of a soul once the physical body expires, explore this portrayal of Jim's journey and allow yourself hope. The tender, passionate, unending affection shared between Chris and Jim, however, is a level of love to which we should all aspire; I do."

— JULIANNE COUSINEAU, Elementary Education Teacher

"The soul's ability to continue to expand its consciousness after this life is evident in this book. Like a bolt of light that transcends the readers heart as we navigate through the pages of this captivating book; a story for humanity! A must read for those curious about Heaven, spiritually minded and in need of hope."

— LAURA PONTICELLO, Publisher, Divine Phoenix Books,

www.divinephoenixbooks.com

"Jim's account of the soul's soaring journey and of the destination—the Heavens—is peaceful and reassuring. Jim's wise advice is simple: Be the best you can be and settle for nothing else giving only your best on Earth. It will be good practice when you arrive. The book takes away both the fear and panic of dying and the emptiness and loneliness of being left behind by someone you love."

— DOREEN MIORI-MEROLA, Retired Teacher and Current Director of

Thinking Collaborative, an international educational consulting company

"Jim's Flight is an incredible and true love story. Actually a love triangle! Christine, Jim and God! Christine and Jim's deep faith guides them through the agonizing and terrifying journey that occurs when a loved one is diagnosed with stage IV cancer. While reading this book, you feel like you are sitting with Christine and Jim eavesdropping on the doctor's appointments and intimate moments. Jim's reflections, through Elizabeth, are words that help to lift the veil of life after death. Many questions answered; so many more to ponder."

— FRAN HUDSON, Retired Teacher

"I think this book would bring comfort to those who have lost a family member or friend. Comfort in knowing that our loved ones are safe, comfortable and happy in their life with their soul. It makes me feel happy knowing that once the dead leave this Earth that they are still so much a part of our lives."

— GRACE SMITH, RN, BSN

"This book will be a big help to those who are ill and to their families. I feel it gives hope of an afterlife of love and peace. It was wonderful to know that your loved ones are close to you after they pass on to Heavens world."

— BEVERLY J. PONTICELLO, Former First-Grade Teacher, Secretary,
Reiki Master, Vibrational Healer

"Some people teach us how to live. Fewer people teach us how to die. This uniquely told love story teaches us how to die. Some love stories go beyond death. This is one of them. Sometimes in life there are stories that go beyond the familiar concept of death. This uniquely told story by Christine Frank Petosa and Elizabeth Williams, this love story between teacher, Christine, and pilot, Jim, is one of those stories—all planes landed."

— MARK BRENNEMAN, General Manager/PGA Professional,
Shadow Creek Golf Course, Las Vegas, Nevada

"This book started out as an affirmation that there is life and fulfillment after death. The author takes you through the devastating and painful news of an illness, the inevitable separation from the love of her life, and the wonderful realization that love lives on through his constant reassuring messages delivered by her dear friend. This book would appeal to all ages. It sends a sense of hope and a view into the unknown. I believe."

— KIM PONTELLO, Owner of Benoits Salon/Spa/Store,
www.benoitscoiffures.com

"Grief from the loss of a loved one follows no timeline, nor is there only one way to get through it. Chris Petosa's book, *Jim's Flight,* takes the reader on a journey that touches upon all the elements of a full and meaningful life: love and loss, grief and faith, despair and hope, fear and courage and, in the end, death and healing. With the help of a gifted spiritual communicator, Elizabeth Williams, Chris breaks through the veil imposed by the physical world where death is the end, and enters into the metaphysical realm of the soul, where death is just a new beginning. The reader discovers that even after death the soul learns, heals, loves, finds redemption and reconciliation, but most of all grows. This book is a must read for anyone bereaving and looking for something more than just the traditional formulaic solutions to dealing with grief and loss."

— SUSAN L. SCHAROUN, PHD, Associate Professor, Department of Psychology,

Le Moyne College, Syracuse, New York

"For those of us who were lucky enough to know Jim, his words resonate… both those spoken before his passing and his reflections beyond. Life and death… a beginning and… a beginning of another journey. Jim shares his perspectives at a time when his journey in this life was difficult and then in the place beyond. A compelling read no matter what your beliefs."

— MARTHA M. FRANK, PHD, OTR/L, BCP, AOTA Board Certification in Pediatrics,

Professor at The Sage Colleges, Troy, New York

"I feel gratitude for Jim's message of SOUL LOVE as communicated here through Chris and Elizabeth, and I am at a loss for words to adequately express the soul-knowing that his message has ignited in me. My words are lacking yet Jim's afterlife message of deep, all-encompassing and ever-expanding LOVE has been successfully conveyed and imprinted in my heart. Thank you, Chris Petosa and Elizabeth Williams, for opening to Jim's message and bringing this important reminder of LOVE forward to those of us still in the physical."

— MELINA CARNICELLI, Metatron Travel, Auburn, New York

"This book is a love story in so many ways. It is Jim's tribute to his wife, Chris, and their gift to humanity to remind us all of what we truly know but may have forgotten—that souls and love live forever. Jim's story can provide hope and support to people and families facing difficult diagnoses and reassurance that emergence into Heaven is filled with incredible love. Through their work in writing this book, Jim, Chris and their spiritual medium, Elizabeth, encourage us to live every day with presence and passion in our lives because love is all that matters, now and into eternity."

— CHRISTINA MICHAELSON, PHD, Associate Professor,

Le Moyne College, Syracuse, New York

"Captivating! Engrossing! Are you afraid to 'die'? Missing a loved one? Curious about where they are? What they do—if anything? Chris and Jim Petosa bravely open their hearts with the help of gifted Spiritual Communicator, Medium and Grief Counselor Elizabeth Williams. Jim, communicating from another realm, and his wife share their grief, concern for family members and how they learn to live and grow without the other. We are witness to the remarkable transformation that can and does occur when we leave our bodies … or better yet, right now if we choose! Let the wisdom of Jim's Reflections re-awaken your soul to Hope, Peace, Love and Joy."

— MARY LIA, Special Education Aide, Chiropractor, Author of *Between Two Worlds*

green press
INITIATIVE

FSC
www.fsc.org

MIX
Paper from
responsible sources
FSC® C013483

JIM'S FLIGHT

One Soul's Perspective from Heaven

Christine Frank Petosa
with Elizabeth Williams

FINDHORN PRESS

Published in 2016 by Findhorn Press, Scotland

ISBN 978-1-84409-706-7

A CIP record for this title is available from the British Library.

Edited by Patricia Kot
Cover design by Willow3 Design LLC
Photos: Chris Frank Petosa (p. 291);
David Schweighofer (pp. 12 & 27; front cover);
Portrait Innovations (p. 309; back cover)
Interior design by Damian Keenan
Printed and bound in the USA

DISCLAIMER
The information in this book (in print and electronic media)
is given in good faith and is neither intended to diagnose any
physical or mental condition nor to serve as a substitute for
informed medical advice or care.
Please contact your health professional for medical advice and
treatment. Neither author nor publisher can be held liable by
any person for any loss or damage whatsoever which may arise
from the use of this book or any of the information therein.

Published by
Findhorn Press
117-121 High Street,
Forres IV36 1AB,
Scotland, UK

t +44 (0)1309 690582
f +44 (0)131 777 2711
e info@findhornpress.com
www.findhornpress.com

Contents

Dedication

To all people who are in fear of dying,
may your fears be put to rest.
To all people who are curious of the afterlife,
may you find peace in knowing the truth of its existence.
To all people who do remain after their loved ones have gone,
know that your souls will be reunited.
"I do love the thought that although Jim may not be
flying corporate jets, he does have new wings.
I'm sure they're beautiful, just like he is."

— CHRISTINE FRANK PETOSA

"Wonder what is ahead of you, not behind you.
Ahead of you is an adventure.
Behind you is that which will remain
unless you let it fly away."

— JAMES PETOSA

Foreword

This book is a work of pure, unconditional love. It would seem that all authors feel their books are works of love along with toil, emotion and great effort. However, when I say this book is a work of pure, unconditional love, I don't mean that from my writing aspect, although that is also very true. I mean that the story I tell, the information given and the readings with Jim after his death are truly intended for the benefit of any and all readers because each person shares in the same commonality. We are born, we live, we experience and we leave. What that experience entails is up to each of us.

How Jim's and my lives and experiences could benefit others was the initial reason for writing this book. That it can benefit others in any fashion would be an answer to our prayers. When Jim was alive, we intended to write our story. As he became sicker, of course that story changed. When he passed into the afterlife, the story gained a whole new perspective. The concept that our lives and experiences with terminal illness can help others in any way sincerely comes from unconditional love for our fellow man and woman.

We lose our physical bodies, but our souls live on forever and for eternity. There is a life in Heaven that consists of more than we could ever dream of. Throughout the readings in the last section of this book, I was continually amazed at the transformation Jim went through and continues to go through. In the reading of November 2011, he was the exact same Jim I always knew. By the July 2012 reading, Jim had already become wiser, more philosophical and more introspective about all that he had experienced in his lifetime as well as what those of us here on Earth are still experiencing. I am so fortunate to have been able to learn and share with others because of readings with Elizabeth Williams, a professional medium.

Based on the premise that the soul is eternal, Jim and I want readers to know our story of a serious illness with a terminal prognosis, as well as the process of what the patient and the caregiver may have to endure. But at the end of that ordeal, Jim gives us a glimpse of our greatest reward: living in the afterlife. Since one person is all it takes to make a difference, helping one person would bring great joy and satisfaction. Our hope is that this book will help humanity. Jim's reflections in his own words (in *italics*) and the readings after our story are to help people understand what is coming for all of us at the end of our physical lives. It is certainly nothing to be feared.

It is important that you know I kept a binder of Jim's medical information while he was ill, and recorded readings as I had them with Elizabeth, so every piece of that information is written in truth to the best of my human ability and knowledge. Jim worked with Elizabeth and me in readings for editing purposes after the original readings were done so the wording would flow easily for the reader without changing any of the meaning brought out in the original readings. The parts about our lives were, again, written in truth to the best of my human ability, knowledge and memory.

The Basics of Spiritual Communication
(Channeled Explanation from the Entourage through Elizabeth)

Mediumship can be described as an ability to speak, communicate with or sense souls who reside within the spirit worlds. Organized religion is based on Bible teachings and man's interpretation of those teachings. However, when we delve more deeply into mediumship itself, we see it truly is a gift to be born connected to the divine rather than disregarded.

Mediums are often mentioned in the Bible and other religious scriptures. Education of mediumship is often neither taught nor discussed. It sometimes appears to be evil or without favor in God's eye. It is important to remember that the Bible was written well over 2000 years ago when the world was filled with fear. Anything not directly of God was thought to be bad in this ancient black and white world. Mediums, soothsayers and others who foresaw the future were thought to not be of God and therefore evil.

Professional mediumship is, however, becoming more widely recognized. You must remember that mediumship is not a "craft" or "skill." It is an ability that comes from God. In life, we human beings often fear what we do not understand. This can be said to be true of people who are uneducated or inexperienced about mediumship. Many fear what they do not understand. It is much easier to do the opposite—to understand what we fear. We must remind others that ALL comes from God. A medium is simply an individual who is capable of communicating with the unseen worlds. Put another way, you might say we all have the ability to pray or communicate, yet not everyone is capable of hearing back the answers to their communication or prayer. Mediums are capable of hearing a return response.

The reasons an individual would visit a professional medium run the gamut from healing to understanding, and to some curiosity. Mediums can also be given answers to serious questions of many kinds. Imagine someone you love has been killed and forensic medicine is unable to solve the problem. An authentic, accurate medium is often able to provide information that will help find the answers for which you are searching. Finding missing children, understanding reasons for someone's death, healing grief and settling estate issues are some reasons people have met with a medium.

A medium should be chosen based on their reputation for accuracy and also because of their reverence to God and their lovingness as well as their openheartedness and integrity. A good medium can give answers to questions based on what they know or have read or learned. An authentic medium can provide to you information that comes directly from the soul.

The best way to choose a professional medium is by word of mouth from someone you trust. Ask the person making the referral about the medium's love of God, their faith and spirituality, love for humanity and prayerful practice to Jesus or another enlightened being. A good medium should be someone who studies meditation and who seeks their own inner light. They should have a happy heart, along with knowledge, consciousness and humor. Mediums should respect your privacy, be empathetic to your grief and encourage you to heal your issues through counseling or through complementary therapies. A medium wants very little from you except your healing.

Good boundaries are needed in the client/medium relationship because of the intimate details that are shared during a session. There are two important reasons for this. First, a professional medium will want your emotional healing to be addressed. The second reason is not to allow clients to become too attached to communication. Using Elizabeth as an example, she would direct the one who is healing to look inward and not become dependent on communication alone. A true professional medium would demonstrate these qualities.

Many people don't know what to expect when they visit a medium for the first time. When visiting Elizabeth, you enter into the waiting room of comfortable surroundings and soft music is playing. Prior to the session, you are advised to bring a beverage, a notebook and/or a recorder if you choose to record the session. Many guests are nervous and have mild anxiety that is usually eased once introductions are made to help the client feel comfortable. After your introduction, usually with a hug and a smile, you are taken into a separate room where the reading will take place.

Elizabeth explains to you that because she does not generate the thought, she will remember very little of her time spent with you and encourages you either to take notes or record. It is important not to be agenda-driven. Many times souls that are unexpected, such as neighbors who have passed on, a workmate who lost someone close or people who you may not have been thinking of may attend the session. The point is to keep your mind and heart open so that all who wish to speak with you may have the opportunity to do so.

After the explanation is given, a prayer and blessing of the space is said. Elizabeth may begin to yawn. Although it appears odd, the yawn indicates that visitors are arriving. Elizabeth will take a list of your questions to pose to your loved ones or guardian angels. Often you realize questions you did not verbalize are answered without asking. When the session begins, frequently Elizabeth's mannerisms will change and she will imitate those who are talking from the other side. Elizabeth will then give you an idea of who is in the room. She can see them and hear them just as she hears you. At times she can smell scents such as a perfume or cigarettes.

It is important to stress that you must keep an open mind and heart. Be aware that anything is possible and can be expected to happen during a session. Often the temperature of the room will change from very warm to very cold as those who are no longer with us do not have physical bodies and therefore, they do not generate body heat as we do. An actual conversation can continue anywhere from 90 minutes to two hours based on how long the soul(s) can tolerate being in the mortal world.

After the session is complete, Elizabeth thanks the souls for coming and asks Mother Mary to return them to the Heaven worlds. She offers gratitude to the Angels for their protection, and thanks is given to God for all things that are provided in our lives. Elizabeth will ask what you, the client, will be doing after your visit. The reason she asks is sometimes during the drive home, clients become very emotional. Elizabeth wants to know you will only be alone if you choose to in order to process what you have learned. Elizabeth respects that you are prepared to deal with information presented during the session. She ensures that you will have her assistant's phone number in the event that you need to talk further about your reading. If necessary, Elizabeth will return a phone call to you.

The entire process can be an enriching one for many reasons. Mediumship, although not a conventional therapy, often provides comfort to clients due to being able to communicate with souls in the afterlife.

Glossary
(A compilation of channeled information through Elizabeth)

AFTERLIFE VS HEAVENS – When a soul leaves his or her body, the soul will enter into what is known as the afterlife. The afterlife is considered a "place" or realm. Within the afterlife there is a board, or group of elders, that shows a review of the soul's life to the soul who has just entered. It is here that any acts that benefitted others are recorded. Conversely, it is true that acts that were intentionally committed against another are also recorded. It is within this place that the souls who enter are given time to right the wrongs committed in this lifetime. The soul is given the opportunity to heal what needs to be healed with the help of Angels and divine masters and teachers.

The afterlife is also a place of rest for many, especially after long struggles that take vital energy from an individual soul. These struggles may include emotional, mental or physical ailments such as cancer, sudden death or suicide. It is a place where fear is dispelled from the soul.

There are many levels of Heaven. The next "assignment" of what will take place for the soul in the higher realms of Heaven is given and the soul's journey is launched into those higher realms of Heaven.

The physical body is a precious commodity that many take for granted. At times, a soul enters into the afterlife and is directed to return to Earth and complete that soul's mission in the physical body, for instance, what many refer to as a "near death experience."

ANGELS – Angels are beings of light that exist in the Heaven worlds whose one true purpose is to provide unconditional love to those willing to receive. Every human being has at least one Guardian Angel. This Angel, through intuition, provides guidance, insight and direction. Many believe we cannot hear the Angels speak and yet the opposite is true. We must be quiet and listen.

ASTRAL PLANE – After a soul leaves the physical body, at times it may linger in what's known as the astral plane. There are several reasons for this occurrence, one being the soul is so attached to the earthly realm that it refuses to let go, move into the afterlife and transcend through the Heaven worlds. The astral plane is a space of existence that is described as a lower realm where souls who have left their body remain. The world around us that we cannot see with the naked eye could be considered the astral plane.

AUTOMATIC WRITING – Automatic writing is a form of channeling where those in the spirit world speak to the medium using writing. Inner quiet after meditation allows the medium a means to communicate with the spirit world through writing that is not from the medium's mind, rather from the spirit world. It is fascinating to observe as it often appears on paper as though it is scribble, with no true formation of words. As the medium takes time to decipher words and correct punctuation, a message from the spirit world can be received. During the writing of this book, automatic writing was used frequently for some in the spirit world to share their messages with the medium. Automatic writing is often used when those in the higher realms wish to speak and distinguish themselves from those from the lower realms. It is incredibly accurate and can also be used to diagnose ailments.

CHANNELING THROUGH A MEDIUM – Channeling is the process that takes place when the medium receives information from higher levels of existence such as Angels and heavenly masters. It is when information is moving through the medium by a flow of energy and the medium is speaking the information that is received. It is usually done in the form of telepathic means, especially as the vibration of Angels and heavenly masters is much higher than the vibration of physical people on the planet. How open the heart of the medium is relates to the soul from whom the information is received. Often souls who are no longer physical speak *to* the medium rather than channel *through* the medium.

CO-CREATED PLAN – This may be an unfamiliar concept to many. Traditionalists often don't recognize this concept because it is not in the basic framework of most religions. Prior to physical birth in the heavenly realms, a soul makes an agreement with the Creator to come to the planet in a physical body. It is during this time a plan between a soul and God is developed and the human being agrees to carry out this plan. Every individual on the planet has a co-created plan. There is a mutual need for one another. Usually this co-created plan involves others who we encounter as a means to carry out the plan.

While the soul is in a physical body, the mind might ask, "Why would I choose this sometimes painful situation?" We must remember that every situation is an opportunity for each of us to show gratitude, heal and learn. Sometimes those opportunities feel difficult. Each soul's plan is to be carried out in accordance to God's will. God's will is that each person be unconditionally loving but because we live on Earth, the circumstances may not feel unconditionally loving. On the Earth plane, people don't always behave in an unconditionally loving way. Because of this fact, many do not embrace the idea of the co-created plan. Often due to painful situations, many find it difficult to believe they would choose the circumstances they are living with.

ENDOSCOPY – An endoscopy is an upper GI procedure during which a tube with a camera is inserted into the patient's mouth and extends to the esophagus and upper gastrointestinal tract. The purpose of this test is to photograph the esophagus and the upper gastrointestinal tract, done either as a baseline or to determine or diagnose gastrointestinal complaints. The patient is under sedation for this test. In Jim's case, the endoscopy was what determined his diagnosis of esophageal cancer.

ENLIGHTENMENT – Enlightenment can be described as an individual soul's total awareness of God, either within the physical body or within the Heaven worlds. Our goal as humans is to have an awareness of God while remaining in our physical body. We are currently reaching an age of enlightenment where many souls are becoming aware of God and oneness while in the physical body. There are various paths to enlightenment. Some consist of meditation and some of knowledge and wisdom. Religion often can begin our journey toward enlightenment. Any religion that encourages oneness and unconditional love of yourself and neighbor is suggested. It is important not to confuse enlightenment with religion. There are many people who never attend church yet are fully aware of God and universal oneness.

ENTOURAGE – About two and a half years after he left his physical body, James (Jim) began "working" with a group of Master souls that he termed the Entourage. The Entourage and Jim work together to impart unconditional love, higher knowledge, wisdom and insight from the Heaven worlds in many of the readings. Jim briefly explains those among the group without giving a clear definition of who these beings are. Saintly in nature, Jim and they walk together through the Heaven worlds and work together on this project providing information to the author.

FAITH – Faith is the constant ever knowing belief and intuition that God the Creator, however you frame it to be, is always there in the worst of times, in the best of times, in all of time. It provides strength and unconditional love. It's a knowing at an intuitive level that God exists everywhere within everything. It is

Truth, ever constant, absolute and within all human beings when focused upon it. It is, in fact, what sees us through the good times and the bad.

HUMANITY – The ultimate definition of humanity would be human beings coming together as one people. No classes of gender, race, ethnicity, social status or spiritual and religious separation would be known. Humanity involves all of mankind coming together as one.

INTUITION – This is a term used to describe a sense of "knowing" that does not involve logic and reason.

KARMA – This term is used to describe the idea of cause and effect. When an individual intentionally commits an act against another, a record of what this individual does is kept. Put simply, what goes around comes around. What we as individuals put out to the world—good, bad, et cetera—will always come back to us.

MUSCLE-TESTING – Muscle testing, also known as kinesiology, is among the healing arts used as a means for diagnosis for emotional, mental and physical issues. Information and stimuli are received through neuro-receptors in the brain and spinal column. This information is stored in the muscles of the body. Usually the arm is the muscle that is used. A statement is made concerning the body. Whether the statement is true or false is determined by the strength of the muscle while being tested. This technique is used often in the healing arts as well as during chiropractic adjustments, where it originated.

PET SCAN – PET is an acronym for positron emission tomography. This is a scan that is done to see the inner functioning of the body, usually done through the upper torso and trunk of the body. It shows three-dimensional pictures on a screen after scanning to help doctors be aware of any dense areas or areas that are not fully functioning. In Jim's case, the testing was done roughly every six weeks to determine his progress related to the treatment he was receiving.

REALMS – Realms exist in the Heaven worlds. The afterlife is the first realm of existence after the soul leaves the physical body. It is best to imagine Heaven as many realms, levels or heights that can be traveled. The soul, once it transcends through the afterlife, grows and acquires knowledge that allows the soul to ascend higher and higher through the Heaven worlds. What puzzles the human mind is that Heaven exists to infinity. Heaven goes beyond what is imaginable with the human mind.

REIKI – Rei means universal energy. Ki is a life force energy that moves through every living thing. So Reiki can be described as a universal energy that moves through everything. Initially formed as a system in Japan, Reiki was brought to the United States as a complementary therapy—a therapy which can, when coupled with medicine, help enhance the effects of modern treatment. Not religious in nature, Reiki is now a widely used therapy that can be found in medical institutions across the United States. No matter the ailment, Reiki promotes a deep relaxation allowing the body to rest so that healing can take place. It is done with a practitioner or can be done on oneself, fully clothed. Hands are placed gently on or above the body and a natural loving energy begins to flow, helping the receiver to relax.

REINCARNATION – It is in many belief systems that reincarnation is the soul returning back into a state of physical existence. Prior lives are not always complete with the lessons needed to be learned. "Carne" simply means meat. When an individual is incarnated, that simply means the soul is in the body (or in the meat). When the soul returns back from another lifetime and is in a physical body, the soul would be known as re-incarnated. In other words, the soul is back in meat, either to bring back prior knowledge and wisdom or learn through a lesson which was not fully learned during the soul's last physical existence.

SOUL / SPIRIT – The study of anatomy describes the human body. A human body requires conception, which is when an egg from a female and the sperm from a male create a human body. In addition to the body, a soul is created by God and deeply rooted within the heart of every human being. The soul is an invisible substance that cannot be seen, touched or felt. It is within the soul that spiritual knowledge is gained and stored. This knowledge is accessed by using intuition, usually during meditation.

The soul has an energy known as the spirit. The spirit is the essence that brings the soul to life. The spirit is from God. As the soul is fully activated by God, it develops an awareness or consciousness of God, also known as "enlightenment." It is the soul's highest goal to become enlightened while still in the physical body. Every soul has the opportunity to become enlightened either within the body or in the Heaven worlds after physical death. (See definition of enlightenment.)

SPIRITUALITY – It is described as an active seeking to know God. Many confuse spirituality with religion or faith. Spirituality can be prompted by religion but religion does not define spirituality in totality. Spirituality is an innate search for God within each and every being. The spirit always seeks and recognizes God. Spirituality can also be described as the study of spirit.

TELEPATHIC COMMUNICATION – Telepathic communication can best be described as communication that takes place through brain wave activity without words. Typically people receive telepathic messages on a regular basis and do not recognize the point of origin from which they come. Many mediums communicate telepathically to souls that are in the Heaven worlds as well as Angels and other beings of light. Specific details can be received by the medium from the souls that are communicating with them. This is just one source or way in which information can be received from the higher realms.

TGA (Jim calls them **"episodes"** in the book) – Transient Global Amnesia – During the first session after Jim's passing, Jim mentions an "episode." The Christmas Eve prior to his passing was the first time these episodes began with Chris. At first she had confusion. Then she repeated the same four or five questions for almost eight hours. The doctor is unclear as to exactly the physiological cause of these occurrences. Rather, they seem to be brought on by high levels of stress and emotionality. TGAs can last anywhere from one to eight hours. Each of Chris's lasted seven to eight hours.

THE PROJECT – There are times during a session when Angels, also known as the beings of light, request the receiver of the information to carry out what is known as a divine mission. During this book, the Entourage refers to The Project as actually being the book. The Entourage provided the name during a session to help the reader gain understanding that this book is a work of unconditional love rather than one driven by ego. The Project will actually consist of a total of three books.

TRUTH – Truth is a law of the universe that God is constant. In this instance, God is equated with unconditional love, spiritual light and is ever present in the spirit of every human being. Truth is not the difference between telling the truth and a lie, rather the difference between what is temporary and what is constant.

UPPER GI PROCEDURE – GI refers to gastrointestinal, said simply stomach and intestines. Initially the patient drinks a substance that will allow any areas within the GI tract to be highlighted. The patient is put in front of a screen. This is the beginning of how gastrointestinal disorders are usually diagnosed. In Jim's case, because of his age, diet, et cetera, the doctors passed off his symptoms as acid reflux disorder. He was prescribed medication prior to the testing to help. It was only due to Chris's insistence that this test was performed. There was a mass in Jim's esophagus and stomach.

VIBRATION – Perhaps the best and most appropriate way to describe vibration is to describe what it isn't, which density is. When the soul lacks faith, intuition, realization and unconditional love or is unaware of such things, we can then say that the density of a human being is more prevalent. When the soul begins to recognize God within, love unconditionally and develop faith, it is said to lose its density and vibration of the soul will increase. Imagine dust on a light bulb and the light is shining through the dust. The light would be considered God's love and the dust the density. As the dust begins to dissipate the light shines brighter, thus the vibration of light radiates at a higher level. The same is true with the soul. As the soul loves, lives, learns, grows and deepens faith, the light within the soul becomes brighter.

PART ONE

Prologue

*M*y name is James Petosa and I'm speaking to you through the medium Elizabeth Williams. Elizabeth and I were introduced shortly after I was diagnosed with esophageal cancer at age 47. I left my body at age 49. All of my words and reflections in this book were channeled through Elizabeth by me three years after my physical death. It's great to share with you all that really does happen, or at least what happened to me. That "dying," or as I call it, the journey through the afterlife, is a process just like living.*

Elizabeth knew very little of my life before we met for the first time. It is imperative to mention this fact prior to you reading further. She knew minor details of my personal life and history. I share this information with you to help you understand the validity of her ability to communicate between your world and the Heaven worlds. My words are the exact words spoken from me to Elizabeth after my physical death. Only grammatical changes have been made and that is because my wife, Chris, is a school teacher, and she insisted upon it.

My greatest love in life was my wife, Chris.

Seven days prior to my diagnosis of cancer, Chris saw Elizabeth for a healing session and asked Elizabeth if she had any insight of what the outcome would be. Elizabeth stressed during their conversation to make it an absolute priority to go for more testing for what was initially diagnosed as acid reflux. Elizabeth is not one to purposely instill worry, but she made it quite clear that this was an issue that needed to be addressed quickly. Once the diagnosis of cancer was given, I was no longer a skeptic about Elizabeth's intuition or abilities. As you read on, you'll understand more about what I mean.

I know when many of you read this—those of you who were close to us—our family, our friends, people from church, my colleagues from work, my fellow pilots—none of you would believe the new and improved "me." You have to clean up your act here. I could swear with the best of them. There were many times when I was judgmental. I complained a lot. I was grumpy. At times, I was even a recluse in my man cave. Now that I look back, not only did Chris not know why, but I didn't either. I was really moody. That's the Jim Petosa most people remember. So as you read this, keep in mind that even the worst of us can change. You will be witnesses to the extraordinary changes within me that have taken place since I left my body.

My goal in life was, is and always will be to share as much as I know, feel and have with the rest of the world. It was my lifelong dream to become a pilot, a dream that took true persistence. No matter how broke we were, with my wife, Chris, and my faith, I never gave up. If I could live my life all over again, I would still do everything the same. I would not change one thing. I mention this because as you read further, you'll gain an understanding of what I witnessed while flying the friendly skies. The reward I felt inside myself was far greater than the hard work I had put into achieving my goal of flying.

My life really began when I met Chris. She was pretty, funny, upbeat, smart, sometimes mouthy, kind and loving. She came from a good family and had good values; there was just something about her from the very moment we met ... the way she laughed, the way she carried herself, her good humor and her spontaneity.

When I was diagnosed with cancer, as everyone would imagine, I was in total shock. Sometimes even denial. "The perfect textbook case," as they would say. I would like you all to know above any and all things, I believe now that what helped the most was being surrounded by my wife and those who I love.

We tried everything to fight the cancer. I say "we" as Chris did everything possible to be sure I had all I needed. There is no humanly way possible I could ever repay her for that.

I had the good fortune the last five years before my death to have a job that afforded me what I would need medically and the use of all aids in the non-medical world. Few people probably have anything close to what I was given or at least it seemed that way at the time. That alone made all the difference in the world. I learned a lot, more so than any other time in my life. To have gratitude, not for what I wanted but for what was happening. Even when the treatments were bad, I was grateful to have something that might save my life.

For the most part we didn't talk about dying; we talked about living. The curiosity and fear of what really happens after you die were always there, for me. Yet I found out much later that I could still partake, be a part of, be one with all of those I knew and loved as we are one with everyone in our universe.

This book not only speaks of what happens in life... real life, what happens when we die, but most importantly what happens when we are born again into the new world which we enter.

I learned so much by being a part of this project. I did not know that I would go through the same feelings and emotions as the ones I left behind. It is my hope that the readers understand every word as the truth, just as it happened, just as it continues to happen. If there's one thing that's true, love really doesn't end when you leave your body. It only gets stronger and our soul seeks to grow.

It's hard to believe the amount of love, peace, tranquility and adoration that exists here in the Heaven worlds. Most people believe that they are forgotten or left behind but nothing could be further from the truth.

Please read every word with an open mind and an open heart.

There will be more to come. That, every soul can be sure of. Life does not end after physical death. Rather a truer, more authentic life is lived and the soul continues to grow, learn and seek God.

Do not fear—ever—leaving your body. Concern yourself with matters as to whether you lived a good life on Earth, whether you were honest, clear and true to your heart.

There are some things I miss of the Earth such as my wife, my family, friends, and the fun things that I did. I loved flying, airplanes, making love, the outdoors, good food, wine; everything that every other human being would love. To give it all up and believe that you go in the ground and that's where you stay is a ridiculous thought. "Life" continues. This you can believe.

Remember this closing thought: that what you do not do in this life you take with you. Make every moment of your life matter. Have gratitude for the smallest of things. Love with all your heart and be open to bounty, goodness and, mostly, love.

I had great fortune when I was there on Earth. It may sound unbelievable, but here in the Heaven worlds I have been introduced to those who were waiting for me all along—the Entourage, a new and different kind of fortune. This group of divine loving beings is now my heavenly family. I have the great privilege to walk with them, to learn, to grow, to share and to communicate with all of you. Power-

ful love, knowledge, insights of Truth, God the Creator, Angels and Saints truly do exist. Our departed loved ones including myself take on a new form. We never, ever, ever die.

May the pages that follow bring you insight, guidance and direction. If you haven't done so, start now: live a good life and life will give back to you a hundred-fold.

May the best be all you receive in your life.

We're headed in for a smooth landing, ladies and gentlemen. Thank you for flying with us today. May our paths cross again in your journey across the friendly skies.

— *Captain Jim Petosa*

Jim's Story

Jim was raised in a very well-respected family. He was the middle child of five children. His father was a dentist and his mother worked part-time at his office. However, Jim's father was ill for many years and died at the young age of 61 leaving his mother to manage the household, have sole financial responsibility and raise five children on her own. Jim told me it was a tough life for the whole family.

I never knew Jim in his younger days before age 30, but from my eighteen years with him I heard story upon story that very quickly taught me what "Jimmy" was like. Jim was always and will always be "Jimmy" to his family and hometown friends. People always talk of that twinkle in his eyes—sometimes mischievous, sometimes just a "smiley twinkle," but always a twinkle.

Whether he was playing with siblings, cousins or the neighborhood kids, he got along with most everyone. Stories tell of Jimmy the instigator. At times he instigated games in the house when the kids weren't supposed to be playing in the house. At other times Jimmy instigated family conversation that purposely led to a harmless family bickering session or someone starting a rant on a controversial topic. That trick was used throughout Jim's whole life. He'd get someone going and once they started on their soapbox, Jimmy would laugh and laugh while the rest of the family groaned and accusingly yelled, "Jimmy!" Along with their accusations, though, came a smile or a smirk because that's what Jimmy was known for—"stirring the pot" and loving every second of it.

Jim's brother, Paul, was eight years younger than Jim. "Paulie" admired his older brother and followed him around as much as possible. They had the usual sibling teasing and arguing and one of Jimmy's actions toward Paulie was one I wouldn't wish on anyone. Jimmy would sip some milk from a glass, pin Paulie down on the floor and let some of the milk mixed with spit drip out of his mouth as if he was going to let it fall on Paulie's face. At the last minute Jimmy would suck the milk back up and Paulie was saved from certain misery and disgust. Sibling love at its best! (I recently found out from Paul that there were plenty of times when Jimmy wasn't able to suck the milk back up in time. Apparently Paulie didn't escape the misery and disgust every time. Somehow Jim failed to tell me about those times!)

Paulie loved hanging around with Jimmy's high school baseball team and became the honorary mascot. The boys on the team loved teasing Paulie and played numerous jokes on him with Jimmy joining right in on many. One day some of the boys decided it would be funny to tape Paulie's hands to the back of the bus so he couldn't get free. Jimmy wasn't involved with that stunt so when the teasing became scary for Paulie, Jimmy came to Paulie's rescue, told the guys to knock it off, untaped Paulie and let his friends know that this time they had gone too far.

The Petosa house had a huge basement in it—the kind of basement that all kids want to be in, play in and probably a place from which they could escape their parents. Because it was so big, it was a basement that could be very scary if you were in the dark. The siblings would play in the basement, probably playing those games they weren't supposed to be playing in the house. Jim often thought it was funny to run upstairs, shut off all the lights and make a scary Frankenstein-type laugh at his brothers and sisters who were left in the scary basement. Yes, he was an instigator!

Another "Jimmy" action was the Train Wreck. A train wreck is what you see when someone (Jimmy) has a mouthful of food, chews it up so it's all blended nicely together and then that someone (Jimmy) opens his mouth as wide as he can and lets out a huge laugh purposely so that everyone can see every morsel of food in his mouth. Such a classy and lovely (but fun) behavior!

Grandma Vanetti was within walking distance from the high school, so Jimmy went to Grandma's for lunch almost every day on school days. She served him soup most days, which is probably the reason soup was always one of his favorite foods. He never stopped telling stories about going to Grandma's for lunch.

Jim's mom, Joanna, his sisters, Marianne, Roberta and Theresa, his brother, Paul, and all of his extended family could tell you story after story about the funny, mischievous "Jimmy" behaviors that he showed throughout his life. They would also tell you stories about what a nice guy Jimmy was. As he got older he was the responsible "go to" guy. His mom knew she could call him for advice on house repairs or to actually do the repairs. If his mom needed a remodel or repair job done on the house Jimmy would get the estimates and talk to the contractors.

He loved his siblings and whether he consistently showed them or not, he was always concerned about their well-being and happiness. He was close with all of his siblings' spouses—Rod, Mark and Leslie. He considered them almost siblings as well.

Jimmy didn't wait until family functions and holidays to talk to his relatives like so many of us do. He was the one to call his aunts, uncles, cousins, nieces and nephews just to say hello and see how they were doing because he hadn't talked to them in a couple of weeks. It was almost as if Jim knew he had to stay in touch and show his love to his family because he wouldn't be on this Earth for a typical full lifetime.

As each niece and nephew was born, Jimmy was the little kid again, playing or wrestling on the floor and inevitably teaching them little tricks their parents wouldn't have taught them. Uncle Jimmy was a favorite with Brian, Jessica, Eric and Daniel. Just a few short years ago, Paul and Leslie had their first child, Olivia. Uncle Jimmy didn't have much experience with babies but he sure loved little Livy. Unfortunately, he didn't get to meet Paul's and Leslie's second baby but she is his namesake—Ava James. Although Jim didn't meet our nieces and nephews on my side until they were older, he loved every one of them with all his heart, and I know they felt the same about Jim.

From the time he was a young boy Jim knew he would have a career as a pilot. He didn't just want to be a pilot—he knew he would be a pilot. He knew which aeronautical university he wanted to go to for his degree in aeronautical science, but he knew as well that he couldn't afford to go there directly out of high school. His parents certainly would have paid for college if they could afford to but with his dad being ill, his mom became the sole breadwinner and simply couldn't run a household and pay for college for five children. Jim decided to enlist in the Navy, assuming that would help him pay for college later.

Although Jim had his choices planned out, the beginning of his enlistment in the Navy was more difficult than he expected. For one thing, he was actually seasick for the first three months deployed at sea. In fact, Jim was so dehydrated from being seasick that he had to have intravenous hydrations to keep him healthy. Along with that, he was tremendously homesick for family and friends for the first six months of his enlistment. His sister, Marianne, was his rock during that time. Jim talked to her quite often because he was depressed due to being so homesick. He told me many times that Marianne was the one who got him through that time period successfully. One of her suggestions was to talk to the priest on board the ship. He was grateful for her wisdom because counseling sessions with the priest helped Jim deal with his feelings of homesickness. After the first six months Jim actually enjoyed the remainder of his five-year enlistment.

Jim's plan of being in the Navy to help pay for college did not come to fruition, but the lack of money didn't keep him from attending the college of his choice. With strong family support, Jim was off to Florida. Along with taking classes, Jim worked various jobs throughout his college years in order to pay for college. All of his hard work was well worth it; five years later Jim graduated with an aeronautical science degree. Without his family's support, encouragement and visits, he would not have achieved this goal in his life.

After college Jim worked in North Carolina for a time and then moved to Michigan. Following a long illness, his father passed away two days after Jim's birthday in 1991. Jimmy came "back home" after working in Michigan two more years and never moved away again. He had decided he wanted to be near family because that was what was important to him. I know his family was thrilled; Jimmy had been gone for a long time. He had often gone to his big sister, Marianne, for advice on all sorts of things but I noticed that he became the one to give advice for most of the years after coming home again. If an argument developed during dinner, Jimmy would often try to put an end to it. If someone started gossiping or mentioned a rumor they heard, Jim would often "do the right thing" and defend the person.

Jim was most interested in securing a job with an airline, particularly Jet-Blue or Southwest Airlines. He never acquired that "dream job" with an airline, which ended up being a blessing in disguise. After a long time of looking for any type of aviation job, Jim flew mail for the U.S. Post Office six nights a week which led to a job chartering clients to various destinations. Following that, he flew corporate jets for three different companies. The last company he worked for truly was his dream job. Jim had made it to the position he wanted in the career he loved!

Spirituality was always important to Jim. He was raised Catholic, went to mass every week and attended a Catholic school through eighth grade. Going to church and attending Catholic school doesn't automatically make a person "spiritual"; sometimes that can actually make a person denounce spirituality. In Jim's case it may have helped, but he told me he always felt spirituality was important starting at a very young age and would have whether he went to church and Catholic school or not. He said it helped him learn about religion and that was a good thing for him, but he would have felt that "spirit" without it.

I know from friends that Jim always tried to be the best person he could be; it was important to him. "Doing the right thing" was how Jim tried to live his life. He said he knew he didn't always get it right, but it was tremendously important to him to try. Prayer was another huge part of Jim's life and spirituality. He felt that prayer was the contributing factor that recreated his faith so many times in his life when he started to feel less faith due to going through difficulties and hard times. He was fascinated by the Saints in the heavens, loved ones who had left this Earth, everyone and everything that had to do with God. He wasn't one to talk about it much because he felt that spirituality was intimate and private between God and him or sometimes God, him and me. Jim didn't want to talk to others about his spirituality; he felt it was sacred and dear to him. Because he felt such a strong faith he didn't feel he needed direction from others—it was already in him. He believed what he believed.

Jim did become very close to several priests in his life, and he loved and respected the guidance, ideas and advice he received from them. Another beautiful thing about Jim was that he believed in "tradition." He loved the concept of tradition in all aspects of his life whether it was about family, holidays, ceremonies, military ... all of life in general. Later, when we were married, I felt blessed to be married to a man who felt so strongly about tradition. We had our own traditions or practices as a married couple, we both loved attending any and every event and activity possible that had to do with our families, even the "tradition" of being ethical people in all parts of our lives.

Jim wanted to be sure I would always be taken care of in case something ever happened to him. In that way he was old-fashioned; he believed he needed to be the primary provider for me and tried to take care of others, too. He was generous to me, to our families and to people he didn't even know. He was a person who felt that if he was blessed enough to have "a little extra," then he wanted to be the one to treat people to dinners, events, et cetera. We regularly donated money to charities because we were blessed with each other and enough money to pay our bills and have fun. That's all we needed.

Jim's Reflections

Watching Chris from the Heavens and viewing her go through the painstaking process of remembering details as she recalled and researched was bittersweet for me. At the time Chris wrote my story and remembered every detail, I was still close by feeling the loss and remembering how much I truly missed her and my family. Even the nicest of memories have an effect on all of us—those in the Heavens and those who remain on Earth. For years I watched her as she worked with kids and lesson plans. She loved teaching school. She was diligent and applied herself to everything. This project is different. She was emphatic that my story be told ... her story, our story, be told. She was/is passionate about helping as many people as she can ... as we can. When she gets something in her mind or, better still, when it's close to her heart, she will not give up. For everything she has done she will never know the gratitude I feel toward her.

Family was everything to me growing up. I was thrilled to have siblings to torment and laugh with, loving every minute of it. We enjoyed the entire neighborhood, baseball, life ... it was so easy being a kid. That is what it's like when life will allow. Being here is being with family and loved ones. It is indescribable love.

Remembering my father's illness in my late childhood and watching my mother work so hard was difficult. On one hand it's hard to understand as a kid when your dad is mentally unwell, and nothing seemed to work to get him better. I hated seeing him the way he was when he was sick, not because I couldn't bear to watch him, but because I couldn't imagine what it was like for him. To see a once vibrant, loving, well-respected man who any kid would want to be like change so drastically ... I can't imagine what he had to endure. In those days, nothing seemed to help his condition. It was, perhaps, the worst memory I had.

When you're asked to remember what you remember, it's hard to decide what stands out the most. It's also astounding what I did remember. Mom and Dad, my sisters and brother, my grandparents, aunts and uncles, friends ... so many people I encountered in my life. I never thought for a moment about being separated from them. Much to my astonishment, they are never far away even when we die .We are told this and asked to believe it, but until it finally happens, the reality kicks in that you're no longer physical but reunited with your past loved ones. It takes a while to sink in. Having the realization slowly is probably God's way of not letting us feel the pain of separation from those on Earth that is so emotionally deep. As the process continues it becomes much easier, especially because we're all reunited here. And then the love ... it's amazing!

Ladies and gentlemen, thank you for joining us today. The love you carry with you has been felt by Captain and Crew. Until next time, this is Captain Jim Petosa reporting from the afterlife.

— Captain Jim Petosa

Chris's Story

My family consisted of my parents, Wanda and Bill, my brother, Woody, my sister, Kathy, and extended family. From as early as I can remember I loved nature. It was our whole life. We were allowed more freedoms than most children and taught good morals and respect. Our house was filled with fun and laughter almost continually. I've always been a dog lover but the day my dad brought home Ike, my horse, was like a fairy tale. I loved everything about Ike. I always had an "all one" perception. Family, animals, nature—that was our life and it was especially important to me.

My dad could never say no to anything living. One day he brought home a baby raccoon that had been orphaned and needed a home. We called him Sammy. Sammy quickly became a part of our family. Raccoons use their front paws like hands. You've probably seen pictures of them catching fish from a stream or washing their food with their paws. Sammy used his little paws to go digging in our pockets for whatever treats we put in there for him. He would sleep in the bathtub at night, wake us in the morning by licking us and sit with us at night just like a dog or cat would.

After about two years, Sammy suddenly started becoming aggressive and spent more time outside than in, and he was growing bigger. Looking back it's funny how we don't discriminate whether animals are boys or girls. Imagine our surprise when Sammy became pregnant! Oops! Sammy was a girl. Even though we grew up on a farm, we hadn't had a discussion yet about the birds and the bees. This was our first lesson. This was the kind of life we lived; living in the country was full of surprises on a daily basis.

We rode our horses practically every day. On weekends and in the summer we would be out riding and away from home for hours at a time and often for a full day. As long as we were home in time for dinner, all was good. Chief was Woody's horse, Stormy was Kathy's, and mine was named Ike. We would take them swimming in our pond, travel almost every inch of our 120 acres, ride them in our local parades, set up jumps to practice jumping and even held "horse shows" for our parents or anyone else we could get to watch. We rarely had an audience but still had the shows. We were truly the stars in our neighborhood! Our grandparents had a camp named Lost Valley on the Schoharie River, twenty-two miles from our house. Like an old movie, one time Woody, Kathy and I rode our horses to Lost Valley and spent the entire weekend there. We had a blast! I could go on for days about the great times we had at Lost Valley.

Ike was my best friend. It was never a problem taking care of Ike, and we never got tired of each other. I would spend hours brushing and grooming him, riding him or just talking to him. One day I did something that caused my parents to be upset with me, although I can't remember now what that was, and I went straight to the barn to vent to Ike. I complained and got my anger out while Ike just listened and twitched his ears once in a while. Luckily he wasn't like Mr. Ed, the TV horse; Ike just listened and didn't talk back.

Like most kids do, I decided to run away from home once. I knew I'd need supplies because I would be gone for a long time so I packed up some food and water, tied a blanket on the back of my saddle for the cold nights and left. I got pretty hungry so I was back by dinner. But Ike would have gone wherever I wanted for as long as I wanted. Everyone loved Ike, especially me. If it's true that animals are like their owners, I must really be something!

When I was 15, Ike was killed when our barn roof collapsed in a heavy snowstorm. Our other two horses miraculously were not even hurt, but my best friend was gone. Losing Ike and my very own first dog, Sandy, were the first times I remember feeling devastating pain. As you read further, you'll find out that animals really do go to Heaven. My dad mentions Ike and our other animals several times in readings.

To give you an example of how silly and goofy we acted, although we were completely serious, I have a chicken story for you. Kathy, Woody and I were given baby chicks one Easter when we were quite young. Kathy and I wanted them to lay eggs but nothing was happening. So we decided to help them along. We made nests for them and pushed them down in the nests, fully expecting to see eggs pop out. Maybe we had spent too much time on the farm. No eggs ever came out, and that's when we discovered that chickens could be boys, too!

It's interesting how certain events in our lives shape our personalities, character and sometimes even our future. In first grade, I was in the top reading group along with my best friend, Carol. (Ike couldn't go to school!) Our reading group would sit around a long, brown table and our teacher would give an instruction such as, "Read pages twenty-five and twenty-six to yourself and look up when you're finished so I know when you are done." That was what we did every day. Carol and I had an unspoken competition going on, or maybe it was just me, and I would read as fast as I could so I would be the first to finish the assigned pages. I read every single word on the pages but getting finished first was all I cared about, not what the words actually said.

Down the road, especially in high school, I had to work very hard for just so-so grades. I knew I was smart but I would see friends around me who didn't seem to work nearly as hard as I did and yet achieved better grades than me. During my first semester in college I took a required Western Civilization course that I hated. I attended class two times a week, and we were quizzed on a great deal of reading material every single class. I failed quiz after quiz after quiz and quickly realized I would fail the course if I didn't do something to turn my reading around. I was doing all the assigned readings but could not pass those quizzes.

It dawned on me one day that I was doing exactly what I did in first grade; I was reading every word—quickly—but not a single bit of it was being retained. I realized that day that I had trained myself way back in first grade to decode words perfectly, but unless I was interested in the material, nothing stuck with me. I had to teach myself to read all over again, this time for comprehension. I would read a paragraph, cover it up, see what I remembered and if I didn't remember much I would read it again and again until I remembered what I had read. I passed that Western Civilization course but only because of my desire to do the best work I was capable of doing.

That experience greatly influenced my future. As you will read, I became a teacher. I taught in a typical elementary class for the first five years. During my first year of teaching I had so many students with learning difficulties that I was driven to figure out how best to help them learn, so I got my master's degree in special education. Twenty-eight of my thirty-three years in teaching were spent teaching special education students. I didn't have a learning disability or any kind of learning difficulty other than being careless, but I did know what it felt like to be unable to retain information in school. I told my "first grade" story to every class every single year of my career, hoping that it would inspire at least a few students during those years. More important, I was better able to understand the realities faced by students with learning difficulties because I had walked in their shoes.

I was always a person with a positive attitude. When you were a kid with my kind of upbringing, it was easy to keep a positive attitude. Throughout my school years, I was always concerned that others thought I was a Goody-Two-shoes because I wanted to do the right thing. I developed that attitude from my parents. Please don't misunderstand; I was far from Miss Goody-Two-shoes. My rule was as long as I didn't hurt myself or somebody else, it was okay to have my share of good fun.

We went to church every Sunday, and I continued to learn the importance of having that attitude. Turn the other cheek, pray for your enemies, honor your mother and father, treat your neighbors well ... I did my best to practice those things. For a time when the priest spoke of vocations I even thought I should become a nun even though I didn't want to really be a nun.

The fleeting thought of becoming a nun changed very quickly because I knew I loved family and in my heart I knew I wanted marriage and children. I realized I didn't have to be a nun to be spiritual, thank goodness! I was always spiritual but I called it religious then. I couldn't wait to go to the Stations of the Cross during Lent and I wanted statues of saints when I saw them in stores. What I put on my Christmas and birthday lists, though, were statues of horses. I wanted the cross with Jesus on it that belonged to my grandfather. It was all so important to me for some reason. I was drawn to all of it, even though I didn't know why.

As I got older, I fluctuated between careers I thought I'd like, but what I really wanted most from the time I was in sixth grade all the way through high school was to become a flight attendant. I knew I wanted to travel and thought that would be the easiest way because I knew that, otherwise, you needed a lot of money to travel. How ironic, I thought years later, that Jim was a pilot and I wanted to be a flight attendant. I researched what I would need to do at that time to attain that career, and it was essentially required to have a college degree before I could even think about applying for that training. Oh yes, a college degree was required by my parents, too!

I went to St. Bonaventure University thinking I would major either in education, journalism or social work but then become a flight attendant after graduating from college. During my first semester, I took an Education 101 class with a fabulous professor who I credit today with my becoming a teacher. He arranged for each of us in the class to be placed in a local school once a week, working with early adolescent special education students. That did it. I was sold on teaching and knew that was what I was meant to do.

St. Bonaventure was the most wonderful college for me. It was small, provided a good education and was located in the middle of nowhere so there was very little to do socially except spend time with friends. I made such good friends that, forty years later, I still see and talk to so many. We share the same values, support each other in good times and bad and are now attending weddings and baptisms of children and grandchildren. My parents loved St. Bonaventure. My father always joked that it was a good thing I didn't want to become a lawyer because after having attended Bonaventure I would never be able to pass a bar. Yes, the beer did flow easily there!

Bonaventure was the place where I started learning about "spirituality" as opposed to being religious, and I found the Franciscan philosophy to fit me perfectly. I just knew that I understood more about God, the mass, and that going to church could be so informal that we could sit on the floor. It was the mass that was important; where it was held and where we sat didn't matter. I always attended mass not because I had to but because I wanted to. Even as a student who acted like a typical college kid, going to mass made me feel close to God and I craved that. One of the scheduled masses at the campus ministry was at 10:15 p.m. on Sunday night.

Why so late? Because the Rathskellar, our bar on campus, closed early on Sunday night. If you were at the Skellar on Sunday night, you would leave when it closed and follow a hundred students to the Campus Ministry building to go to mass. Something which could seem irreverent to many, taught us students what being Catholic and spiritual was all about. It changed my spiritual life forever.

Choosing St. Bonaventure University had nothing to do with the fact that it was a Catholic school. I knew when I applied to St. Bonaventure that I would be required to take three theology classes. The anticipation of that felt like torture because after all, I was a college kid, but the course choices were many and varied. I learned about other religions of the world, about "spirituality" and even about the spirit world, which I used to think was taboo. We nicknamed that class "Spooks!" What I thought would be torture instead opened my mind to a much larger world than the small one I was in.

I graduated from college, moved back home to live with my parents and acquired a teaching job at the same elementary school which I attended. From the day I was offered that first job and shown to my classroom, I knew I was right about my career choice. For the next thirty-three years, I loved teaching and spending time with my students in my classroom.

Each age level brings its own excitement to teaching. Teaching second grade, I loved the innocence and interest shown by the children no matter what I was teaching. Budding independence and desire for knowledge were my favorite characteristics of the fourth graders I taught.

Teaching middle school special education children brought unique challenges to my career. At that age, students are trying to figure out who they are and what they will become. One day they might bring a teddy bear to school and the next day they carry the problems of the world on their shoulders. I loved being a guide who could help them figure out what life was all about. I found that almost all children will do their best if they know they are loved and supported by those around them. Often that simply means lending an ear and listening to what they have to say.

We all need validation in our lives.

I taught in that school for four years before being married and moving to Syracuse, New York. My former husband and I met in college. We had a long distance relationship before being married four years later. We were both good people, had our share of fun but also had some difficulties. We ended up getting divorced and having our marriage annulled. I learned a great deal from my former husband and our marriage, from both the good times and the difficult. Now I know that was all a part of the plan to get me to where I am now.

In 1981, I accepted a teaching position at a small school district in Solvay, New York, near Syracuse. Everything happens for a reason, as I have learned and witnessed time and time again. Jim and I were married in 1994. I spent twenty-eight wonderful years teaching in Solvay, loved my job and worked with people who were, and still are, like family to me. I'm sure that to others I didn't seem like the teacher who would want to retire at age 55, the age teachers were first eligible to retire without a pension penalty if they had taught at least thirty years. I was good at what I did, I wasn't "burned out" and my husband wouldn't be retiring for several more years.

But as I got closer to age 55, I started to have a very strong desire to retire as soon as I was able. In 2009, my superintendent put out a memo that as a one-time event, anyone who turned 55 before Labor Day would be able to retire before the school year began and be able to receive the financial incentive defined in our current contract. At the time, as strange as it seemed to others and maybe even to me, I was driven to retire. I knew it was the right thing for me to do. I had no doubts and no sadness about ending my career. It didn't seem to make sense but that's the way it was.

Synchronicities happen. In May 2009, one month before I would retire, I had an "episode" in school where my short-term memory gave out on me for a while. I couldn't give directions to a student taking a test, couldn't remember how to use my classroom telephone and was confused about several other things. I probably should have called 911 in case it was a stroke as the doctors reprimanded me later, but I knew Jim was home so I called him to take me to an urgent care facility. Jim and I had such a bond that I may not have been able to remember many things at that moment but I knew how to reach my husband, the one person I wanted at my side.

The Monday after my last day of school, I had a follow-up visit at which the neurologist told me I had a seizure disorder and couldn't drive for six months. From the day of the original episode I found I had lost some short-term memory ability and also had some times of confusion. In August 2009, I had a bout of severe vertigo and lost all functional hearing in my right ear. The vertigo became less severe, but I continued to have some vertigo all day every day from then on. Retirement wasn't starting out so well!

A good point to mention here is that we need to be responsible for our own health. I was not satisfied with the results that the hospital on-call doctor had given and decided to take a new approach which meant choosing a new neurologist. The new doctor and I had a much better working relationship. He diagnosed me with active Epstein Barr Virus (EBV). He was sure but couldn't prove that the virus caused the loss of hearing and, therefore, the vertigo. I continued having episodes of confusion.

Believing there are no coincidences, I decided God knew about my health issues and pushed my desire to retire because of them. I was soon to find out that my medical issues, significant as they were, were only a small part of the reason I was driven to retire.

Jim's sister, Marianne, gave me a gift certificate to have a Reiki session and recommended a local Reiki master, Maryann. Reiki is a hands-on healing energy. "Rei" means God, or universal energy, and "ki" means an energy that moves through all living things.

What I already knew was that it was a complementary healing therapy using either light hand placement on the body or no touch at all. I learned that we have what are called meridians in our bodies that are unseen by the naked eye, yet are actually what connect us to the universe. As unbelievable as this might sound, and was to me at first, I would later learn that this is a concept of modern science. Unfortunately, as a society, most of us know very little, if anything at all, about this. Through these meridians, Reiki can affect our energy fields and, therefore, promote stress reduction, deepen relaxation and enliven our cells, thus awakening the body's natural ability to heal.

Reiki is now widely accepted in medical institutions. It is considered an alternative or complementary therapy that enhances medical treatment. Since I was struggling with my own health issues, something inside told me that Reiki would help improve my health issues. My intuition proved to be correct. In time to come, Reiki helped me heal numerous physical, mental and emotional issues. Imagine a light as bright as the sun moving through your whole body. Reiki feels similar to a wave of sunlight that moves through your being. I also found that it strengthened my spirituality by helping me look inward where God really resides. It has a similar effect as meditation does for us.

In November 2009, I spoke with someone who had a reading with a medium named Elizabeth Williams. A medium is a person who is able to communicate with souls who have passed on from this physical life. Jim and I had had numerous conversations about this type of thing before. Although I had been to many "psychics" and Jim had a friend who had received very accurate information about Jim from a psychic she had visited, neither of us had ever had a reading with a medium. We were open to hearing about information we could learn from a medium, particularly Jim's father who had passed away in 1991.

I decided to give Jim a reading with Elizabeth as a Christmas gift that year (still 2009). However, with his busy schedule and maybe because of a bit of fear of the unknown, Jim never got around to using it. I, however, decided that I would make an appointment with Elizabeth for two reasons: I wanted to see if I could have contact with my father who had died in 2000, and I wanted to see if I could gather some input regarding my health issues.

February 1, 2010, was a day of major change in my life. That was the day of my first reading with Elizabeth. I went to the session not knowing what to expect, but I was not a skeptic in this area so I was very open to whatever happened. Elizabeth's assistant, Betty, had told me to prepare ahead of time by telepathically calling out for the people I might want to talk to during the reading. Of course, my father was the primary person I wanted to hear from. Not knowing what to expect, I came up with a list of questions to ask my father. I was curious to see what had happened with his soul since my father wasn't a religious man. I know that to this day, my father probably still laughs about the fears I had since he died. He was a real jokester with a dry sense of humor and everyone who knew him was always ready for him to come out with some pun, funny comment or "questionable" humor.

When I was growing up, my mother took my brother, sister and me to church every Sunday. It was mandatory; we didn't skip church. But my father only went with us on Christmas and Easter. As we got older, he stopped going altogether. You know from what I wrote previously that I was a rule follower and I listened intently to everything in church. After my father died, I prayed and prayed to dream about him when I went to sleep at night, and in all the years between 2000 and 2010 I had two dreams that I remember with my father in them.

People pray in different ways. Some recite prayers learned in religion class or church, some sing or chant their prayers, some just talk to God. There are so many ways to pray. I'm one who talks to God. When I was young I learned to recite many prayers. I always said my prayers at night and recited several in a certain order. Even then, though, I talked to God. I had my time for recitation of prayers but the rest of the day, if something came up that I felt I needed God's help with, I just told Him what I needed and asked Him to help me with it.

For me, that is the best way to pray. When I recite prayers, it reminds me of my first grade story. I can recite the whole prayer, be done with it and then have to think back to where I was in my prayer list. When I pray that way, it's not coming from my heart but rather my head. Talking from my heart to God is what is important to me. In the later years of my life I do still recite some prayers, but if I choose to do that I slow down and think of every word as I'm saying it. If I'm not thinking about it and feeling it in my heart it doesn't have enough meaning for me. That's why most of the time, I just talk to God. And talking to God has gotten me through some mighty tough stuff in my life. That's because I *do* believe He listens, I *do* believe He knows me and I *do* believe He helps and loves all of us.

Knowing my religious background and how I took everything to heart about what I was taught, you can imagine that because my father didn't go to church and I had only had two dreams about him, I was worried that he might not be in a "good" place since his death. I didn't believe in a burning hell, but I did believe there could be suffering in the afterlife in one way or another. I didn't know what I would find as far as my father was concerned.

I went into my reading with a page full of questions to ask my father just in case he really was there. Like most other people, I thought to myself, even if Elizabeth says it's my father, how will I really know? Again, I'll tell you I was not skeptical about the possibility of hearing from loved ones who had passed, but still, how would I really know? I was open to anything I would hear.

I also was hoping to find out some information about my health. I had numerous issues and wanted to know if Elizabeth could possibly help with seeing if there were underlying problems. As it turned out, the beginning of my reading was all about my health issues. The Angels suggested to Elizabeth that my health issues were primarily due to a virus that I contracted years ago.

The Angels were correct. Elizabeth knew nothing of me so she couldn't have known that I had already been diagnosed with EBV. Elizabeth suggested that Reiki or "energy work" might be able to help me, especially the vertigo I had from the hearing loss.

So far she was right on target, but I hadn't heard from my dad yet. Suddenly my father came into the reading. He spoke with me for at least thirty to forty-five minutes. My question of "How will I know if it's really him?" was out the window in no time. He talked about very serious personal events that had happened to a certain member of my family that no one could have known about, especially him because he had died years before we even knew the extent of the atrocity. He talked about my worries regarding this family member and that I needed to know that I couldn't do anything about that; the problems had to be fixed by those involved. He was so right. I spent so much time worrying about this particular situation and felt that I had to "fix" things.

There was more. He joked several times in the way that was clearly my father and when I told Jim and my family about the humor, they said, "Yup, that's Big Bill!" He told Elizabeth to tell me about the dog that was sitting next to him and that it would be important to me. He was right. Out of all the dogs we'd had as pets over the years, this one was Lieba, my dog that had died several years before.

What struck me the most because of my worry all those years that Dad might not have ended up in a good place was this comment to Elizabeth: "Tell her I went up; I didn't go down. That's a trick they play on you." That did it. My father knew of my worry about him all those years … what if he wasn't in a good place because he didn't go to church? And he did it in the way that my wonderful dad would do it—by joking.

Dad told me he's very happy on the other side, that he's been many places and "traveled across the universe." He said some "over there" feel he's "stuck" because he spends so much time here on Earth with us instead of staying on the other side all the time. He said he always watches over us all—my mom, his children and his grandchildren. There was no question after this reading; it truly was my dad I was talking to! I asked questions and he answered them. Specific names of family members came up. He talked about my mom and some health issues she now had that she did not have when he was alive. There were so many things that finally gave me actual proof that my dad was not only okay, but he was with us and participating in our lives.

After our reading I asked Elizabeth what my father could have meant by the word "stuck". She explained that many people, when they hear the word "stuck," think it means something negative. I knew from the way my dad talked and the way I felt inside that "stuck" was just a word and I shouldn't be influenced by the connotation of it. When souls leave their body, they may stagnate and not transcend to the higher realms because they're firmly attached to our earthly realm. The key here is not that communication or "visiting" Earth is a concern as much as the soul choosing not to grow, learn or discover because it is too attached to our earthly realm.

For many people, hearing from their dad and knowing he was in a "good place" on the other side would have been enough to call it a life-changing experience. But for me it was even bigger than finding out that my father was doing well. I had just found out that there is truly "life" on the other side after we die or, I should say, after we lose our physical bodies. Hearing from my dad and all he knew of what had gone on in my family over the last ten years was proof to me that there is not only life after we die, but they have the freedom to do what they want. Those who have died are able to travel, have jobs and stay around us. They do their best to help us through our difficulties and rough times.

Please don't misunderstand me. Remember, I have always been a religious person and I have always believed in life after death. The problem was that I didn't know what life after death really meant. When I thought of it and visualized it, I pictured little harps with wings floating around on the clouds with everything perfect for eternity. But what would be perfect about being a little harp floating on a cloud?

This may sound silly, but I'm willing to bet that many of us think this way. Talking to my dad through Elizabeth had proven to me that we aren't those little harps, but real people, or rather, souls. Believe me, if everyone who passed on to the other side looked like harps, my father would have made some joke about it. But he didn't. That's why February 1, 2010, was a life-changing day for me.

After my reading with Elizabeth, I decided to use my gift certificate to try a Reiki session. The emphasis of being "healthy" is usually placed on the physical, yet it is so much more. Healing is a term that usually implies physical cure. However, healing can occur on many levels. For example, emotional, mental and spiritual health are not often addressed in the medical profession when we think of good health, yet I was soon to discover how much this healing therapy would help me in all of these areas.

Since 2010, I have received Reiki from several practitioners. I began having weekly sessions, hoping to lessen my vertigo and give some healing to my

47

body in general. The possibility of getting rid of my EBV and restoring hearing in my right ear had me excited. I didn't know what to expect. I found it to be very relaxing and although I didn't know if it was doing any healing, I did know I felt good during and after each session. This was an experience for me that I knew I would continue simply because I liked it and felt it was having a good effect on me.

I've told you about my life and how I've lived it, and by reading this, you would be led to think I'm all serious, spiritual and maybe even boring. If I've given that impression, it was unintentional. Yes, my life has been filled with numerous serious issues since 2009, but it was not always so. If you asked family and friends who know me well to describe me I'm sure they would say I was always serious about my career and the students I taught and that if I attempted any project, I would give it my all and do the best job possible.

What they would first say, however, would most likely be that I am fun, outgoing, a good friend, love to have a good time, tell horrible 'punny' jokes and that I can be pretty goofy. Just ask Jim. My family gatherings are filled with "one-upmanship" on who can come up with the best—or worst—play on words. I constantly get teased about the silly things I've done over the years by both friends and family.

Most recently, as I have taken much time to write this book, I've had friends tell me that I need to get back to going out, having fun and "being" fun. It's true that I've been very serious about writing this book and have given it the majority of my attention. That's because I think it's tremendously important that people hear the story Jim and I are telling about the circumstances surrounding our lives, his death and the afterlife.

I will get back to meeting family and friends for breakfast, lunch and dinner, go to more movies, shows and concerts, and I'll be more punny than ever before. I love being out in nature, spending time at the camp Jim and I used to rent on DeRuyter Lake, listening to country music and driving Jim's big-ass Silverado around town. I'm a country girl at heart, am spontaneous as long as my animals are taken care of, and I love to travel. That's the "real" me. Jim liked the real me and that's all that ever mattered to me.

Jim's Reflections

It would take all day to describe the "real" Chris. She's always coming up with new, bigger, brighter, better ideas. The day-to-day fun that we enjoyed is never forgotten.

Watching her work on this book, sometimes to the point of "maniacal," is both heart-warming and gut-wrenching. I know her true intent because I know her so well—to tell people the truth. Life is what you make it. Life doesn't make you, you make your life.

I have to admit, when she first suggested I go to Elizabeth I thought she was a little nutty because she had had so many ideas before that were just as crazy. However, my sister, Marianne, couldn't have made up the messages from my father that she described, and if it made Chris happy, that's all I cared about. I was glad to give her my gift certificate (although I did want a new gift for Christmas!). After she came home and actually began to execute a plan for her own health and I could see the difference it was making, I became interested.

To know Chris is to love her easily. To really love her, you must take what you get because you never know what you're going to get. That was what made life so great. I know she writes this book as we planned, but I know my wife and I know it's because she believes in what she's doing that it will make a difference and that it will matter to somebody. It matters to me, our families and our friends. As you read further you'll be able to see that even the worst of situations can be made better with a little laughter, a little fun and a whole lot of crazy ideas.

Ladies and gentlemen, thank you for joining us today.

— Captain Jim Petosa and Co-Pilot Chris Petosa,
preparing for the next flight ahead

Our Lives Together

I was connected to Jim Petosa from the minute I met him at a bar in Solvay, New York. It was 1985 and I was out with friends. Jim and I were introduced to each other by our mutual friend, Chris, and if we said two sentences to each other that was a lot. But I said to my friend KC, "That man is the most handsome man I've ever seen!" Jim had just been discharged from the Navy and was going to attend an aeronautical university in Daytona, Florida. Of course I didn't think I'd ever see him again. All I knew was that he was the most handsome man ever, and I developed a crush that I knew would never come to fruition.

Jump ahead several years to 1993. I was teaching in the middle school in Solvay as was my friend KC. A student came into my classroom and handed me a note. The note was from KC and it said, "Guess what—Jim Petosa is subbing in our school today!" Well, you can bet I'd never forgotten who Jim Petosa was, and my heart actually did a flip-flop or two. Soon enough, I saw him in the teachers' room and in no time at all, we were chatting and flirting. He only subbed in our school once in a while but when he did, my heart was all over the place.

I found out that he had been living in Michigan after going to college. He was a pilot looking for "the" job, but up to that point had been a flight instructor. Jim's dad had passed away in 1991, so in 1993, Jim decided to leave his job as a flight instructor and come back home to Solvay where most of his family still lived. That's why he was subbing at school; he needed money and would do anything as long as he had work. He worked construction, subbing … any jobs that would give him a paycheck.

After Jim came home he joined a softball team on which Jack, a mutual friend of ours, also played. What a coincidence—I played softball as well, and Jack and I often met up after games with each other's teams. Jack started playing matchmaker and before long, Jim and I both looked forward to our Thursday night softball outings.

A couple of weeks into this, Jim told me he was going to Boston that very weekend (Memorial Day weekend) to visit the friend who had originally introduced us and he asked me if I would go with him! I couldn't believe it, but had to say no because I was having a deck replaced on my house. Jim thought I said no just because we didn't know each other well and I didn't think it was "proper." He was so sweet; he said, "We'll be sleeping in separate rooms if that's what you're worried about." I have to say, I respected the fact that he acknowledged that. But I really did have a deck being replaced and had to be at home. So Jim went to Boston and wouldn't you know it—my deck work had to be postponed to the following weekend!

After softball the following Thursday night, Jim suggested we go to a nearby diner to get something to eat. After getting into his car he reached into the back seat and pulled out a t-shirt. He had been to a Red Sox game at Fenway Park and brought me a "Green Monster" t-shirt from Fenway. I couldn't believe it. What man does that when we hadn't even dated yet? We went to the diner, had wonderful conversation, and it seemed we were both falling in love very quickly. We finished our early morning breakfast and went back to get my car so I could go home.

After we arrived back at my car Jim asked if I would like to go out to dinner that weekend. (Now this was to be the weekend for the deck work!) I think I stayed quite calm on the outside, but on the inside I was going crazy. I said I'd love to. Jim asked which night—Friday or Saturday—and I quickly thought to myself that if we went Friday maybe we could see each other Saturday, too. I knew I was jumping the gun and wishing for way too much way too soon. But I suggested Friday and Jim agreed.

Getting ready to go to dinner Friday night I was as nervous as a girl going to her first prom. Fifteen outfits later, I thought I was dressed right and nervously awaited Jim's arrival. The minute he arrived and came to my door, I may still have been nervous, but calmness came over me telling me that this was right and good. On our way to dinner I just couldn't stop looking at him—he was so darn handsome! Fortunately or unfortunately, I've never been one to keep much to myself and so I told him exactly that. "Jim, I can't stop looking at you because you're so handsome." Immediately, I was cringing for being ridiculously open way too early, and thinking, "Oh my gosh, why did I just say that????" But Jim just smiled, gave me some compliment, and I knew I hadn't made a mistake. We had a wonderful time at dinner and when he brought me home, we enjoyed more great conversation and company until the early morning hours.

Jim had to work the next day but I asked him to come to my "deck party," which was simply some friends coming to my house for a barbeque while my carpenter friend, Joe, worked on the deck. He did come over, to my great excitement, and if he was trying to melt my heart, he succeeded; he brought me a single rose! Not only did Jim come to the barbeque but he took over the grill and helped entertain my friends. It was our second "real" date and I already felt like we were a team.

From that day on, Jim and I saw each other almost every single day and most of the time he stayed at my house instead of going home. Yes, our relationship was moving incredibly fast, but we both knew it was the right thing. During our second weekend of dating Jim took me to his mom's house to meet some of his family. I was extremely nervous. I knew his mom was a strict Catholic and here I was a divorced (but annulled) woman, eight years older than Jim (I found out later that no one knew back then!), and they had barely even seen Jim since we had started dating. So I guess nervous wasn't really the word; I was scared to death that they would have already formed opinions of me and wouldn't want me for their son. Luckily, I couldn't have been more wrong. A beautiful family relationship began that day.

One of the things that I absolutely loved about our second weekend of dating was that we went to church together on Saturday evening. Going to church was very important to me and to have the man I was falling in love with feel the same way was just incredible. From that day on, every time we stood in church with our hands on the pew, either Jim's hand was over mine or mine was over his. That was one of the most beloved acts of our relationship and continued for our eighteen years together. What a beautiful, sensitive man Jim was.

Our relationship moved along very quickly. We said our "I love you's" after two weeks and during the third week we drove to Michigan to visit wonderful friends, Emily and Charlie, and to attend the wedding of Jim's good friends, Carey and Scott. After a few days in Michigan, we drove back to Syracuse, changed the clothes in our suitcases and drove to Virginia Beach to spend a few days at the ocean and visit my cousin Bill and his wife. Here we were, three weeks into our relationship and I was already feeling like we were a forever couple. Little did I know then that we really were a forever couple.

As I mentioned earlier, Jim's career goal in life was to be a pilot. Still no flying job was coming along but every once in a while, Jim would rent a small two-seater airplane and we would go flying, which I loved. On February 12, 1994, I went to the gym to work out and ended up staying there quite a while. It was a gorgeous winter day with a beautiful blue sky and sunshine which is somewhat rare in Syracuse in the winter! When I got home (no cell phones then!) I saw that Jim had called and left numerous messages on my answering machine asking where I was, when would I be home, et cetera. I called him immediately and he said that with such a beautiful day, he wanted to go flying … did I want to go? Well, of course I did, but I told him I'd need to shower and change my clothes. He told me there wasn't time for that because we'd lose the sunshine if we waited too long. So we went, Jim clean and as handsome as always, and me in sweatpants and sweatshirt with my hair pulled back and no shower. Jim rented the plane and we flew around the area.

As we flew over Skaneateles Lake he told me to fly the plane (clearly just for a minute) and, with that, reached behind our seats. I immediately thought, "Oh my God, is he going to give me an engagement ring and ask me to marry him????" But I quickly saw that the box he pulled out was quite large, certainly not an engagement ring. Yes, I was immediately disappointed, but I realized this must be my Valentine's Day present. He took over the flying and told me to open the box. I read the card first and couldn't believe what it said: "Be my Valentine forever." In the box was a set of champagne flutes that he knew I liked and we could use at our wedding. He really was asking me to marry him!

I was figuratively and literally on cloud nine. My answer? "Of course I'll marry you." Later on, Jim told my father that he asked me in the airplane over a lake because if I said no he was going to throw me out of the airplane. (Did I tell you he was quite the jokester?) He wanted us to pick out my engagement ring together so he chose this way to ask me.

On November 26, 1994, we were married and it was one of the most meaningful days of our lives. Yes, the wedding was beautiful. We picked readings and music carefully, our friend Fr. John performed the ceremony and the reception was great fun, but the real reason it was so beautiful was because we were making a commitment to each other that we knew we would not break. We were truly a couple and hoped to have children to raise and love. Our families were now joined and a new life had begun. I'd never been happier.

Jim continued to pursue a flying job, particularly one with Southwest Airlines or JetBlue. In the meantime Jim worked for a carpet cleaning company, a food warehouse and finally a needle factory. He hated them all but he was a responsible man, had come into our relationship with debt and no assets, and was determined to make our lives financially easier. I was a teacher and, to make extra money, I tutored about ten hours a week besides my full-time teaching job.

One day Jim called me excited about the possibility of a flying job. He interviewed with Rick, a man who became one of Jim's best friends, got the job with a local aviation company and was back into flying! Jim was one happy man and of course, I was thrilled for him.

The job he got was a tough one for newlyweds. He was to fly the U.S. mail six nights a week from Syracuse to Buffalo. I would teach all day, come home after tutoring to spend a couple of hours with Jim and have dinner before he had to leave. He would load the mail, fly it to Buffalo, stay overnight in an apartment set up for him and load and fly more mail back to Syracuse the next morning. He would get home after I had already left for school. Most weekends, I would go with Jim on his mail flights.

In the winter, after he unloaded the mail we would get into a snow covered, freezing car, get something to eat and then go to a freezing apartment. In the summer, the flights were beautiful and we didn't have to battle the Buffalo/Syracuse cold and snow. Jim made a very low salary but it didn't matter. Jim was back into flying. When we looked back on those days in years to come, we always said what great days those were. Cold, snow, blizzards, ice ... it didn't matter ... we were together, and it was always an adventure.

Then a new job came along. Instead of flying the mail, he started making charter flights for the same company. He was now flying to destinations where other people wanted to go. It could be a day trip, a couple of days or a week at a time. Not only did this make Jim happier in his career but it was great for us as a couple because we now got to spend more time together.

He loved making charter flights. Flying with Rick meant so much to him, partly because they were friends and partly because it was Rick who got him back into aviation. We never forgot that. Over the years we became great friends with Rick and his wife. We even vacationed at camps next door to each other for twelve years.

If there was one thing that Jim and I valued, it was work ethic. I totally supported Jim's persistence and determination. Our ultimate goal was stability in both of our careers so that we could start a family. Before Jim got the job flying the mail, some friends and even family members tried to talk Jim out of continuing this pursuit of his career. They felt he was wasting his time and should be looking for something else. Some people even came to me and suggested I try to talk him out of it. My response? No way. If this was what my husband wanted, then I fully supported him going after it.

With each new position Jim took in aviation I was able to tutor fewer hours after school. More time at home for me made both of us happier. Jim's next job was flying corporate jets for a local businessman and this opened up a whole new world to both of us. Jim loved learning to fly new airplanes, and I loved that I was invited on several trips to places I'd never been before. Most of all, we loved the fact that we were doing this together.

After a few years of flying for this company word came out that the business was going through some difficulty and the jet would be sold. Many pilots would have immediately looked for another job and left to protect their own financial interests, but not Jim. He thought the world of Michael, his boss and owner of the jet, and would not leave Michael and the company until there was no plane to fly. Again, some people would have opinions that he should leave but loyalty was one of Jim's best qualities and he wouldn't leave Michael in the lurch. When the jet was finally sold Jim was again out of an aviation job.

Jim didn't think of this time off from work as a vacation. Because he didn't want to get into a financial bind Jim started pounding the aviation pavement. As hard as he looked there were no flying jobs to be had in the area He took advantage of everything the local unemployment office had to offer and he received a training grant to learn to fly a 737 jet. The grant didn't pay the full shot but it helped out tremendously. We both felt that this was the avenue to take to secure a permanent job. Jim received his 737 rating and we thought that was the next path in his career.

Meanwhile, we wanted very much to have children. I was 40 and Jim was 32 when we married. Yes, I did rob the cradle. I had already had a miscarriage in my previous marriage but Jim and I were hoping that miscarriage was a one-time event. Unfortunately we had trouble even getting pregnant so we started seeing a fertility specialist the year after we were married. After several attempts at artificial insemination, nothing happened. The doctor suggested we take a break from it as people sometimes get pregnant during the break. That sounded crazy to me but what did I know? We did as the doctor suggested and hallelujah—I got pregnant! We were ecstatic. Life was just getting better and better.

I was about seven weeks pregnant when I started showing signs of miscarrying. I left school immediately and went to the doctor only to find out that I had, indeed, miscarried. I came home devastated, called Jim to tell him, and went to our bedroom to cry, cry and cry some more. When Jim came home, he held me and cried with me. More visits to the doctor, more tries at artificial insemination, and then I got pregnant again. We were somewhat hesitant and nervous as would be expected, hoping so desperately that this time I would be able to carry the baby to full term. Again in my first trimester I miscarried and our dreams of having a family were shattered.

I just didn't understand. At that time I thought that if you were a good person and you did what you were "supposed" to do, good things would come your way. I got mad at God, didn't go to church for a few weeks and even talked to our priest. People didn't know what to say to me after my first miscarriage let alone after having three. I had had enough of, "It's for the best," and "Something must have been wrong with the baby," and "You can borrow my kids any time you want." Then I had to hear things like, "I get pregnant if my husband even comes near me," or "Oh, I hate being pregnant; I wish I could just get this thing out of me!" I know in my heart that people don't intend to be harmful with their words. I can only speak for myself but after going through this experience, it was better for me when someone just listened or simply said they were sorry for my loss.

Jim and I decided we still wanted to try to have a baby, so we went to a hospital in Rochester for in-vitro fertilization (IVF). We tried two rounds with the daily shots and everything else that goes with that procedure. We were disappointed beyond belief. I wasn't able to produce enough eggs to harvest in either cycle of the IVF. We were devastated by the finality of this news.

I became obsessed with getting pregnant and being able to hold a pregnancy without miscarrying. I felt like a failure because I couldn't do what most women can do ... produce a child. In my eyes, Jim was being gypped out of one of the greatest joys of life ... having children. So the IVF procedure wasn't our last attempt. We decided to look into egg donor programs. After quite a bit of research I asked my friend, Judy, to drive with me to a clinic in Cincinnati that had an excellent egg donor program. She was willing, so off we went to find out about the next procedure in the long line of What People Do When They're Obsessed About Having A Baby.

The people I spoke to at the clinic thought I was a perfect candidate for egg donation. I filled out the necessary forms, we did a lot of talking about the logistics of the procedure and Judy and I headed back to Syracuse. But somewhere along the way, either on the trip home or after having conversations with Jim about this or maybe it was in my subconscious all along, I began to have doubts. Although egg donation looked like the most promising possibility, something inside told me this was not the way we were supposed to have a baby. I remember so clearly sitting at my mother-in-law's kitchen table with her and all of Jim's sisters, talking about the situation and crying the whole time. Something didn't feel right. I realized that attempting to have a baby this way was taking it out of God's hands too much for our comfort. We had already tried so many routes to having a baby and if it wasn't happening, then maybe it wasn't supposed to happen.

We did believe that we each have a plan in life, and a baby didn't seem to be a factor in ours. The worst part for me was that now we finally found a way that really might allow us to have a baby and we were actually making the decision not to proceed. It was so difficult to make that decision and stick with it, but we both felt it was the right thing to do.

I was so obsessed with having a baby and what I was taking away from Jim that it was all I could think about. It seemed as though I thought about it every minute of every day. It depressed me, and although Jim never acted like not having children was important, I felt sure it would have an effect on him. Could he love me as much if I couldn't give him children? But that thought was an effect of the obsession to have children. Jim made that clear to me one day while on a drive.

I asked Jim if he regretted marrying me since I couldn't give him children. He repeatedly assured me that we married one another because we loved each other, not simply to bear children. He told me that of course he wanted children with me and was as devastated as I was about our situation, but that didn't change what he felt about me nor would it ever.

We had discussed adoption but we didn't have any money for that. We also wondered (like the egg donor option) if that would be the right thing to do, given that Jim was gone so much for his job.

One Sunday morning in church, I knelt before mass began and talked to God with tears running down my cheeks. I told Him that if He didn't want us to have children I understood that that was His plan, but asked that He please, please help me to accept it. Suddenly it was a week or two later when I realized that I hadn't even thought about having a baby since that Sunday morning, a true miracle in my eyes.

Now the year was 2004, and Jim had been without a job as a pilot for more than a year but was diligently following his dream. Then Jim was offered a new job! It was in Ithaca, an hour and a half away, but the distance didn't make a difference to us. This was another company for which he would be piloting charter flights on corporate jets. With this job, he was gone even more than the previous one. The trips weren't always long, but they were pretty constant. Being the new guy, he had to be away for lots of holidays, even Thanksgiving and Christmas, which was hard on us but probably harder on him; at least I could be with our families. I did a little whining and complaining, but was appreciative that Jim had a job. Jim never complained.

In 2005, Jim met a man named Bruce, for whom he flew charter flights several times. Jim thought Bruce was a wonderful guy and admired him a great deal. Bruce was personable, outgoing and a devoted family man. In September of 2006, Bruce offered Jim a full time pilot job with his company! We were ecstatic, and after a short time working for that flight department, Jim came home one day and said, "This is the company I want to retire from." He had truly found the job he had been looking for all these years.

He had been devastated when he didn't get hired by an airline years before, but now we both saw that everything had fallen into place and this was what was meant to be. Within the next two years, Jim became the Director of Operations for the flight department. It was more responsibility and Jim was honored that Bruce and Rosemary (both owners of the family company) wanted him to do the job. As Jim often told me several times later on, he was married to me, we had two loving families, and he had the career of his dreams ... that was all he wanted in life, and he had achieved it. Now was the time to just enjoy it.

And so we did. We truly loved our life together as a couple. In many ways, Jim's career was tough on our family life. He could be gone for a week or two, or more, at a time. He often had to miss family gatherings, birthday parties, music and sporting events of our nieces and nephews, and sometimes even Thanksgiving and Christmas celebrations. But even though he loved his career and was away from home a great deal, I always knew that he wanted to be home for all of those things. I always knew he wanted to be home with me. Jim would call me every single morning, we would talk every night before the first one of us went to bed, and often many times in between. Our families understood this was his job; he couldn't be home for everything, and I represented us well at as many family gatherings and kids' activities as I could.

One of the great things about Jim's career when it came to our marriage was that it was always so fabulous when he came home. Our relationship didn't ever get old or boring. We also loved to travel, and we did a lot of that. Sometimes it was a cruise or beach vacation with friends or family, sometimes by ourselves. Bruce and Rosemary were so kind and generous to us that I was invited on flights several times. Because of this, I was able to join Jim in California, Las Vegas, Italy and France ... wonderful trips with so many memories. Work trips for Jim but total vacation for me. For this we were so grateful.

We also started taking annual trips to Aruba with my brother, Woody, and our sister-in-law, Martha. On our second one, in January 2010, we decided to buy a timeshare so we would be sure to get away together at least once a year on a "non-work" trip.

To many, trips, vacations away and travel in general would be the greatest thing a couple could share, but I think Jim and I were different there. Don't get me wrong … we loved to travel and loved our trips together, but I think most of our best and most beloved times were while we were home together in our house. Our house is a very modest townhouse that I bought four years before we started dating. It needed work, and I had done very little to it prior to Jim moving in. Since that time, it is a totally different house, and that is all due to Jim's vision, our planning together, and gradually making updates as we earned the money. Our happiest times were those when Jim would come home from a trip. We would enjoy wine or cocktails and hors d'oeuvres as I cooked dinner and just talk. We talked and talked about anything and everything: his day, my day, family, house … everything. Those were precious times.

We eventually remodeled the basement and put in a gas fireplace with beautiful leather chairs on either side for our "talk time." Sometimes we'd go to the basement and have our cocktails and hors d'oeuvres and it turned into what we called "crap night"—just appetizers but no dinner. It was always spontaneous and always fun.

Some couples dread the work that has to be done around the house, but Jim was gone so much that we treasured a weekend when we could just do jobs around the house together. It might not sound like fun, but we enjoyed it. That was what we both loved about our life, practically everything we did together was fun. That might sound hokey and as though I'm making it up as I look back, but it really was true. Even sitting watching TV together wasn't just passing time … it was quality time spent together.

Was this because of the career he'd chosen and the time we spent apart? Maybe. However, the divorce rate for pilots is high, so for some couples, that would have driven them apart. In short, we loved each other very much, and had so much fun in our lives.

Jim's Reflections

Chris thinks I remember nothing from the time I met her in the bar in Solvay. Quite honestly, I do. I remember every little thing. She was pretty, funny and had eyes that shined, and despite the amount we had to drink, a mind as sharp as a tack. I was the one who felt like an idiot because I was, well ... slightly intoxicated. I knew if I acted like that then, she might not think I was so great.

When Chris and I were reunited, I played dumb ... so I didn't feel like a fool. How was I supposed to forget those bright blue eyes? When I went to Boston, all I could think of was, "What do I bring back to a girl like her?" All I could think of was to give her a t-shirt. Most girls would probably have rolled their eyes, but not Chris. She was so excited over a stupid t-shirt. I knew at that moment I wanted to know more.

I came to her with nothing—no money, no job, nothing but my family and, of course, the crazy love I had for her. Chris is funny. When you do even the smallest thing for her, she makes it out to be the most amazing gift she ever received. She talks about being nervous the night of our first date; that doesn't describe how I felt ... showing up at the house of the sweetest, prettiest blue-eyed girl with nothing to offer ... talk about nervous!

The second happiest day of my life, other than the day we were married, was to take her flying and propose. I was never more nervous or afraid, but when I asked her to marry me, I felt like I was insane. I had to be out of my mind. Indeed I was completely out of my mind, insane with the idea that she might say no. I knew, despite anything I was told about flying, getting a job, everyday life things ... nothing would be harder than asking her to marry me, especially if she said no. It's funny how women have no idea of the fear of being rejected that lies in men's hearts. When I look back now and see the pain of cancer, the turmoil, the gut-wrenching pain of finding a job, of losing pregnancies (that Chris wanted so much), nothing bothered me more than being afraid that she would say no.

Chris, through our entire life together, never ever considered that I would feel worse without her. The life we led after I became a pilot, my dream job for Bruce and Rosemary, was nothing compared to what I wanted to give her. I loved flying, people, laughing with our friends, but never do I remember a sweeter, more lovely, happy, grateful (I don't even know the words) look than when I told Chris I finally had my dream job. She deserved the best! That was all she ever would know from me ... my best!

On behalf of the flight crew, we give special thanks to Co-Pilot Chris Petosa for helping us arrive safely at our destination.

— Captain Jim Petosa

Cancer Hits – Diagnosis

Jim had been having backaches for a few years, and had been seeing a chiropractor regularly. I also had back issues once in a while, probably from stress, and I generally felt better receiving chiropractic services once a week. Jim, however, was seeing the chiropractor at least twice a week and often three times when he was home. Somehow, it seemed to make sense that his back would hurt: first of all, his drive to work was two hours, four hours if he didn't have a trip and came home the same day. Second, as a pilot, Jim was in the cockpit for many hours at a time. He often flew coast to coast, and sometimes even to Europe. With all that sitting, whether in a car or a cockpit, whose back wouldn't hurt?

He also seemed to get sick quite often with colds, sinus infections and bronchitis. It seemed like it happened too often, but then again, we rationalized that he was in a cockpit or jet cabin for hours at a time. The pressure may have been affecting his sinuses and he was around many different people a great deal. It all seemed like reasons for getting sick more than most. Then he developed a cough that never really went away. At first it seemed like maybe it was one of those illnesses hanging on in the form of a cough, but we gradually realized it wasn't getting better.

Jim decided to go to his doctor to have the cough checked out. His doctor knew of his history of frequent illnesses. At the end of 2009 and the beginning of 2010, Jim had several tests done, including a chest x-ray, stress test, Doppler, ECG and an EKG. The doctor didn't find anything unusual. He diagnosed Jim with asthma and prescribed medication. Based on symptoms, testing and medical knowledge, asthma appeared to be a logical diagnosis. Since Jim was still young, the diagnosis seemed to correlate with the symptoms. We accepted the diagnosis, yet there were still episodes of doubt. Something just didn't feel right to either of us but we both felt a sense of relief that we at least had a diagnosis of Jim's problems.

In January 2010, we went on our annual Aruba vacation with my brother and sister-in-law. Like any other couple, we were excited to go on vacation, be with family and enjoy one another's company. In my heart, I felt this would be the perfect opportunity for Jim to get some rest, relaxation and feel better. But while sitting at the pool, it was obvious that Jim's cough was not getting any better and was actually becoming constant. My sister-in-law even mentioned that Jim was clearing his throat quite often, something I hadn't realized, probably because it had crept up gradually in our lives. I soon realized that Jim had also begun losing weight. When I inquired, he mentioned he felt as hungry as he typically would at mealtimes, but felt full much sooner than usual, and therefore wasn't eating as much.

At about the same time, Jim started to have chest pain. Knowing I would nag him about it if I knew, he kept it to himself until he came home from a trip one night and said he wanted to go back to the doctor because of chest pain.

On February 12, 2010 Jim went to the doctor for the chest pain and I went with him. An EKG showed a very slight change from his previous one, but since they were finding nothing else, they decided to send him to the hospital for a cardiac catheterization and an MRI of his head.

Let me interject here that Jim had been told he'd had high cholesterol for at least a few years. He tried the medicine the doctor prescribed, but it made him feel terrible because of the side effects. Jim was adamant about not taking the cholesterol medicine. He told the doctor he would prefer to tackle the problem through diet, exercise and a supplement suggested for lowering cholesterol. His cholesterol numbers never really improved and as it was a genetic trait in his family the catheterization made sense. After the test, the cardiologist asked me to come to the nurses' station so he could show me the pictures from the catheterization. He said Jim had textbook perfect arteries … no plaque or blockages at all. The MRI showed nothing out of the ordinary. All good news, but still not an answer.

This cardiologist prescribed a medicine for acid reflux in case that was the problem. Jim was only 47 years old at that time, so given the results of the tests, acid reflux seemed a logical diagnosis.

After that visit to the doctor, Jim was out of town on quite a few trips, for about three weeks. In early March he got sick again and felt like it was a combination of bronchitis and a sinus infection. He told me on the phone that when he got home from this trip he had to get right to the doctor to get an antibiotic because he felt so terrible and he didn't want to lose time from work.

Jim frequently minimized his health issues. He didn't want to worry me, he didn't like being sick and having to go to the doctor all the time and he especially didn't want to lose any time from work. For Jim to address this with me on the phone before even arriving home was monumental.

I told him I would be going with him to the doctor. I felt like the pieces of the puzzle weren't fitting together and we had to get to the bottom of his problem. Jim came home from this trip on the evening of March 9, 2010, called his doctor's office first thing the next morning and made an appointment. This office had several doctors, and Jim had seen different ones previously, but on March 10, he saw a doctor who was new to his case. As always, Jim tried to lessen the seriousness of how he felt or the condition causing the reason for his illness. His primary concern was getting an antibiotic to get rid of his current infection.

I also explained to the doctor that it was very obvious to me that the discomfort Jim felt behind his breastbone was now becoming more frequent and increasingly painful. There were even some nights that I would wake and find Jim sitting up because he said it seemed to make his chest pain better. So although Jim's main concern was to get an antibiotic, my main concern was to get to the bottom of all his symptoms once and for all.

An unexplainable feeling inside of me told me this was something much more serious. Logic and reason never surpass what we feel in our hearts to be true. I knew something was not right. At this point, the doctor suggested that these classic symptoms indicated acid reflux. I'd like to vehemently emphasize that, as you read this, besides listening to the information provided, take into consideration that you, walking around in your own body, are the best judge of your needs. If something persistently gnaws at you, address it, no matter how insignificant it might seem to someone else.

The doctor prescribed two medicines and thought the visit was over. I asked what more was going to be done to find out what caused the rest of Jim's symptoms. The doctor said that it was probably just acid reflux. Probably. The word grated on my nerves and I quickly became a bitchy, pushy wife. I said we wouldn't accept "probably" anything, and I requested that an endoscopy be done to rule out anything with Jim's esophagus. The doctor said that was "way too invasive," but that an upper GI could be done, did we want to schedule one? We absolutely did want to schedule one and as immediately as possible. Before leaving the office, we had an upper GI scheduled for Jim the following day, March 11, 2010.

Keep in mind that doctors are trained to treat based solely on data collected during doctor/patient interaction. Remember when working with doctors that a partnership is created. They must work with the information provided by the patient and treat according to that information. The sole responsibility does not lie completely on the doctor but on the patient as well. It's a partnership.

At 10:00 a.m. the following day, a Thursday, Jim had the upper GI. We left the doctor's office and went to a nearby grocery store to pick up a couple of things. Within twenty minutes, Jim received a phone call from the doctor's office. Jim was told that the upper GI showed a large mass on his esophagus and he would need to have an endoscopy immediately. He got another call later saying that he was scheduled for an endoscopy on Monday, March 15. We now had to wait through Friday and the whole weekend.

I knew in my heart that this was terribly serious. A friend's father had recently passed away from esophageal cancer and I knew it was one of the worst cancers to have due to its high mortality rate. Jim knew it was serious and was scared to death, but I don't think he was as familiar with esophageal cancer, and I certainly didn't tell him what I knew. Of course, we told each other that just because it was a mass didn't mean that it was cancer. Little did we know what we were about to face.

We stepped onto the roller coaster.

The message here is that it is extremely important to advocate for our own health. I'm sure that because of Jim's age and the fact that he "looked great" influenced the doctors not to push to find an answer to his symptoms. It seems simple and obvious to know that if you put all of Jim's symptoms together, something was definitely wrong, yet if we did not push for an endoscopy, we would have gotten nothing except, "It's probably acid reflux." Again, the message is that if you feel deep inside that something is out of kilter, address those feelings with your care provider. Listen to your heart and follow your intuition. The worst you could be is wrong.

On Monday, March 15, Jim had the endoscopy. The doctor performing the endoscopy was personable, discussed the procedure with us and we felt like we were in competent hands. Although Jim was still somewhat groggy after the procedure, the doctor called me in to be with Jim and told us he would be back to talk about the results. I sat with Jim, nervous as could be, and was feeling glad that Jim was somewhat groggy; maybe he wasn't feeling as anxious as I was.

When the doctor came in just a bit later, he sat down with us and told us straight out: Jim had cancer. Cancer. The "C" word. Esophageal cancer. A very large tumor. At age 47. Our worst fears had been confirmed.

Jim didn't smoke, wasn't a heavy drinker, wasn't in his 60s or older, wasn't obese … none of the risk factors fit him and this diagnosis. We asked what I'm sure everyone does when they hear this news: "Doctor, are you sure?" He was sure. He wanted Jim to have a CT scan right away. We didn't even leave the building; he was sent to have the CT scan immediately. The doctor said he'd call us with results as soon as he knew for sure the extent of this cancer.

Suddenly I knew the reason I was driven to retire from a career I loved. I felt this was the plan that was chosen for us. (At a later time, I learned of the co-created plan for all people.) I didn't like the plan, but I was so grateful to have been able to retire at the beginning of that school year. I believe this was God's way of giving me precious time with my husband. Otherwise I would have resigned immediately after Jim's diagnosis. Perhaps some would not consider this a matter of importance, yet a diagnosis like this causes such a ripple effect, even my students' education would have been disrupted. So many others are barely able to take time off from work, let alone be a full-time caregiver. Being grateful doesn't even begin to describe how I felt.

On Wednesday, March 17, the doctor called to tell us the mass involved the lower third of Jim's esophagus, extended through the gastroesophageal (GE) junction and into his stomach . It also looked to be in at least one lymph node. That made it stage III. The doctor saw a spot on his liver, but said it could be a hemangioma, which is a harmless, benign spot. He told us we'd be assigned to an oncologist and it would be investigated further.

And so the roller coaster was in motion.

We had our first appointment with the oncologist on March 19. You'll notice that I say "we" because I went with Jim to every or nearly every appointment, infusion, procedure, et cetera and was involved with every aspect of his illness. At Jim's first appointment with his oncologist (to be called Dr. from this point on), she discussed possibilities, answered questions and ordered an MRI of Jim's liver to be done that day and a PET scan to be done on Monday, March 22.

Jim had both tests done and we met with Dr. again on Tuesday, March 23. She told us that the PET scan and MRI showed that there were at least two metastatic cancer spots (cancer that has traveled to a different area from the original primary cancer spot) on Jim's liver. That made it stage IV. Stage IV is defined as cancer that has traveled to distant organs, in this case his liver. She told Jim he most likely had six months or less to live and that he should get his affairs in order.

No words that have ever come out of someone's mouth have been as devastating as those words: Six months or less to live. Get your affairs in order.

As we listened to her, we were in shock. Because we knew this could be a difficult appointment and did not want to miss any important information, we asked a third party to join us for Jim's first few appointments. She asked the necessary questions which eluded us at the time.

The doctor suggested that Jim have both chemotherapy and radiation for two weeks, and then switch to just a chemo regimen. However, three days later we met with another doctor, a radiation oncologist who said the only benefit of radiation at that point would be to help Jim with swallowing, and that was not a problem for him. So now radiation was out and the plan was to just have chemo treatments.

We put the word out right away to family and friends that Jim was diagnosed with stage IV esophageal cancer (EC). I know some people would want to keep that information private for a while, but because both of us believed in the power of prayer, we wanted as many people praying for Jim as soon as possible.

You know that Jim and I both believed in the tremendous power of prayer. We believed that individual prayer held great power and that group prayer held even more power. We believed that if the group of prayers was large, there was a better chance of getting an answer because God could see how important it was to so many. We started by putting Jim on our church's Prayer Line and after that found numerous ways to ask people to pray for Jim's health and a positive outcome of the cancer. We asked everyone we knew to pray for a miracle.

Along with that came people calling with unsolicited advice. Advice from people who have "been there" is good, but when you're so confused, shocked and devastated, it's overwhelming. At first Jim didn't want to leave Syracuse for a second opinion because he was worried that he would then have to have all treatments away from home. After agonizing over options, he decided to get a second opinion at a well-known cancer center in New York City. Jim's brother and his cousin were able to provide information that helped Jim secure an appointment in NYC on March 29. We couldn't believe it! Moving this quickly had to be good, right? We figured we had a fighting chance since everything was happening quickly. We assumed we were on our way to Jim's recovery.

Just an observation from me at this point. As I said in the last paragraph, because we got the word out about Jim's cancer immediately, we were overwhelmed with advice from people. One person said to do this, another said to do that, go here, go there, go somewhere besides Syracuse, et cetera, et cetera. When you've just heard horrible news and then you're getting too much advice from extremely well-meaning people, it almost makes you not want to hear it, not want to answer the phone, yell "Leave us alone!" and wish you hadn't said anything to anyone.

However—and this is so important—even though Jim and I hadn't even had time to process all of this yet, the advice and suggestions were good to have. When you find out that you or your loved one has stage IV cancer, you do have to move fast. You do have to get a second opinion, and maybe a third and fourth ... whatever it takes. If we just sat and processed the whole situation, Jim may have had a shorter life. If you're reading this and it is happening to you now, or if it ever happens in your future, do your best to keep a level head. Discuss your options, and if it's at all possible, get a second opinion. It doesn't mean you have to do what they say, disrupt your whole life and move to a different city ... none of that. It's simply a second opinion. And if it's at all possible, a major cancer center would be the place you should go.

During the course of Jim's cancer, we went to several major well-known cancer centers for opinions and/or procedures. Each place we went had something different to offer. What it really boiled down to, though, was not just the suggestion for treatment that made the impression good or bad; it was the way we were treated that made the difference. For example, the compassion shown to us, the knowledge made available to us, the respect shown to us as people and potential patients was noteworthy. The important message here is that being more scared than you have ever been in your life cannot stop you from taking action. Act, don't react based on fear. Speak to the professionals who deal with cancer on a regular basis.

We were thrilled that Dr. J could get us in as early as March 29. She was a member of the medical group that came highly recommended to us, considered to be the best in treating esophageal cancer in NYC, so we felt very blessed.

The roller coaster was headed upward once again.

We had no idea what to expect, but when we walked into the medical building for our appointment, we were shocked. There was a different floor for each kind of cancer, and the waiting rooms were packed full. We couldn't believe what we were seeing. From what we saw it seemed that cancer is "big business" and it didn't give us a good feeling.

We had to wait about three hours for our appointment but when we finally got in to see Dr. J, we were very pleased with her. She was all business, but she seemed thorough and competent. Thankfully, Jim's cousin, Stephanie, was with us for this consultation. She lives in Manhattan and came with us for moral support. For something so difficult and emotional, it was helpful to have another set of ears.

Treatment suggestions were cut and dry: three drugs were discussed, and we were happy that the treatment the doctor suggested was the same one that Jim's doctor in Syracuse recommended. Dr. J was adamant, though, that Jim needed to get an MRI of his liver. It was suggested that a PET scan wasn't always reliable with cancer in the liver because sometimes spots looked to be cancer on a PET scan when they really weren't, and that the spots seen could be due to an old infection. We took every bit of hope with us that we could because most of the news at the consultation wasn't terribly hopeful. Jim would be getting three chemotherapy drugs every two weeks, with scans every two to three rounds. This would continue for at least a year. If there was some improvement seen, then "maybe" they would consider a break from the chemo, but most likely Jim would be on at least one drug forever because his cancer was so aggressive.

We felt like we kept getting slapped in the face over and over again … bad news, bad news, bad news. But we always tried to keep a positive attitude. I asked about numerous (eight, to be exact) therapies and procedures that I had researched before coming to the consultation, but Dr. J said she wouldn't even consider anything but her recommendations until we found out more about the spots on Jim's liver. If the cancer hadn't metastasized to his liver, other possibilities could be considered. Although the suggestions weren't what we had hoped for, we had to put our trust in the doctors and our faith in God that the path we chose was the right one. After all, that's why we had gone there.

Jim had an appointment with Dr. back in Syracuse two days later. We were happy things appeared to be moving so quickly, although that was to change a bit. Later on, we also realized that when you have a tumor as large as Jim's in his esophagus, GE junction and stomach, the doctors have to work quickly. So Dr. ordered a liver biopsy (instead of an MRI of the liver) to be done the next day, and scheduled Jim's first chemo treatment the following Monday.

Before Jim's first treatment, we had to go through something called "chemo teach" to learn about the chemo drugs and the possible risks and side effects. For example, one of the drugs could affect the heart, so Jim's heart had to be watched carefully. Another could cause diarrhea, as well as rash on his hands and feet. With the third, Jim couldn't touch, eat or drink anything cold for the first five to seven days because it could cause pain to the touch or spasms in his mouth and throat. They even suggested keeping an oven mitt on the door of, or in, the refrigerator to make sure he didn't forget that he absolutely couldn't touch or have anything cold. Sound a little scary? This was just the beginning.

We were so grateful that Jim's liver biopsy had been scheduled for the very next day so there was minimal waiting involved. This couldn't have been more frightening because the result meant the difference between stage III and IV. Obviously, we knew that was tremendously important, but soon we were to find out how very important that difference was. I haven't mentioned yet that along with everything else going on with Jim's body, he also was born with only one kidney. With one kidney, we and the doctors needed to be sure that anything they prescribed or did would not damage Jim's right kidney; there was no room to play with there, which was a major concern to us. We had to reiterate to every professional involved that Jim had only his right kidney and we had to trust that every move they made was done with that in mind. It was very difficult to keep up that level of trust. We kept ourselves very well informed. We documented every appointment. We brought "extra ears" to appointments when we knew we might not understand the information presented. We documented everything. Despite the feeling of helplessness that remained, our underlying faith never wavered.

On Monday, April 5, we had our "chemo teach" class at 9:00 a.m., after which Dr. told us Jim's liver biopsy was negative!!! We were so thrilled and felt so blessed … finally a piece of good news!

The roller coaster was on its way up!

Four specimens were taken from Jim's liver, as specifically as possible from the spots that had appeared on the PET scan. The report read, "There is no evidence of metastatic adenocarcinoma in this specimen, either by morphology or by immunochemistry. Multiple levels examined." (Medical terminology for "There was no cancer present in Jim's liver based on the results of the test.") Through the whole treatment period, we certainly learned new medical terminology and lingo; this was just the beginning. Of course, we were ecstatic about the news! This meant the cancer would be considered stage III, and radiation and surgery would be possible.

Jim started his first chemo infusion (which was to take three to four hours) right after that. However, just after Jim had started the second of the chemo drugs, a phone call came to the infusion room telling the nurses to stop Jim's infusion immediately! Apparently, Dr. had called Dr. J in NYC to tell her of Jim's negative liver biopsy. Dr. J didn't believe it was negative and asked Dr. to stop the infusion; they wanted Jim to come back to NYC to have a laparoscopy of his liver there. It sounded like they meant immediately, so Jim and I went home and made arrangements to go to NYC the next day, even though we didn't have an actual appointment yet. It sounded so immediate that we wanted to be there and ready so that this could get done as quickly as possible.

Another dip on the roller coaster.

After arriving in NYC, we waited for an appointment we thought to be immediate but there was none. They did try to schedule us so we didn't have to go home and come back, but it didn't happen. We returned to Syracuse with an appointment to go back to NYC on April 13 for a consult before the laparoscopy on April 16. The directive to get back to NYC had sounded so immediate to us that we did what we thought would improve Jim's chances the most. He was diagnosed with cancer on March 15, and we already knew that the earliest we might know any results of the laparoscopy would be April 16. One full month without any chemotherapy starting … all the changes with test results … all the stopping and starting … truly, it was a roller coaster. The situation was worrisome to us, but what choice did we have? Like it or not, we were now part of the cancer system. We knew we needed a definitive answer to the question of whether or not the cancer had metastasized to Jim's liver.

At the consult on April 13, Jim and I were both very impressed with the doctor (Dr. S) who would be performing the laparoscopy (especially Jim … the doctor was beautiful!). She was a gastric surgeon, and explained the reasons for having the laparoscopy. She said this procedure would allow her to look at Jim's liver closely in order to perform a much better guided biopsy of the suspicious spots on his liver. She would also look for "peritoneal spread," or tumor deposits in Jim's abdominal cavity, and if any were present, they would be biopsied as well. After the laparoscopy, a more complete staging would be done and better-informed decisions about treatment.

We both felt quite confident that we were in good hands with Dr. S doing the laparoscopy. The procedure was performed on April 16, and Dr. S came to talk to me immediately following the procedure. They would do biopsies on two spots on the right lobe of Jim's liver, and she took "washings" from various spots of his peritoneal cavity. She was sure there was cancer in his liver, but the biopsy results would take approximately five days, and if these biopsies showed malignancy, Dr. S said the cancer would need to be treated very aggressively. We knew that already but … five days until the results of the biopsies? That seemed like forever! Again, what choice did we have?

We received the results on April 23. Both spots biopsied on the right lobe of the liver were malignant, and microscopic washings from Jim's peritoneal cavity were positive for cancer in the pelvis, left upper quadrant and right upper quadrant. The results were worse than either of us had expected and we were devastated. All we could hear were Dr.'s words from March 23 ringing in our ears: Six months or less to live. Get your affairs in order.

The Cancer Experience – Part I

We looked at each other in disbelief. We were shocked and terrified. Tears poured from our eyes as we clung to each other. We were already emotionally exhausted and mentally distraught. As we looked at each with complete dismay, we were both asking the same question. How could we ever be separated? It took all of our strength to hold ourselves together, to regain our composure and hear what the doctor was saying. I took notes as accurately as I could. Jim stared at the doctor with a "deer in the headlights" look. Dr. started talking about medicines that Jim should take to coat the lining of his esophagus … vitamins to take to try to prevent neuropathy in his hands and feet from the chemo drugs … medications to help constipation … it was all a big blur. Could chemotherapy do its job and get rid of this horrid disease? Did we have a chance of receiving a miracle from God?

The roller coaster flew down the biggest dip yet.

On this same day, April 23, 2010, thirty-nine days after Jim's original diagnosis, Jim had his first full chemotherapy infusion. He would be infused with drugs every three weeks and take a chemo pill two times every day. In the weeks, months and year to come, Jim and I would often wonder if anything would have changed for the better if the original biopsy had not come back negative, and he was able to start his chemo treatments a full month earlier. On the other hand, if it hadn't been for the laparoscopy, we wouldn't have known of all the cancer in the liver and peritoneal cavity. As of this day, April 23, Jim had lost thirty-two pounds, and he was just beginning his chemo treatments. We drove home in complete silence. We couldn't even look at each other knowing the sobbing would start all over again. We were in such a daze that neither of us could tell you a thing about the rest of that day and night.

Just as you always hear, there were so many side effects from chemotherapy. Jim was always given preventive medications for nausea, et cetera, right along with the infused chemo drugs, but later, the effects were felt at home. As mentioned before, one of the drugs Jim took in his first chemo protocol makes the patient very sensitive to cold. We didn't have to worry too much about the weather since it was April, but for five to seven days, Jim couldn't drink any cold drinks, couldn't use ice, and couldn't touch anything cold. If he did, he could have spasms in his throat which could have been very dangerous. It was suggested that we put an oven mitt on the refrigerator door so Jim would remember not to open the refrigerator door as he would normally do automatically. We did that, and it worked well.

We were repeatedly informed of the importance of knowing the symptoms Jim was experiencing, so more medications could be given to counteract side effects. Doctors prescribed chemotherapy medications to cure the cancer and more medications to treat the side effects caused by the chemo medications. I kept a diary as best I could of his physical condition, when and how he was eating ... anything that we were told to do in accordance with treatment. All these things were reported to Jim's medical team.

Anyone who knew Jim was familiar with his positive attitude, his joking personality, his silliness and practical jokes, his huge smile with the twinkling eyes and his loving nature. No matter how lousy Jim was feeling during the chemo treatments, he was a man of dignity and did his best to present a strong front. He did this especially at his medical appointments, when we went to church and at work. At home, though, it was a different story. Jim was able to express how he really felt about everything, whether it was good or bad. For example, a usually talkative, goofy Jim would often sit in silence, withdrawn, trying to preserve his energy. Sometimes I would come home to find him crying in his chair. He became easily frustrated at something as simple as my encouraging him to eat.

Jim, who used to be a person who wouldn't even take an aspirin when he had a headache, came to have a basket of medicines he would or could take. In some people, one of the symptoms of esophageal cancer is difficulty swallowing. For most of the cancer, Jim said that wasn't a problem, but swallowing pills was a problem just because he didn't do well with it and never had. He had trouble swallowing one or two small pills, let alone the number and sizes of some of the pills prescribed to help him. He did fine with liquids, so for some meds, he would take a liquid form rather than the pills.

When I look back on the diary I kept of Jim's symptoms and how he felt, it sounds like he was in torture most days, regardless of the meds to help the side effects. Since Jim was not a complainer, you'd never know he was feeling as badly as the diary stated. Women often say that when men get sick, they act like babies, they complain and need to be waited on hand and foot. That certainly was not my husband. The opposite was true for him; he probably tried too hard to stay strong, for himself and others.

We also met with a nutritionist who would give us suggestions for foods and liquids to eat and drink to try to help Jim gain weight. Jim had tried some of the nutritional milkshakes and breakfast-type drinks, but none of them really appealed to him during chemo treatments. We understood that lack of appetite is a typical side effect of chemotherapy treatments, so we were determined to help him gain weight. Having heard from the nutritionist that there were many types of milkshakes and high calorie drinks that could assist in weight gain, we found one in particular that Jim liked. He liked the flavors and, with eight ounces of whole milk, one shake was 600 calories. I also found a recipe for some banana muffins that, if made in the largest muffin tins, could have 1,000 calories in them! We were so grateful for the nutritionist's suggestions like these.

A once strong and robust 220-pound Jim now weighed 170 pounds. He had lost fifty pounds in less than four months! You can imagine how noticeable this was. Many who knew Jim wanted to contribute and make a difference. His mother and Aunt Paula made soup. Theresa researched to find anything with enhanced nutritional value that would help him gain weight (ie: nutritional superfoods). She even gave him a toothbrush sanitizer to prevent sores from forming in his mouth due to chemotherapy drugs. Whenever our busy schedule allowed, Roberta and Rod would cook dinner for us. We were so fortunate to have so many people wanting to help. Even when we were on vacation at camp, our neighbor, Rick (the same Rick who hired Jim to get his pilot career going), would make breakfast for Jim on a daily basis. The point is, cancer affects everyone, but most of all, it affected Jim.

His appetite was so poor that no matter how hard anyone tried to help Jim gain weight, often he just couldn't eat. Jim, once a lover of great food, lost his taste for all foods. The loss of taste, let alone the difficulty of swallowing, was bad but even the smell of food and the vomiting and dry heaves that often came with it simply destroyed something he once enjoyed so much.

We met with either the nurse practitioner or Dr. every week, whether Jim was having a chemo treatment or not. Jim's physician group at the oncology center kept a close eye on everything and we all had a wonderful relationship with each other. Jim said through his whole treatment that his goal was to be Dr.'s "star" … he wanted to be her biggest success story. We knew she had a patient who was doing very well with cancer and was three years out from diagnosis. Jim had somewhat of an internal competition going with that patient. Good for him. Anything that helps make a patient strong and keeps them fighting is a great and necessary thing.

Jim often stated that he felt he was treated like a king at the center. Everyone from the front desk staff and schedulers, to the nurses, nurse practitioners and doctors provided great care. The infusion nurses were fabulous. As crazy as this sounds, after a time, it started to feel like a family in that infusion room, not only with the nurses, but with some of the patients with whom we were on the same schedule. Cancer is difficult enough, so those pleasant, happy experiences were important.

Keep in mind though, that Jim was a kind, friendly, sweet man. It certainly wasn't hard for everyone to love him. We know it's not like that for everyone. Some people just can't muster up the energy to be happy and friendly and act like chemo treatments are "all in a day's work," like Jim did. Some people had no one to come in and sit with them during treatments. Some had to come and leave by cab or hired van, and others looked so sad and without hope.

When a person is diagnosed with cancer they hear from others to stay strong, to keep fighting, to imagine those cancer cells being eaten up by the chemo, to pray, pray and pray some more … the list goes on. It is so true, at least in our case, that all of those suggestions were not only good thoughts, but necessary. The patient and those that love that patient must have hope. They must have faith that the patient can be cured of this disease. As I said earlier, we chose to tell people right away about Jim's diagnosis so we could get people praying and sending positive thoughts and love Jim's way. People sent cards and notes to let Jim know they were behind him all the way.

I had been on the receiving end of a website called CaringBridge when two people I knew were seriously ill. CaringBridge is a free site, funded by contributions, which a person designs for their own personal situation (www.caringbridge.org). Several people suggested that I might want to start a site for Jim so that I could put news about Jim and true information out to people, rather than make and receive a million phone calls about him. I especially liked the idea because by using CaringBridge, I would be the only author, so I knew that only true information was going out to the world, not rumors that might turn into misinformation.

It was during this time that Jim started having weekly Reiki sessions. Jim wasn't sure he even understood what Reiki was. All he knew was that during and after his Reiki sessions, he felt relaxed, comforted, calmed and reassured. He knew something was working.

Back to the medical happenings. Jim's second round of chemo was on May 14, and the plan was to have CT and PET scans done at the end of that three-week period to see if this treatment plan was working. We felt, along with Dr., that if a particular set of drugs wasn't working, why keep using them? That would be the time to switch to a different chemo protocol. If the drugs were working then—hallelujah—let's keep using them! Jim's first scans after this treatment were done on June 3. We were to get results the next day, which is soon, but the waiting was still torture.

Results: Main tumor in the esophagus/stomach greatly reduced. However, the liver was worse. Now four spots were clearly seen and both lobes of the liver were involved.

Jim was scheduled to have a chemo treatment that day so Dr. immediately changed the chemo drugs to the new combination and he started the new protocol. The new chemo protocol was to have two new drugs infused once every three weeks, and Jim also had to start wearing a pump which pumped a chemo drug into his body through a port five days a week, twenty-four hours a day. Five days later, Jim would go to the center to have the pump disconnected and get a shot of a drug which helps make more white blood cells in order to prevent infection in people. While necessary, the shot always caused body aches for several days afterward.

The pump had to be worn around Jim's waist in a fanny pack. It was like an appendage for five days each cycle, which meant no swimming or anything that could damage it, showering by hanging it on the cabinet door next to our shower and sleeping with it, which was uncomfortable and made noise every time the pump put the chemo drug into his body. Nothing was easy.

On the Saturday after this new drug-combo infusion started, Jim began to feel extremely weak and tired, with no strength, and was also light-headed, with a rash and no appetite. In addition, he was experiencing vomiting and diarrhea. The on-call oncologist said to go to the emergency room where we found out it was all primarily due to dehydration ... our first experience of what dehydration can really do to your body. Jim stayed in the hospital for two nights to get fully hydrated and have his symptoms calm down.

From that point on, Jim's nurse practitioner suggested that with this chemo protocol, Jim schedule regular hydration infusions at the cancer health center. So in the first week of the treatment, Jim would have three hydrations, the second week either two or three, and by the third week, he could usually go with only one or two. We felt like we were living in the infusion room.

This chemo protocol worked for Jim from June 4 until September 17. Scans were good and the tumors in the liver had all shrunk. Two even "disappeared," or at least didn't light up on the scans.

Jim was able to celebrate his 48th birthday with new hope! We thought we were on our way to a new life … one without cancer. We sure enjoyed that summer! Jim was even able to attend his thirtieth high school reunion and rejoice in the fact that he was alive to celebrate with old friends. Was Jim finally in that two to three percent of people we kept hearing about who make it out of this disease alive?

The Cancer Experience – Part II

We were beyond ecstatic that this treatment was working for Jim. How great it was that right at the time of Jim's 48th birthday, everything started going in the right direction and the roller coaster was definitely on its way up. All too often in life though when all is going well, "the other shoe drops," as they say. This time it was me. In October 2010, I had a couple of days of severe pain in my lower left abdomen. I doctored myself all too often as Jim would be quick to tell you, and I assumed I had an ovarian cyst. I had also been diagnosed years ago with Irritable Bowel Syndrome but it hadn't been a problem in a long time. I didn't feel too worried about this.

The pain became worse and spread through my whole abdomen. One evening, I knew I had to go to the emergency room. I had put this off because I did not want Jim in a hospital where he could easily contract a virus or infection because of his compromised immune system, and I knew he wouldn't let me go to the ER alone. I was right. We went to the ER and a CT scan confirmed the diagnosis of diverticulitis which is an infection in the intestines, sometimes due to diet and often induced by stress. The doctor said worrying about Jim may have brought this on. I would most likely be fine and may never have another again. Time would tell.

Stress certainly can play a part in our health, especially during times of emotionality. I had five diverticulitis attacks between that time and October 11, 2011. Don't ever let a doctor tell you "it's all in your head," just because you happen to be in a stressful time in your life. Stress can and does cause physical problems.

Jim started to develop neuropathy in his hands and feet (damage to nerves which could go away with time or be permanent) in September. Dr. wasn't comfortable continuing one of the drugs because she felt it was the drug responsible for the neuropathy. Jim started his third chemo protocol on September 29. This one was infusion of two new drugs every two weeks with the pump again. Luckily, the pump was connected for only two days at a time this time … nicer for Jim. Scans on November 22 showed that this protocol was also working … No cancer lighting up at all!!!!! Jim had this treatment every two weeks for months.

Once again everything was going well. We were thrilled! And again, the "other shoe" dropped. Christmas had always been our favorite holiday and was very important to us. Our tradition every year was to spend Christmas Eve with my family and Christmas day with Jim's. On the morning of Christmas Eve, 2010, I remember coming downstairs to the kitchen. That's the last thing I remember. Jim later told me I acted strangely and didn't know about or remember things I should have known. I didn't know it was Christmas Eve even though we had opened our presents to each other the night before. I kept asking the same questions over and over, questions that didn't even make sense to Jim.

Thinking I could be having a stroke, Jim called 911. He explained why we were going to the hospital and said he knew the situation was serious when I didn't understand that there was even a problem. For approximately eight hours that day, my short-term memory was permanently erased.

We spent the day in the hospital with me asking the same several questions over and over and over. Jim told me afterward he was terrified not only of what was happening to me but because he was worried that if he died from the cancer and this happened to me again, what would become of me? Who would take care of me if he wasn't there? He said he was also scared because I was the one who took care of everything—this kind of thing wasn't supposed to happen to me.

My neurologist was kind enough to come to the hospital on Christmas Eve to help determine what the problem was. While he was still there, my memory began to return. Numerous tests were done and all were negative. The on-call doctor wanted to admit me for observation but I fought that because I realized Jim had been in the hospital all day with me and just like the last ER visit, I was concerned about Jim's exposure to infection and viruses. My doctor understood that and took responsibility for discharging me. The on-call doctor did not know what was wrong with me but my neurologist had seen this before and knew what it was. He explained to Jim and me that I had an episode of Transient Global Amnesia (TGA), a sudden loss of memory not caused by epilepsy or a stroke, but often seemingly caused by acute emotional distress.

Jim and I went home and spent Christmas Eve by ourselves for the very first time. As it turned out it was also our last, so spending it by ourselves was a great thing.

Jim had scans again on January 18 which showed one liver lesion had increased again, but it wasn't lighting up, so maybe it wasn't a cancerous lesion. Along with these treatments, Jim received Reiki at least once a week and sometimes more often.

In the meantime, we went for consultations at three major cancer centers. We were treated differently in each place and preferred some over others, but in the end, the results were basically the same. Jim had stage IV esophageal cancer and we were reminded every time that only two to three percent of cancer patients lives through that cancer. Because the current chemo protocol was working for the most part, none of the cancer centers we consulted with would do any of the other procedures or treatments that were being done on stage I, II or III patients. One center even forgot about us! We waited two and a half hours before we were even seen by a resident! Some visits gave us hope of at least having the possibility of keeping the cancer under control, while others were just downright depressing. We were highly disappointed that none of the centers would perform any targeted treatments due to Jim's having stage IV cancer even though he had already surpassed the "six months or less to live" prognosis that was given when diagnosed. One center told us they would not perform these treatments because they would not be covered by insurance.

Jim's neuropathy was extremely bothersome for him. Even though it improved somewhat after stopping infusion of the one drug, it never went away. He had a combination of pain and numbness in his hands and feet, and sometimes it went up his arms and legs. It was very frustrating for him. We saw a neurologist, Dr. T, who did nerve testing, and Jim tried taking a couple of medications for the neuropathy, but they didn't help his condition.

Jim tried so hard to wear a happy face and put on a strong front, but from the time he started all the chemotherapy treatments and taking all the medicines to help the side effects, up until the very end, he rarely felt well. We would go out with friends, spend time with family or attend some social event, and he would socialize and act like he was doing fine, but as soon as we would get home, Jim would have to lie down due to tiredness, sit down because he was in pain, often had to rush into the house because he was about to have dry heaves. The issues he had to deal with were endless. We knew from friends or relatives who had cancer in the past that current medications for side effects were better than ever before, but that didn't change the fact that Jim rarely felt well the way most of us feel well.

Although he had all of these issues, we were happy because since June 2010, his condition seemed to be improving and, for a while, cancer lesions didn't show up at all. What more could we ask for? Jim had already passed the "six months to live" prognosis. He and I stayed positive, had hope, acted strong and things were looking good. He continued to receive Reiki on a regular basis.

Jim continued this chemo protocol. He had scans done on January 17, 2011. Results showed that one liver lesion had increased by about one third in size, but it did not light up on the PET scan. Of course we didn't like the growth of the lesion, but it wasn't lighting up, therefore the cancer wasn't back. Right? That's what we grasped onto. Otherwise hope starts to fade and we couldn't let that happen.

I had heard of a procedure that the Mayo Clinic was performing to ablate liver tumors even on patients with stage IV cancer! The doctor from the Mayo Clinic said this was a brand new procedure (MRI-guided laser ablation) and that interested patients had to be approved after the Mayo Clinic doctors looked at required scans and tests. We spoke to Dr. about this and she thought it was certainly something to consider if Jim's liver tumors got worse.

We had been told from the beginning, and by every cancer center we consulted with, that cancer cells often "get smart" when they've been treated with the same drugs for a length of time, especially in certain types of cancer. Esophageal cancer is one of the "bad" cancers to have because often by the time symptoms become a problem to a person, the cancer has already metastasized. So even though we knew the odds, even though we knew what happens with most stage IV esophageal cancer patients, even though we knew that the cancer cells would probably "get smart," we continued to hope that Jim would be in that two to three percent that make it out alive.

We continued to pray and ask for prayers. We went to healing masses. At two of those masses at least two thirds of the church was filled with our friends and families because our friends, Carrie and KC, made a point of trying to get as many people as possible to come, support Jim and pray together for him. At the first healing mass we ever attended Jim fell back ("rested," as the priest called it) and lay on the floor for a few minutes. I'd seen this happen before, but I never knew what people go through when it happens. When the service was over, I asked Jim what he felt like when he "rested." He said it was the most beautiful thing. He saw the brilliant white light that people talk about and had the most peaceful, calm feeling during the experience. He didn't want it to end, as it was an extremely spiritual event for him.

Reiki, or energy healing touch therapy, became a very important part of Jim's life. Jim's sister, Marianne, whose career had always been rooted in science, shared her own personal benefits of receiving Reiki. Jim had always admired his big sister's guidance and direction. Because he held Marianne in such high esteem and knew some change was happening within him, he followed his intuition and continued to receive Reiki. Jim mentioned several times that Reiki was the one thing that seemed to bring him the most comfort, the greatest benefit and was the most soothing. He didn't know the words to describe it; he just knew that during his sessions, something was happening to help his overall well-being. Since Jim and I were both seeing positive results from Reiki, we encouraged others to do the same.

One of our practitioners, Elizabeth, constantly encouraged Jim to "rest," almost to the point of ad nauseam. Jim would jokingly say, "I can rest when I'm dead," or "If I rest any more, I'll be dead." However, to Jim, resting meant sitting and watching TV. That was not Elizabeth's definition of resting. We were to find out later, according to readings through Elizabeth, a professional medium, that resting really meant being meditative and quiet within oneself. During numerous Reiki sessions with Elizabeth, Jim's father, who is on the other side, referred frequently (channeled through Elizabeth) to the need for Jim to rest. She was hesitant to say this information was from his father, but she continued to encourage him to rest. With the stress Jim was going through, feeling relaxed was enough for him to keep going for the sessions.

During this time, Jim began to express what he really thought of Reiki. As mentioned before, he couldn't explain it, but he knew something was happening right from the beginning of his Reiki treatments. It was very relaxing for him. Sometimes he fell asleep or something "like" sleep. For many months, Jim went for weekly sessions with Maryann and/or Elizabeth. It was evident that both believed in the power of Reiki and hands-on healing, and are grounded in their faith and spirituality. Because of the healing benefits of Reiki that I witnessed and that Jim mentioned so often, I became a Reiki practitioner. I did this to continue to be an active participant in Jim's healing as well as to relieve my own "caregiver" stress. I highly recommend that other caregivers do the same.

During the nineteen months that Jim had cancer, he had other tremendously spiritual experiences. When Jim wasn't feeling well or was too tired to drive, I would drive him to his Reiki sessions. One night, Maryann and Jim walked out together, came up to our truck, and Maryann said, "Well, do you want to tell her or shall I?" I didn't know what to expect. Maryann proceeded to tell me that during Jim's session that night, as Reiki was being offered—specifically around Jim's feet—Jim raised both arms as if reaching upward.

Maryann stated that his arms remained like that for twenty-five minutes. Who can hold their hands in the air that long without putting them down, especially a tired, weak cancer patient?

Afterward, Jim and Maryann spoke about the session. Maryann explained to Jim that in her mind's eye she saw Jesus. Remember, both had much love and devotion to Jesus. Maryann felt compelled to kneel, completely in awe. Maryann stated, "Jesus said to me, 'If you feel compelled to kneel, I will kneel, too.'" The look on Jim's face as he was speaking of the experience was enough to show both the amazement and his disbelief that he was worthy of this happening. For many sessions afterward, his hands would rise up, but never as high as that first time when Jesus appeared. During other times with Maryann, Jim would come home and say he felt that his hands were being held by someone during the session and it was not Maryann.

After a Reiki session with Elizabeth, Jim came home and when I asked how his session was, he seemed very tentative, as if he was hesitant to tell me something. He said, "Chris, I felt like I was actually up off the table." When I asked if he meant literally off the table, he said yes, and that when he asked Elizabeth about it after the session was finished, she confirmed it ... Jim had actually levitated off the table.

To some readers, these three spiritual experiences might seem unbelievable, but Jim was not one to exaggerate anything like this. Actually, the opposite is true. It would be more expected that Jim wouldn't mention them for fear of not being believed. However, I believe this is what faith is all about. Can we always understand it logically or prove it? Certainly not, but there is no doubt in my mind that all of these experiences happened.

Do these spiritual or remarkable events happen to everyone who is on the receiving end of Reiki, or energy work? I don't know, but Jim was certain that these were actual experiences. It could also be said that all people who go to healing masses do not see the white light that Jim saw, either. But I do believe it had a great deal to do with Jim's innate spirituality and that a great amount of healing was going on during his sessions with both Maryann and Elizabeth.

This is why I became certified in Reiki Level I—so that I could give Reiki to Jim on any days that he wasn't seeing Elizabeth or Maryann. I believe so strongly in the healing power of energy work that I have energy sessions (Reiki) every week for my own health and well-being, and have since become certified in Reiki Level II.

Back to Jim's medical treatment. We knew from the scans in January 2011 that there was a lesion showing on Jim's liver, but it wasn't "lighting up." Again, were we to be disappointed because there was a lesion, or happy because there was no lighting up (which would be indicative of cancer) on the scan? Jim was not in any pain and had even stopped taking hydrocodone.

Jim continued the same treatment until the next scans in March. From our past persistence we knew it was important to insist the doctors listen to Jim because he knew his own body better than anyone. That certainly was the case here. Ironically, exactly one year to the day of having to push for more testing, we found that the PET scan showed the cancer was definitely back. What was believed to be acid reflux one year prior had turned out to be something completely unexpected. Now the cancer was in the left lobe of Jim's liver and an MRI showed six small spots in the right lobe. Had we not pushed for more testing originally, Jim probably wouldn't be alive at this point.

There are no coincidences. As you read further in this book and as you reflect on your own life, you will most likely find similar synchronicities. These "coincidences" can't be proven yet certainly are difficult to ignore.

The roller coaster dipped again.

Dr. changed Jim's chemo protocol once again. This time to two drugs to be infused once every three weeks. I also found out more information about the MRI-Guided Laser Ablation being done by Dr. W at the Mayo Clinic. We chose to go to the Florida site rather than the Minnesota location, because we felt the climate would be easier on Jim's body. We discussed the information with Dr. She thought it was a good idea to have the procedure done and Jim was willing to try anything that could help. After preliminary testing, Jim was approved for the procedure, and we headed to Jacksonville on March 29, 2011.

We were highly impressed with everything to do with the Mayo Clinic in Jacksonville. Every person we dealt with was extremely professional, every appointment for testing and procedure were kept on time, the procedure and everything about it was clearly explained, and the hospital room Jim stayed in the night of the procedure was unlike any we'd seen. There was a pull-out couch so I was able to be with Jim following the ablation. Dr. W did tell us that when he actually performed the procedure, he would make decisions based on what he felt would attain the best possible results. For example, if he felt ultrasound guidance made the tumors easier to see than MRI, he would do that. If he felt that using microwave antennae was better than laser, he would do that. It would all be dependent on what Dr. W saw when he was performing the procedure. He would also look for the spots that the MRI showed on the right lobe of Jim's liver.

On March 31, Jim was put under general anesthesia and Dr. W ablated two tumors on the left lobe of the liver using ultrasound and microwaves. There were no complications. When we asked about the right lobe spots, he said he did not see anything that he could ablate. After surgery, when asked if he knew this would kill the tumors, Dr. W said it probably worked, but we wouldn't know for sure until the next CT scan in three months. Dr. W said that the tumors would still be in the liver, but without blood flow they should die and that they would gradually shrink. Jim had a great deal of pain coming out of anesthesia and the doctor said he would likely have pain for about a week after surgery.

We flew home on Saturday, April 2, and Jim started his fourth new chemo protocol on Monday, April 4. Jim did continue to have pain in his liver area, and now with a different chemo protocol, a whole new set of side effects. This was all so horribly difficult on Jim, yet he rarely complained.

With this chemo treatment, on Tuesday he again had to have an injection that helped to keep up his white blood cell count. With this injection came a couple of days of muscle aches and overall malaise. Jim drove to Elmira the day after the shot, but felt very poorly and felt worse as the day and evening went on. The pain on Wednesday, Thursday and Friday was bad enough for him to go back to taking hydrocodone. He had no appetite, had extreme fatigue, pain, constipation due to pain meds, and developed a sunburn-like rash and mouth sores.

By the next appointment with the nurse practitioner (a new person this time) on April 13, he was beginning to feel better. Jim said he had "discomfort" now, rather than pain (although I always felt that he downplayed his pain rating when asked how bad it was on a scale of zero to ten), he had a bit of an appetite, but not much, was less constipated, but was still fatigued and continued to have the mouth sores. This overall feeling continued, and from this point on, Jim never felt significantly better. Some days were better than others, but I don't think he had any days that a typical person would call a day of feeling well.

Various treatments were tried to combat side effects and the way Jim felt overall … medicines, steroids, vitamins, et cetera … but nothing ever really made him feel good except his Reiki sessions. A bone scan was done to see if Jim's pain was caused by metastases to his bones, but that came back negative. From what we knew of bone pain, it was horrible and neither Jim nor I could bear his having to go through even worse pain than he had now.

Jim was scheduled to have another CT scan and his next chemo treatment on May 16. His CT scan came back showing a new tumor in the left lobe, and the two ablated tumors now appeared to have coalesced into one larger lesion. There were also new tumors on the right lobe of Jim's liver, and the celiac node which was of normal size before was now enlarged.

Again … devastation. Another dip on the roller coaster.

We were now at the point of not having many options left to get rid of this cancer, but still we tried to keep hope and not give up. It's impossible to imagine how devastated Jim felt as he kept his feelings to himself, but it was gut-wrenching to me.

Dr. talked with us about different chemo possibilities, looking again for clinical trials that might be appropriate for Jim, consulting with the doctors from the other cancer centers. We knew we were running out of options. As far as chemo drugs, Jim could go back to some of the previous ones, but they either hadn't worked or they caused Jim's neuropathy to worsen. There was a drug that hadn't been tried yet, but it wasn't a drug that had been used very successfully for Jim's situation. As far as clinical trials, most have requirements of not having used chemo drugs at all or a minimum of one or two. Jim had used so many that he wouldn't qualify for most trials. The one he did qualify for was a "Phase I" trial and would be performed merely for toxicity levels. Unfortunately, it was not appropriate for Jim. Clinical trials were out.

After consulting with doctors from the various cancer centers, it was decided to try one more drug, this one with few side effects, if any. The pump would be used again, this time for four days before being disconnected. One doctor suggested that Jim should wear the pump for seven days, but there comes a point when you have to consider quality of life and Jim and Dr. decided on four days instead of seven. This protocol would be done weekly for three weeks and then Jim would have one week off before starting the series again.

Earlier I wrote about how close Jim was to his employers, Bruce and Rosemary. They were always thinking about Jim and what they could do for him. A very sweet example of this is when Jim first started his chemotherapy treatments. Apple had just come out with the first iPad and Bruce and Rosemary sent him an iPad to use while he was in the infusion room having his treatments. They are such kind, generous people. At some point around this time, Bruce had a talk with Jim and strongly suggested that Jim needed to go on disability so that he could rest more and concentrate on healing rather than being stressed out by work. There was that idea of REST again … sitting quietly, accepting the moment.

We all knew this was the right thing for Jim to do from a health stand-point. However, I worried about what this would do to Jim's spirits. He loved his work, he loved being busy and I knew he would have a difficult time giving up his work. I'm sure we all knew that this would present a mental and emotional setback for Jim, but it was so absolutely necessary. He needed to concentrate on healing. When I would say to him that he needed to rest more, he would again say, "I can rest when I'm dead!" I'm sure that sounds shocking to some people, but that was an irreverent "humorous" comment that was typical of Jim. And as much as none of us in Jim's family or group of friends wanted to hear that kind of talk, when he made a comment like that, we just had to laugh. That was his way and a big part of why we loved him.

I was so thankful when Bruce had the discussion with Jim about going on disability. It did make Jim depressed, very much so for a while. He was unusually quiet, didn't feel like doing much of anything and most of all, it made him go inward. That's probably exactly what he didn't want to do, but I believe it was very necessary for him to do. The cancer was getting worse, and he had to deal with that. I would have liked to believe I could help him deal with that, but the fact is that sometimes it's just too hard to discuss the cold, hard facts with your love and best friend, especially when every single piece of this was physically gut-wrenching.

On May 23, Jim began his fifth new chemo protocol, yet another drug with the pump. This drug supposedly wouldn't cause any side effects, but Jim was so tired, had no energy, very little appetite, was constipated and had dry heaves fairly often. This treatment had to be done every week for three weeks. Jim would get one week off, and then start all over again. By June 6, Jim had lost seven pounds in three weeks.

At Jim's appointment on June 24 to disconnect the pump, he was lethargic with no energy and no appetite. He had a hydration infusion and began wearing a patch for pain along with taking a drug for nausea, even though he was eating very little food. On June 27, Jim was to have another infusion, but after talking to Dr. about how terrible he felt, he hydrated again and Dr. ordered a CT scan for the next day. Results showed some improvement in the celiac node, but the tumors were the same in the left lobe of the liver and bigger in the right lobe. We still prayed, we still had hope and we were still expecting a miracle. I could not seem to allow myself to see the situation for what it was … this cancer was continually getting worse, Jim felt horrible all the time, and the unthinkable could happen.

Due to the results of the CT scan, it was decided to make yet another change to Jim's chemotherapy protocol. It was to actually be a repeat of drugs he had used before. Two drugs to be infused once every three weeks. The new regimen was begun on July 5, just after a Fourth of July weekend that was full of pain and misery for Jim. He had now lost seventeen pounds in less than two months. Jim had the second infusion of the current drugs on July 26, as well as hydration infusions on July 26, 27 and 28. Jim had lost twenty-four pounds since May 16.

Jim was continuing his Reiki sessions with Elizabeth and Maryann, as well as with me when we were home. One day Jim and Elizabeth talked about his quality of life, or lack of it, and discussed the possibility of stopping his chemo treatments altogether. Jim decided to schedule a reading with Elizabeth to see what the Angels suggested about continuing or stopping the chemo. Jim also wanted to speak with his loved ones on the other side.

On the way home that day of their discussion, Jim asked me how I would feel if he decided to stop having his chemotherapy. As you can imagine, some part of me inside was screaming, "No, no, no ... you can't stop the chemo ... it's our only chance for you to live ... and I can't live without you!" But those selfish feelings didn't come out of my mouth. I knew how horrible Jim felt every day that he lived. I knew this whole ordeal had been terribly difficult for a long time, but now it was torturous. I knew that asking me that question had to be one of the hardest things Jim ever had to do. And I knew that this was Jim's life. He had the cancer, and I would support the man I loved no matter what that meant. I told him I was behind him a hundred percent with whatever decision he made.

Soon the decision about continuing or stopping the chemo treatments became a moot point. A CT scan on August 15 showed that everything was worse: more tumors in Jim's liver, more nodes with cancer, and the cancer had now spread to his lungs. Talking with Dr., we saw the lost hope in her eyes as she told us there were no more drugs to try, there was no more chemotherapy to be done. I now know that seeing the lost hope in her eyes was the day Jim lost hope, too, and knew he would die.

We did still have the reading with Elizabeth, even though it was no longer about whether or not to continue the chemotherapy. Perhaps some people would be afraid to have a reading with a medium at that point, but Jim's faith was so strong that he needed to hear what was said and from whom. I'll never forget that reading. Jim's father was the person who spoke the most, but all of the deceased members of his family (grandparents, uncles and aunts) were there. They were all trying to talk at once and sounded very excited to be talking with Jim. They told him they were waiting for him, and his grandmother told him that they don't miss us because they're around us all the time.

You might think that this reading with Elizabeth would have been depressing for Jim because it really did sound like they were expecting him soon. But it wasn't depressing at all. It was comforting for Jim to know that his loved ones were really on the other side and couldn't wait to see him! The reading offered validation and a sense of peace for Jim.

Unless you've been through this, you can't imagine how absolutely horrible it is to go through each day knowing that Jim didn't have long to live. We went through the motions of each day; we didn't know whether to talk about it or not; we knew we needed to talk about plans and the future after he would be gone, but we couldn't. It was a devastating, heart-wrenching time.

It was the lowest dip of the roller coaster.

Yet, as awful as it was during that time, we loved each other more than ever. We cherished every second, and Jim visited with family and friends to the best of his ability. And as only my Jim could do at a time like this, he was able to continue his practical jokes like he always had. Jim and I had visited the rectory of the church that owned the cemetery where we wanted to buy plots for both of us. That day was extremely difficult. We scheduled a time to meet Barbara, the woman from the church, to look at and pick out our plots.

The day we met Barbara, our emotions were a little better and Jim was determined to make light of what we had to go through. We did pick two plots next to where Jim's Aunt Angela is buried. When the woman asked if we were sure we were happy with what we'd chosen, Jim said, "Well … wait a minute … I'd better make sure this fits," and he proceeded to lie down on the plot to see if it fit. Then he said, "Come on, Chris, let's see if you fit next to me." I couldn't believe it and would have nothing to do with lying on the ground next to him, but I admit Jim had us all laughing.

But the best was yet to come as far as practical jokes that day. Jim's friend, Joe, played jokes on him regularly and Jim tried to get back at him as often as he could. Joe usually got the best of him. Not this time. Joe's mother is buried in the same cemetery. After we got home that afternoon, Jim called Joe on the phone and told him we had bought a piece of property that day. Joe was very surprised, of course, since he knew how serious Jim's illness was, but asked where the property was. Jim gave him bits and pieces of information. "It's in Lakeland. The address is 499 Garden View Lane," which really was the number of our plot and the name of the area we picked. Joe grew up in Lakeland

and had no idea where that address was. Jim finally said, "It's just a little way from your mother!"

Joe was speechless, swore at Jim and hung up on him. He admitted to us later that he hung up because he was crying and couldn't stop. Jim had gotten the best of Joe and was so proud of it. Jim couldn't stop laughing, and told the story to everyone. I have to admit, it was great to watch him laugh so much about playing the best prank between the two of them. Only Jim could make people laugh at a time when all we wanted to do was cry. That was my man.

On September 6, we went to an appointment with the doctor. Jim was in great pain and Dr. felt he should be admitted to the hospital to get his pain under control. She also spoke to us for the second time about calling Hospice. We had already met with them once, but hadn't signed up for Hospice yet. Jim was admitted to the hospital that day and stayed there for six days, until the doctors were sure his pain could be controlled at home. During his hospital stay jaundice set in, and on the morning of the 9th I came to the hospital and saw that Jim's eyes were yellow. I tried so hard not to show my shock and I did keep myself from crying. But I knew what the jaundice meant—that Jim's liver was beginning to shut down and it was only a matter of time until I lost my love and best friend. We both knew we would soon be separated. We went home on September 12 and started with Hospice on September 30.

We didn't know what to expect from Hospice. I guess we both thought it would be intrusive on the last days we had together. That wasn't true at all. They were there for whatever we needed, and I knew I could call them at any time for help or to answer questions, but otherwise, our days were as normal as possible. We had ordered a hospital bed and put it in the basement because that was Jim's "man cave," but he didn't want to sleep there at night. He made himself come up to the third floor every night to sleep in our bed. He was eating very little and stopped eating solid food on October 4. After that day, he drank a bit of chocolate milk every day until the 8th, and then just water on the 9th. I knew how these things went ... that he would stop eating a week to ten days before passing and stop drinking two to three days before. I didn't like knowing but I can say now that it did help me prepare myself and just concentrate on loving Jim rather than trying to force him to eat or drink when he just couldn't.

Jim still went for his Reiki sessions even though he had to practically drag himself there. He was scheduled for a session with Elizabeth on Friday, October 7, and Elizabeth had offered to come to our house any days that he felt too weak to go to her office. On Thursday night, Jim asked if I would call

Elizabeth to ask her to come to our house. That's when I knew the time was near. Friends and family had been coming to visit and spend time with Jim, but Jim couldn't visit for long periods of time and often fell asleep. When Elizabeth came to give Jim Reiki that Friday, I went downstairs so they could have quiet and privacy. About twenty minutes later, she came to get me and told me that Jim wanted me upstairs. I thought he was leaving me. I laid with him for a couple of hours, just loving him, talking to him, crying and trying to hold on to every minute and second I had left with him.

When I realized he wasn't ready, I called our families so that they could see him in case he left us within the day. He didn't. We had him for a few more days. Even then, Jim didn't lose his sense of humor. When our brother-in-law, Rod, went into the bedroom to see Jim and expected to say good-bye, Jim said, "False alarm!"

Jim went into a semi-coma state on Saturday, October 8. Sometimes he talked or whispered to us and sometimes he didn't. But I felt that he knew every single thing we were saying to him. The last few days he could barely move.

My brother, Woody, had come up on Friday even though I told him not to come. I had this crazy idea that I wanted to be alone with Jim in our house each night until he was gone. Woody came anyway, and as I was telling him he had to stay at my mother-in-law's, not my house, he told me Jim wanted Woody there with me. Suddenly I realized that I was being selfish; I wanted time with Jim, but if something happened during the night, like a fall, I would never have been able to handle that myself. So Woody stayed with me, and that was when I realized I desperately needed that company and help and that Jim felt more comfortable with Woody in the house with us.

Jim actually kept his humor right up until the very end. Woody's family came to visit Jim on the weekend, and my nephew brought his brand new little puppy, Tugboat, to see Jim. Jim had met Tug before, so when Andrew brought him upstairs to see Jim, Jim brightened right up and said, "Tugboat," in the way he would have said it before he was this sick. It was beautiful.

My sister-in-law, Martha, suggested we put a recliner in the bedroom so Jim could sit up, if he was able, rather than just lie in bed. We did, and on one of his last nights, when he really couldn't move himself, I woke up in the middle of the night and saw Jim sitting in the recliner. Somehow he had moved himself from the bed onto the chair. Truly, only God knows how.

I knelt next to him and could clearly see that he was communicating with whoever was in the room with us. People? Relatives? Angels? I did ask if they were anyone we knew and he shook his head, no. But he was communicating telepathically. I know that as sure as I know my name. Again, Jim's faith was evident. Now I fully realized how Jim could act so normal as he faced the end of his life as we knew it. He truly was communicating with loved ones on the other side. Several times while lying in bed, he would wave to someone and sometimes get this slight, beautiful smile on his face.

The next two nights in a row I woke up to Jim sitting on the side of our bed, even though he was barely able to move. Again he was communicating. Each of those three nights, I told him if they called him and wanted him, he should go. I knew he didn't want to leave me. I had heard so many times that our loved ones need our permission to leave. That was so true. I gave him permission several times, as much as I didn't want to lose him. But I loved him too much to be selfish and see him continue to suffer.

At this point in Jim's illness, it was not only excruciatingly hard on him, but also on all of us who loved him. He was in a semi-comatose state, and we didn't know if he was aware of his surroundings or not. This is where a cute story comes in. It's hard to believe I can use the phrase "cute story" at this point, since Jim was barely moving and rarely speaking.

One of the Hospice care providers had come to our house to teach me how to bathe Jim without causing him any pain or discomfort. She also showed Woody and me how to change the sheets. Jim was unable to move, so changing sheets with him in the bed was difficult. One evening, the sheets needed to be changed and Woody and I thought we could do it with no problem. Jim's family was all gathered downstairs, and Roberta asked if we needed her help. We told her no, that we could do it. Oh, how wrong we were! Although Jim had lost a lot of weight, moving a man of his size was much more difficult than we anticipated. In addition, Jim's feet and lower legs were very swollen and painful, so we wanted to avoid causing him any more pain. We quickly realized we needed help so we called Roberta to come upstairs.

Now, picture this: We were trying to move Jim to the other side of the bed and put the clean sheet under him. This required lifting him. Woody stood on the floor, I stood on the bed on the other side of Jim and Roberta was at the foot of the bed trying to lift Jim's feet carefully so as not to cause Jim any pain. We tried to move him in two different ways, but it just wasn't working. Trying one way, Jim's arm got stuck and the other way, we just couldn't move him. Now the three of us were standing over and around Jim, openly discussing what we could do to move him. We decided on another way to try and were starting a one-two-three countdown so we would all lift at exactly the same time. Suddenly, in a voice that was strong and clear Jim said, "I don't think this is a good idea!" We stopped … looked at each other … and all started laughing!

Jim was totally aware and obviously concerned that we weren't doing this very well! It certainly gave some relief to a very tense situation, but it also helped us to know that even in his coma state, he knew what was going on around him.

We had reached the point in Jim's illness when I had to give him morphine and Ativan to keep his pain at a minimum. I made sure he had both at the exact times he needed it around the clock. During the night of October 10, Jim had the most peaceful night of sleep. I was so surprised, since during the last several nights he had been so restless. My alarm was set for 5:00 a.m. to give him his morphine and Ativan, but when I woke up, he was sleeping like a baby and not uncomfortable at all. I decided to wait until I saw some movement to give him his morphine. When he made the slightest move, I gave him the meds.

Just a little while later, Jim woke up and his mind was as clear as the time we changed his sheets. But lying next to him with my arms around him, I could feel his heart beating unusually fast. That minute, he said in his clearest voice and very panicked, "Chris, help me … my heart … help me!" He said that several times. I quickly got my brother, called Hospice to ask them what to do, and they told me to give him a bit more morphine. Jim kept asking me for help as I held him and Woody held his hand.

Then he said the sweetest words I could ever hear at any time … "Chris, I love you so much!"

He asked me for help again, and then he stopped asking. His heart slowed down, and within a minute, two minutes … I don't know … my love had passed on and left his body. I just sobbed and sobbed and sobbed and held onto him as tightly as I could. Woody called our families and Hospice and then sat with Jimmy and me.

The roller coaster reached the end of its run on October 11, 2011, and my dear, sweet love was gone from my life, our families' lives and our friends' lives.

Jim's Reflections

I'd like to say that to believe in doctors wholeheartedly would be the best thing to do. I would also say that above all else, I believe that I know my body well, or knew it when I was on the planet. I knew how I felt. I knew what it was like to wake up with that burning feeling in my chest. I was tired of being sick. I was tired of constant issues that would come and go without really feeling as though I had any control over it. I was tired of a lot of things: having to make appointments, having to take time off from work, having to concern my wife. I was tired of being tired.

The major reason I was tired is because I felt, deep down, something might be wrong. Really wrong. I knew what I was feeling wasn't normal. That's as far as I could go. I joked all the time saying, "Mrs. Petosa ... I mean, Dr. Petosa," that she would find out the answer to everything. Although she thinks she was a nagging, pushy wife, I was glad she was there to advocate for me because, to be honest, I was scared so badly that something could be really wrong.

When you're diagnosed with something, you accept the diagnosis because you don't want to believe there's something "really" wrong. None of it made sense. None whatsoever.

We never really knew how my father died. We never really knew, but we imagined. What we thought, what we were told ... an aneurysm, a heart attack ... all the things that come along with "normal" death. High blood pressure and high cholesterol ran in our family; it was easy to assign a diagnosis from symptoms related to that. My busy lifestyle and the fact that I didn't have the greatest diet made the diagnosis of acid reflux seem obvious. Just a quick fix and it would be all better.

The day I had to have the test, Chris went with me, as always. Everyone was ready to call to find out the results. Deep down, I was expecting that it couldn't possibly be that bad—whatever it was could be fixed. That was my mentality. I believed the doctors could fix anything, but I also believed we could fix anything just by being in tune with our bodies. Somehow or other, my belief quickly failed.

When you're diagnosed with a problem like cancer, especially a cancer that was at least stage III immediately ... the first thing I was, I was mad. I was mad as hell. I was mad that the doctors didn't find it earlier. I was mad that they kept prescribing medication to fix the problem. I was mad at myself for not taking better care of my body. I was mad at everyone who was walking around alive and well. People who did terrible things to their body ... smoked, drank ... you name it, they did it, and they were still walking around at age 95.

When I got this diagnosis, I was mad. I never told anyone this, but that's the first thing that goes through your mind. What the f**k. I couldn't believe it. Everything in our lives had finally evened out and now this was happening. I just couldn't believe it. I was never one to feel sorry for myself, never one to look at the world and say, "Woe is me. I want what somebody else has." I worked hard, I did what was expected, I tried my best to be a good person and now this. What the f**k. That's all I kept saying in my mind. I didn't say it out loud; I was afraid that *would make people think I was ungrateful. That's the first thing that went through my mind.*

When we drove home that day, I was quiet. I just couldn't believe it. They told us to put all our affairs in order. This mass, whatever it was, was there. Somehow or other I can't help but wonder, "Could it have been there all along and they just overlooked it?" I can't instill blame now. I can't look back and say, "What were they, idiots? How could they not know this?" What I can say to you is, don't overlook the smallest of things. At the same time, don't be a hypochondriac. Use good common sense. Sitting at the edge of your bed every night because you can't swallow or you have indigestion isn't normal. That's just a no-brainer. Don't overlook the small things; the small things become big things. At the same time, don't be afraid to address the big things because you can make them smaller.

When I was diagnosed, I told you how I felt, I told you what I thought. Little did I know the treatment was going to be so severe. When I would see Elizabeth, she would say, "Sometimes the treatment we have is worse than the problem itself." That sure is the truth. When we were on our way to New York City, when we were on our way here and there and everywhere, I remember Chris telling me Elizabeth said, "Don't overlook the problem. Don't just let it pass by." We took her advice. I'm glad we listened somewhere deep in our subconscious. At least we knew. I'm glad we knew. Not knowing can be better than knowing and doing nothing, and I wasn't about to do nothing.

So we took our train rides, we did the tests, we took the pills. I say "we" because Chris was there every step of the way. My family, my friends, the people I loved and even the people I didn't care much for ... they were all around me. Everyone was there; sometimes that was too much for me.

Please don't misunderstand. I'm not unappreciative. I accepted every moment of their visits with grace, love and understanding because I know that's where it came from. But it was hard. It's hard when you're trying to recover, when you're trying to recoup, when you're trying to regain your strength, when you would do anything to have your life back to normal the way it used to be.

Then I had all these people telling me what I should do. In my mind I knew what to do. I had to fix the problem. We had to fix it. But at the same time, I didn't give a shit what anybody else thought or said. I just wanted the problem to go away.

I'm sure most people who have cancer think the same thing—you just want the problem to go away. I refused to bury my head in the sand but at the same time, the treatments became overwhelming. It just became too much. But we did it anyway ... Chris and I. We tramped to the doctor's office, we waited for hours sometimes, we watched the people go by ... people that were smoking as they left their chemo treatments ... people that you knew tried very hard not to take care of themselves. I didn't judge them. I understood. At the same time, I wasn't like that. I just wanted to live and be happy. I just couldn't believe this was happening to me.

We did the chemo treatments, I ate those gross shakes, I ate the muffins, I ate what my wife made me, my neighbors, my friends, my family. This one said to feed the problem, this one said to go without eating, this one said to eat too much, this one said to eat too little. All I wanted to do was have the problem gone. So I took the damn pills, I got the shots to keep my blood counts up, I smiled my biggest smile, I winked my biggest wink. I did everything I could. I went to church, I prayed, I did everything to the letter. Just like they told us to do. "They" being the ones who didn't have the problem.

The times I felt the best were when I went for treatments. Treatments that had absolutely nothing to do with doctors or nurses or any such thing. I would go lie on the table and get Reiki. I'd come home feeling deeply relaxed and well rested. I now know what Elizabeth meant when she would say, "You need to get some rest." Not with the TV, not with the radio playing, a book in my hand, a computer, a log book, whatever ... but to rest. To really be quiet. To visualize my body completely whole and well.

I do wonder now, if I had listened, would things be better? I can't thank everyone enough ... my wife, Elizabeth, Maryann ... all the people who were involved in helping with Reiki ... all the people who were on CaringBridge who sent their prayers of love ... all the friends who gathered 'round ... the visits to mass ... the people staring ... everyone. All those things made a difference. Believe it or not, it made a difference. I don't know how it made a difference, I don't know why it made a difference—I only know that the times I felt better were the times that I could just lay there, not do a thing ... and receive.

The greatest message I have for all of you reading this book is to receive. Let people help you in ways you haven't heard of before. Use good common sense. Some people lack that, I know, but do your best. Let people help you in ways that they know work—things that have been documented for thousands of years. Chris didn't know, no one really knew that I would check things out when no one was looking. I would try to find out as much as I could, and I knew that what I was trying to do was get better at any cost.

No matter how much money you have, no matter what kind of job you have, the one thing I knew for sure is that I must have a soul. Like every human being does, I must have a soul. And if that soul fills with light, it can accomplish *anything. That was my journey. To find out how to bring more light to my soul. I knew it.*

With all that had happened over all those months, things were quite a blur. This medication makes you sleepy, this one makes you cold, this one gives you diarrhea, this one makes you nauseous. You never really know. You're only grateful that it's there. That's what I was ... grateful for every moment. Even though it was hard, I was still grateful.

You can imagine our elation when both of us found out there were no more tumors on that scan! All we prayed for ... there were no more tumors! There were no more significant factors that showed there was a problem. All things were gone—all systems go! This was on September 24, 2010.

That summer was the happiest summer of my life. I turned 48. We laughed, we joked, we had fun, we did everything possible to enjoy life. More so than usual. We had more to be grateful for. Of all the things that you want in life ... if you're a man, your wife ... if you're a woman, your husband, a companion, your child ... it doesn't matter; you name it. You want someone, but most of all you want "you." You want "you" to be as normal as "you" possibly can.

I knew the cancer treatments had played a number on my body. My hands started to go numb, my feet, too, and my face at times. It was just uncomfortable to be in my body. I figured I could live with the discomfort forever. As long as I was here, that's all I cared about.

When they did the scan and found the tumors, we were in total shock, especially since we had had so much fun that whole summer. We rested, we laughed, we made love, we went with our friends, we did things in our normal way like we always wanted to do. That's what we lived for ... just to be a normal, everyday, happy couple. So when the cancer came back, I have to admit my hope was depleted. I just couldn't believe it. To see the look on Chris's face when the doctor said the tumors were back in the liver ... it was just unbearable to see. She was so good about hiding things, or at least she tried to be, but I knew deep down that when it came back in the liver again ... just from what I heard, what I read, what I listened to, what the doctor said ... it was bad. When I saw the look on Elizabeth's face, she, too, tried to hide it. When I went back for Reiki with Maryann and talked to her, when I talked to anyone, it seemed as though during that time frame, from what I can remember, the fact that it was back in my liver ... that was not good. I didn't know how I knew, I just knew.

But we tried everything. Doctor appointments became frequent again, different chemo treatments, more of those shakes, more people to visit, more prayers were heard ... we tried everything.

The day of Christmas Eve, when Chris had that "episode," my first thought was, "I'm going to kill you! You ask me that question one more time and I'm going to kill you!" Not really, just figuratively. You can imagine my surprise. Here, you think, wow ... the one person you depend on in your life, and they depend on you, too ... that's when it all really started to sink in. There were so many people that I depended on to do "for" me, as well as what I did for myself. However, there were so many people who depended on me. It didn't wear me down; it made me feel good. It made me feel like I mattered. When you're loved that way, that's all that matters.

Standing there next to her in the emergency room, all the time that it took ... sure, it's funny now when we look at it, and it was kind of funny the first hundred times she asked the same questions, but then it grated on my nerves. My biggest concern was if I leave and she has one of these episodes, what the heck is she going to do? Is she going to know enough to call somebody? Are they going to know what to do? All these thoughts ran through my mind. So it wasn't the frustration of having to answer the questions again and again, or finally, "Look at your paper!" which became a big joke later on. It was the idea that if I wasn't there, who was going to tell her to look at her paper? Who was going to tell her how to work the washing machine if the hoses came undone? Who was going to tell her how to fix the back steps? Who was going to show her all these things? Every night when I would go to bed, I would pray that all the people I knew would continue to help her.

I'd like to say that I kept my hope as high as it could be, but every time I would go for a visit ... .not a visit to the doctor ... every time I would go for Reiki and try to ask questions, I always got the "You need to rest, Jim," answer. Then I knew there was more to be said, but no one would say it. I kept up the treatments; I did it anyway. I did what the doctors suggested. What they suggested made me feel worse. I'm not telling any of you not to do what the doctors say. I am telling you that if you have the opportunity, take the opportunity. If someone offers to you to be a channel of light, accept it. Graciously accept it, because it works. It helps. At the very least, you feel better. Even if it's just for a little while. That's all you want ... to feel better just for a little while.

When the days came down to the slower lifestyle that we began to live, friends called on the phone, people were in and out of the house, the house was full, then it was empty, visitors came from far away ... all with that look on their face, that sadness in their eyes.

May I suggest to you if you're a caregiver or a visitor of someone that you love who has cancer or any other problem, get that look off of your face. Be honest and true and tell the person how you feel, whether it's that you love them, that you're mad at them, that you forgive them or that you don't. Tell them you'll miss them if you know they're leaving. Tell them what a difference they made in your life. Put it in a letter, put it in a note, or just say it to them—whatever you feel comfortable doing—but don't sit there and stare with pity in your face. Because I didn't feel pity for myself; I only wanted a way to get better. And I wanted a way to make people feel better who had to sit there and stare at me knowing I didn't feel well.

As the days grew closer ... closer to my exit, when we knew the time was near, my wife took me one day for a Reiki session with Elizabeth. We ran into Maryann. That day was the first time I saw that look in her eyes. Elizabeth and I had talked in the office for quite some time about maybe taking a little break from the chemo treatments and what that might be like. All the things that she said ... she was honest, she was direct. She knew that I felt like shit. There's no other way to say it. It was easy to see. She knew I was tired. Most of all, I knew I was tired. Leaving behind my wife, I knew was inevitable ... leaving behind my family, my friends, the people I cared about, our animals. We did our best to make the house comfortable, getting it ready, doing all the things we knew to do, but that day it was significant. We knew we were all out of hope. Hope for staying in the body, that is. Not hope for the soul's continuation.

What I never told Chris, what I never told Maryann ... Elizabeth and I talked very candidly that day. I said very clearly, "I'm not afraid to die. I'm just worried what it will be like for the others here left behind." Not that I'm a superhero, but I knew that I would miss them, and I knew there wasn't a f**king thing I could do about it. But I knew I would miss them.

So we did my treatment and I had the talk with Chris. We had already made the decision to stop. Once you make that decision, you know you're headed for someplace else. When we finally did the reading ... it's already been explained, it's already been mentioned ... it wasn't just a sense of fear that I had, but a sense of relief. An overwhelming sense of relief because you know that no matter what, there's a part of you that will live forever with people. Perhaps it's the things you do to a home, perhaps it's the difference you make in their lives in some stupid small way, some weird funny joke they remember, a big hug that you gave when someone was feeling down ... those were the things I tried to focus on. Not would I be remembered for my greatness, but would I be remembered for the little things? Because that's what I remembered most from people. I was grateful, yes, for the people who gave me what we needed, but I was more grateful for the things that people don't notice. Grateful for the everyday things in life ... good food, lasting friendships, people around us ... everything that mattered most. That's where my gratitude came from.

When it came really close to the time of exit, within days, we made that call to Elizabeth and asked her to come to give me Reiki. We asked that nobody else come and disrupt us ... just give us a chance to be in our home by ourselves. But we weren't by ourselves. The room was filled with Angels and souls who had gone before me. That was really comforting to me, more so than anything else.

By this time, my brother-in-law, Woody, who was just like a brother to me, had come to comfort Chris and help with whatever was going to happen. Both knew the souls were in the room by seeing the looks and reactions on my face. They really knew. They knew something was going to happen soon.

I wanted to be sure to say goodbye to my wife before what I knew was coming, before I'd close my eyes forever and be gone from the physical body. Those moments are precious, something that you never forget. If you have the opportunity, if you're ever with someone who's going to leave their body, bring them comfort. Sometimes, just sitting quietly with them, holding their hand, letting them know that somebody is there with them is exactly what they want. Don't try to break the silence by making a joke or laughing. That's disturbing. Just keep things quiet, play some soft music. Don't force things down their throat. Don't cause them any kind of disruption, because they're getting ready for a journey. A journey that's hard to describe unless you're prepared to know what will happen. And prepared, I was. Everything was ready and I knew I was on my way.

As I said, in the morning ... prior to my exit ... I knew I was going. It was the saddest and happiest day of my life. Sad because I left behind so many I loved, but happy knowing I'd be reunited with those who would always love me. So remember, if you have the privilege of being with someone when they're ready to leave, just sit quietly. Listen for what you may not always hear, and hear what you may not always listen for.

Be comfortable with the fact that life goes on forever and that the soul's life extends an insurmountable time, a time we can't imagine. Just remember that's coming. Even the smallest of children are the least afraid when it's time to go.

Just remember ... you keep going.

So I say to you, no matter the amount of pills you take or the diet you change, some things are just not changeable. There is no bargaining with God. When it's your time, it's your time to go. That day, I knew it was my time.

So off I went, flying away ... ready, willing and able, like always, to make the best of what a bad situation might be or what the best situation could ever be.

Read on and you'll learn more. Having cancer isn't the worst thing in the world. Healing the problem isn't the worst thing in the world. Trying to decide what to do while you have the cancer is the worst thing. Stop thinking about it. Stop worrying about it.

When the doctor says, "Get your affairs in order," instead of worrying about your finances (yes, that is important), instead of worrying about saying your goodbyes, worry about what you believe. What you believe strongly affects where you'll go and what will happen to you. To "you," meaning your soul. "Get your affairs in order" can mean so many things. If you ever hear those words, find out first what "Get your affairs in order" means to you.

If you're looking for answers, you needn't look further than what your heart will tell you to be true.

Ladies and gentlemen, let us be a part of your next journey. We hope you've enjoyed flying with us today.

— Captain Jim Petosa

Into the Beyond

My father died quickly and unexpectedly from a massive heart attack, and I lost my husband from a nineteen-month ordeal with cancer. I was not prepared for either, and neither is easier than the other. As far as grief and grieving are concerned, there are pros and cons to each way. But I don't believe one is "easier" than the other.

I know there are stages to grief. I don't know them by heart, but I do know that what I felt immediately was probably a combination of shock and denial. It may sound strange to say I was in shock since Jim went through nineteen months of cancer and followed expected steps near the end of his life. But shock is what I felt.

Following Jim's death that morning, my brother called family, and Jim's family came immediately to see him one more time before he was taken from our house. My sister left work and drove to our house immediately. Everything moved so quickly. Several of my good friends came to our house to give support and even cleaned my house for me. It was such a shock that I barely even remember the specifics of the next few days. Jim passed on Tuesday morning, the wake was set for Friday evening and the funeral was to be held on Saturday. We managed to get through those days, although it was quite a blur to me, as I'm sure it was to all of our families.

Jim's wake was simply amazing. I know there are many people who plan ahead and make their wishes known that they don't want any wake or calling hours, but Jim did not do that. We did plan ahead to a certain degree, picked out our cemetery plots, and without talking about it, we did plan for calling hours. There is no doubt that calling hours are for the living, and some truly cannot or do not want to go through that. But I, and I'm sure our families, were grateful for Jim's calling hours. The wake was set for 4:00 p.m. to 7:00 p.m., but the last people came through the line at 8:45 p.m.. It was raining outside, and people came into the funeral home soaking wet because they waited outside in that rain just to pay respects to Jim, our families and me. It was very comforting to see so many people who loved us all and were willing to wait two hours to show us their love and support.

I couldn't imagine that anything could make me feel better than the support of family and friends at Jim's calling hours, but I was proven wrong by his funeral the next day. We loved our church; our church has always been a beautiful community for us, full of love and fellowship. We have a priest who co-celebrated the mass with a friend and former priest of our parish, as well as our parish deacon and another dear friend who is also a deacon. Many priests only allow one eulogy during the mass, but our priest knew how well-loved Jim was, and allowed three people to speak about Jim—his brother, Paul, my brother's wife, Martha, and Jim's boss, Bruce. (These eulogies can be found in their entirety on my website, www.chrisfrankpetosa.com)

Jim was a pilot. He was often gone for a week, two weeks, or more at a time. Although I was devastated, had that constant familiar pain in my stomach all the time and couldn't seem to stop crying, there was a part of me that kept feeling like Jim was away on a trip; he'd be home eventually. That denial passed fairly quickly. Jim wasn't coming home no matter how much I wanted him to, or how much I begged, pleaded or prayed to God. Two of my college friends who didn't know Jim all that well honored him with a comment I feel sums up Jim Petosa to a T. They told me that hearing about Jim at the funeral made them want to be better people when they left that church. What better compliment can there be?

Jim's Reflections

I know how you both love to be so efficient and you like things in steps and direct order, so I will oblige because I've done that for so long and it's what I'm used to! When the reader reads this, they'll laugh because it's really not so cut and dried. But for the average mind, it is cut and dried. I'm not saying that either of you are average; certainly, I would never suggest such a thing. However, I will say that for all people who read the book, we want it to be well understood.

From what I remember, it was really kind of silly. At first I felt like a clumsy baby as it is first born into the world. Everything from the very first moment that you are born—ever—it literally does flash before your eyes. I used to think that was some kind of crazy myth about life, death and near-death situations, but I saw everything. I saw myself being born, I saw what my father was doing and I saw what my mother was doing and the trouble of having me (in a discreet way, Mom, so don't worry!). I remember seeing everything. I remembered being a little child. All these memories just kept flashing up.

Doctors and scientists might say that was just my nervous system reflecting what had happened during life. Our brains and thoughts are so complicated because the brain stores so much information. Call it science, call it what I wanted to remember, call it whatever you want. All I know is that I remembered. I remembered where we grew up, what we did, who we played with, all my old childhood memories, up through school ... I kept going and going. It went very fast—faster than the speed of light, almost, if you can imagine that.

As that happened, I could feel myself, my soul, a part of me that is hard to describe, coming up out of my body. I could feel myself slipping away from Chris. Not slipping away from her in a way that I couldn't reach her, just slipping away from her in a way that I couldn't feel her touching me any longer. That part was very difficult because I remember how much she wanted me to stay and I knew how much I wanted to be there. But my body just could not take another thing.

It was okay. Woody was sitting in the chair. Chris and Woody were in the room, and I saw everyone. I saw everyone around me. They were all waiting with Woody and Chris, just so that they would be okay or at least the best that they could be, given the circumstances.

On the other end of the situation, there they were. They looked like escorts, like if you were going to be using an escort service. Don't take it the wrong way, Elizabeth. We know where your mind goes with these things. We're talking about an escort service to a place that is reputable! They took my hand, and as they did, I was going through the motions of ... I remember I kept saying to them, "I want to go back. I want to turn around. I want to go back to Chris. I want to go back."

They kept saying, "No, it's time to come with us."

There was a woman—several of them—waiting but it was more as though they were a distance away. One I knew I recognized. I was so in awe of her that I didn't go to her. I could hear them all calling me so I went to them. I could see my dad and he was laughing and saying, "We're here for the party! It's time to get ready for the party." Big Bill was there. There were so many people—people I had met from all over the world who had crossed over, people who knew my soul and recognized me somehow. They were all there waiting for me.

When I went to the next level, so to speak, it was as if I knew I was no longer physical. I was up and I looked back into the room. I hovered at the ceiling. I saw Chris lying on the bed and Woody was sitting in the chair. So many were there with the two of them. Then I got up above the house and literally kept going up. It was like being in a hot air balloon. A better way to describe it is "flying," which we've talked about ad nauseam, per other people. However, it was like flying.

So there they were. They were all laughing. And they had it prepared! They were laughing, not at me, but with me because they knew I was coming. They had everything set up. It was like a giant party! (And we all know how much I like big parties!) That's exactly the way that it seemed to me. They were excited. So I was leaving the body, leaving the world, but I was going into the new world.

What surprised me most of all was the fact that there was not a lot of what most people describe as "light" in the very beginning of the tunnel. I could see the light in the distance and I just wanted to go toward it because all of it was so peaceful. When I was greeted, as I got further through the tunnel, I asked them (I don't know how I knew to ask—I just did) if I could stay and be with them until they could be on their own and there was some kind of odd agreement. But I was so tired. My soul ... it was as if I just needed to lie down. I just couldn't take another moment. Fatigue like you wouldn't believe! But the closer I moved toward the light, the less and less fatigue I had.

When I got to the party, I celebrated, I laughed, I relived old memories, saw people I had known ... people that remembered me from other times in my life as well as other lives, people beyond compare, souls that were just as excited. I could literally see a doorway beyond that, as if there were a door casing or a doorway, and although it sounds absurd, it was a place I knew I would go back to when things on the Earth were complete.

So I watched from afar, I watched from that place. We had our party, we had our laughs, we had our talks, we had our good memories that we shared and there I was—just in that spot. And I watched. I watched everything that was going on with Chris ... all the arrangements, everything that was done ... everybody was there. I watched and I watched and I just looked. It was as if looking through a fishbowl or a looking glass where I couldn't really be a total part of it, but I wasn't apart from it or away from it either. And I just watched. I watched when my mother came to see my body, I watched my siblings come, I watched everyone come. I watched them come and take me from the house. I watched how Chris could barely stand up, she was so tired. I watched the whole thing. And there wasn't one thing I could do.

I remember the next few days, but only vaguely. They told me that it would be best to rest because when I would go back "down" or back to the scene of the crime, so to speak, I would be tired once again. I wanted the energy and the ability to be able to go back, so I did just as they suggested. "They" being the ones who were so helpful.

So I watched and I watched some more until I grew tired again, and literally went and rested. I lay down. I was quiet and peaceful, almost as if I was floating. The next day, when people were up and moving around, nobody cared much about doing anything, and quite honestly, neither did I. I just watched. But only for a little while on this day. It is said in scripture that on the third day, He rose again. I imagined that this is what Jesus must have done. He must have rested. It's a lot of work. It's a lot of work for your soul. Knowing you're going to go back and interact ... excited to do so, but not having the energy to do it ... that part was more than I wanted to face at that time.

The next day went much like the first. I saw Chris; saw that she couldn't stop sobbing. I saw her family. I saw Kathy trying to find a dress to wear. I chuckled to myself a little bit and wondered why they didn't just go shopping. I guess they just didn't feel like it.

So I just watched. I watched my mom. I watched Paul and Roberta, Theresa and Marianne ... I watched them all. I watched everybody that I knew. The good part was that I was there with people that I loved beforehand ... my grandmother, Carmen, various and sundry aunts, uncles, cousins and people that weren't my family but people who remembered me. Right now, I can't tell you how they remembered me. I can only tell you they said they remembered me from a long time ago.

I watched them writing furiously ... Paul trying to find the right words, Martha always having the right words and knowing exactly what to do or say, and Bruce so kind in his words. I watched my friends. I thought Rick would pass out when he heard the news. I couldn't tell if it was relief or just pure sadness. Everyone ... the nieces and nephews, the family ... everyone ... I just kept watching.

The morning of the wake, I was somewhat prepared. Why? Because they coached me. They showed me what would happen, explained to me a little bit about what I would do, what I wouldn't do, what I would be allowed ... almost as if I had boundaries as to what was going to take place next. So there we were—it was time for the wake. It was pouring rain. I was laughing because when I left, I didn't have much on! So I was curious as to whether anyone would be able to see that or not. I knew Chris wouldn't care! But I tried to look my best.

I watched as they all stood by the casket and stared at my dead body. I say it like that because that seems so morbid now that I've had the chance to see it. Just a dead body lying there. Some good memories, some people trying to smile, people not knowing what to say. The whole time, I stood right next to her, sometimes behind her. She got very weak in the knees. All I was worried about was getting her through the next few hours.

I stayed and I watched the people coming in. I had no idea, for such a jerk that I could be sometimes, that I had so many people who really loved me that much. They actually waited in the rain. I just kept shaking my head at some, thinking, "Are you foolish? Come in out of the rain!" Then I felt this sense of honor that was beyond belief, a sense of gratitude knowing that we had so many who cared about us. My one big hope was that they would all be there because I knew once this was over, I would have to go back and I wouldn't be with her. But I picked out from the crowd who was going to help, who she would never see again, who was helpful, and I waited until it was done.

Now when you don't have a body, you feel like ... eh ... it makes no difference. You can just wait there as long as you want. But I remember feeling how cold it was. I don't want to go into the drastic measures that they do when they change your body to "prepare" it for the view. That seems senseless at this time. But they do. They take great care. They make you wear this ridiculous suit. They do all things that ... well ... you can use your imagination with that part.

At any rate, back to the topic. When it was all done and we could leave, they all just stood there staring. I kept saying to Chris, "I'm right here! I'm right behind you! I'm right here!" Everybody just wanted to stand there and stare. They waited and they waited, and I didn't get up from that casket, as much as they all wanted me to. As much in my heart as I wanted to, I didn't get up. The funeral director did all he could to be cordial, be appropriate, do and say all the right things.

There I was, just standing there wondering, "Well, what the hell do we do now?" My mother invited everyone to come to her house for something to eat so we all went there. I decided I'd go along for the fun. They ate food and tried to have a good time. They tried to muster up conversation ... cold, wet and tired. To all those who read this and will be leaving their body, never think those things are fun. They're not fun. Everyone was exhausting and exhausted, including me. I thought for sure that I would have much more energy than I did at that time, but I was exhausted.

When everyone left, and the last goodbyes were said, I was so glad for Chris so she could go home and maybe rest a little bit for the next day. I was never sure when I had to do these things on Earth which was worse – staring at the dead body or listening to the boring things that we say about each other, sometimes true, sometimes not ... when we do the eulogies, when we do the services and our ceremony. If I could do it all again and plan a little better, I'd make sure they had one party of a lifetime instead of a funeral. A time they would never forget! Because I was so sick, and I really didn't care about food or drinking or any of those things, we didn't have a party before I left. So then you get the tradition, the norm. My suggestion? Have a party instead. Have a party when you first find out whether you live or die, because, well, you could still have a party, regardless. So do what you want, but do it well. Really live it up to the best that you can possibly do.

Chris went back to the house and I went back to where I needed to go. They were waiting for me when I got there, knowing I would need the rest and that I wouldn't rest if I waited there with her. So, away I went again, back to where I started ... way up inside, but not high enough to leave completely. Just long enough to rest.

The next morning was okay. We all knew what to expect. We all knew how to behave. Everybody did what was appropriate. And then they show up. And they read these stories about you. I remember feeling so sad. When they say that people die and they go to this wonderful paradise, they should probably get their stories straight, whoever "they" are, because you still feel. It takes a little while for that feeling to go away. I'll tell you I'd rather have that feeling than not be able to feel at all. At least at that time, that's what I remember.

I sat with her, right next to her, as usual. I can't remember who sat next to her physically, but I sat on their lap. (No offense to whoever that was!) I listened to my brother. He's quite a character! I opened my mouth to show him a Train Wreck, but that didn't matter. He didn't see me. I made faces at him, danced around him and laughed my ass off. It was pretty funny!

I guess the lesson here is don't wait until someone leaves to tell them how much they mean to you. I did that when I was alive, or at least I tried to. I tried to make the calls—not just the "owe to" call or the appropriate calls to make, but the calls because I wanted to. Because I loved very easily, I wanted to call people and say, "How ya' doin? What've you been up to? Where'd you go?" To my nieces, "Who've you been with?" To my nephews, "I hope you did the right thing!" To my siblings ... well, I could just say whatever I wanted to them because they just said anything they wanted right back. So I did whatever I could—all the time.

Here we were at the funeral. We were sitting there and listening. Chris was sobbing. It was the worst sob I ever heard in my life. All her friends were around. Her mom was there.

Her mother. I loved her so much and still do. She's with me now, here, when you can pin her down for a minute! She's usually off exploring or doing something. We all know how Wanda was. I heard what she said. She insisted that she didn't belong in the procession in the same spot as my mother and Chris. Then she said she was willing, and I was so honored. She could not see; she could barely hear. But what a woman. She waited. She stood right with Chris. She waited every minute with her. She did the absolute best she could. That was a sweet, sweet honor—one that I will cherish for all of eternity.

My mother was there. She is such a strong woman who I deeply loved and admired. My siblings were there. They listened as everyone said the good things. I listened, too. I was deeply touched and honored by each one. I found it absolutely unnecessary at the same time. But still, there's something inside of every one of our souls that says, "Wow, maybe I did do okay after all. I wonder what's next."

We went through the whole process. We finished up the services, the mass was said, the songs were sung and we had to leave in that long line. Nobody was laughing, nobody was carrying on and having a good time. Despite my effort, nobody did anything but cry.

We got to the cemetery in the pouring rain. My first response was what the f**k! Everybody's going to get soaked and they're not going to stand out here in the pouring rain. Now, most people wouldn't like that language, but the reality is it's just a word. It's not directed at anyone. It was just upsetting the way it all turned out. Not because I cared or wanted some big salute, but because I wanted people to be able to sit down and stay dry for at least a little while. For God's sake, everybody stood out in the rain the night before. So we waited and we waited. Eric played Taps and I applauded. I know you're not supposed to do that, but gosh, I just couldn't help myself. Everybody stood there with their head down, nobody making eye contact, nobody able to look at one another. My mother on one side of Chris, my mother-in-law on the other side. Everyone gathered around and there they stood in the rain, waiting. For what, I'm not sure, but we were all there waiting.

Then, it was the most amazing thing. They were there again, the same ones who helped me leave my body before, the same ones who told me it was time to go. They surrounded my family, my friends, the people I knew and the people I barely knew. There was this ring of light all around them, and there were these "beings" for lack of a better word to call them—not like Martians, so don't get too excited. They were light beings. Giant beings. Hard to tell if they were male or female, but they kept motioning to me that it was time to go. At least for then, it was time to go. At first, I was not happy, wondering what was everyone going to do without me and what I would do without them. I knew somehow we would all manage. They'd all stick together, and we would all manage.

And so I followed the light. It was absolutely amazing! This light and this sound that was unbelievable. I was so grateful I could stay and be with them. I just turned around with one last look and decided I'd better go now while I have the chance. Who knows what will happen next? The whole time, I kept hearing Elizabeth say, "When they come for you, you have to go." I thought she meant the first time. I had no idea this is what she was talking about.

So I did. With one on either side, I left, as if I was floating, flying as free as a bird ... going higher and higher, still watching them. But this time it was different. I was looking ahead. I was waiting to see what would come. As we went higher and higher and higher, we ended up at this space—that's the only way I can describe it to you—a place of pure, white, beautiful ... the most peaceful place you can imagine.

My eyes were open and there she was ... the woman who greeted me the morning I left my body. I sort of recognized her, but not in the way that you recognize an old friend—more of an image you create in your mind. I knew in one tiny split second, in your time, it was her. Mother Mary. I stood there and gazed in amazement. The one we ask for protection of our children. The one we are grateful for when we pray for our mother. It was her, right there, telling me it would all be okay. She smiled the sweetest smile I have ever seen on anyone ... difficult to explain. What was so significant is that there was a body but not a body like you would imagine, not a body like you would think or guess or one you can even make up in your mind. It's more as though it's an image.

Then they were all there. Saint Francis who I had prayed to for so long and Jesus, of course. They were all there. They were all telling me that this time I was going to be here for good, or at least for now. Until they give me my next tour of duty! And the sound ... I went with them toward the sound. It was indescribable. It's not a sound you hear on Earth. Literally, the Heavens opened and the sound was so loud and clear, unlike any sound you can ever imagine from Earth.

I'd like to say I was sad, I'd like to say that I missed the Earth, that I missed my body, that I missed everyone. But I didn't—not in the way you might think. The love was so great. Imagine you can love someone and then multiply that by a million; that's a lot of love! It was so serene and peaceful—absolutely unconditional. You're not asked to describe it, nor are you quizzed on it, how much you knew about, how much you didn't; you're just grateful. There's no other way I can describe it. Just grateful.

Then the doors opened. I forgot to tell you about Saint Peter. Sometimes I used to think those stories were big jokes, but there they were ... all standing, holding the space, just waiting for me to come, expecting the best. And here I was, all this time concerned about whether I was going to make it through or not, and then it was time. It's as if you walk into a kingdom but it's so peaceful. It's indescribable. It's not a big castle or a wide open space. It's hard to describe. All I remember is how I felt and how much of my life was going to be spent here instead of on the Earth. I was so happy! So much love surrounded me, filled me. Absolutely spectacular!

Just like I was told, we never really die. When you're a kid, you think you're going to live to be an old, old, old, old man. Ancient. That's not what it means. We continue to grow. That's when all the learning started—right then and there. You can still see the Earth, but you don't really think about it. And it's not up or down;

it's everywhere. It's a space of existence that's all around. It's hard to describe. All you do, though, once you're here ... all that you can ever imagine is possible in terms of love and peace. That's the way it is.

And so they start to condition you. It's not just the Catholics that are there, either! So please get that out of your head if you have it in there as you're reading this. It's not "just" the Protestants or "just" the Methodists. It's those who truly work on your soul, those who truly seek what else is available, what else is possible and what isn't possible.

There I stood wondering what to do, and I was guided every step of the way. I did ask questions about Chris and every time I did, they were avoided. It was as if I was being prepared. Prepared for my new home. And so I waited. But this time not with sadness ... just joy. I waited, excited about what was next.

You lose track of time when you're here. The only way you know that time has passed is that we can see the difference in people when you go back, if you go back. I don't want to jump ahead of myself. I want to stay in order. God only knows Chris likes order.

It was time for our first visit. I'll never forget the look on her face. She walked in. It was close to Christmas time. I remember seeing the date Chris wrote on her paper: 11-10-11. Elizabeth was her usual self—calm, easy and waiting—just making sure everybody was okay. When Chris couldn't stop crying, she hugged her. She commented on the red sweater. Elizabeth kept trying to ask me, "Jimmy, should we talk now or should we wait?" I just stood there and asked Elizabeth to help make her ready. I knew it was going to be a long night. At first Chris thought she was coming for a Reiki treatment. She just stood there and couldn't stop sobbing. I didn't laugh at her, nor did I laugh at Elizabeth. Elizabeth cried, too. She tried not to, but she did. She held Chris's hand and said, "Do you want to talk to him now? He's here."

They left the Reiki room and walked down the long, winding hall to get to Elizabeth's office. It was like a maze back there. She sat down in the chair and helped Chris get herself together before she started. As you can imagine, I was a little apprehensive knowing how fragile Chris was, knowing she had just come from the doctor, knowing that she was just a mess even after a month. When I say "mess" I'm not trying to tease her, just give you an idea. She was a wreck. She looked like she hadn't slept in weeks. She was tired but she kept moving.

There I was, standing in the purple room; lavender really, if you ask a girl. There I was in the room, looking at both of them, waiting for Elizabeth to start ... saying her prayer as usual. Now I know why she does it. It's formality. It's respect. We do have to have tremendous respect for the other world. That's where we're all going someday.

Then she let me talk. At first, I kept trying to tell Chris to calm down and that it was all going to be okay. I told her who I saw and who I didn't see when I went to the afterlife. Elizabeth had her eyes closed. She sat there, listened to what I was saying and told Chris every word. I never did thank her for that ... sitting with her and not getting mad at me when I yelled at her and said, "Open your eyes! Open your eyes, for crying out loud!" So she did.

Chris was confused. She was having another "episode." I waited right there with them. We did all the things that were necessary. Elizabeth found Chris's phone, called the doctor—everything that was supposed to be done. I just sat with Chris. Elizabeth wouldn't leave her alone; she wouldn't even let her go to the bathroom by herself. She walked her to the bathroom and made sure she had her attention, waited for her to come out, helped her wash her hands, went back to the room and got on the phone and started calling people.

The office was downstairs in a medical building. Right upstairs was Urgent Care. Off we went to Urgent Care. And we waited. We waited like all people do, in the waiting room. Elizabeth was sitting there with Chris, holding her hand, and Chris kept asking the same question over and over again. I kept laughing, saying, "See? See what it's like?" But Elizabeth felt sorry. Not sorry for her, just sorry with her. She answered the question eight million times, at least, and waited for the doctor to come. They called her name and took her in the back room. Elizabeth sat on the table with her. When the doctor started asking questions, Elizabeth answered for her. Then she was embarrassed because the doctor told her to be quiet. That kind of pissed me off—she was just trying to help. I realize he was just doing his job but Elizabeth was very concerned and was just trying to help. They didn't believe Chris at first, which really frustrated me. But we went through everything we needed to go through, and we waited.

Elizabeth left the room and went to call my sister, Marianne, to let her know what was happening and ask her to come for Chris. Then Elizabeth waited in the room until Marianne came for her. The doctor asked a hundred questions. Chris just kept asking, "Did Jimmy come? Did Jimmy come? Did Jimmy come?" No one really knew what she meant except Elizabeth, which was kind of funny in and of itself because everyone should know that, yes, we do come. That yes, we do care.

We do watch. We do wait. We do listen. Not because we're made to, but because we want to. "We" being those in the other world, on a different plane, so to speak.

Then it was done. Chris went home with Marianne. Elizabeth waited and called later to check on Chris. Marianne went through a lot of trouble to figure out what medicines Chris was taking, what she had taken and what she still needed to take. She called everyone in the book. And all would be okay for one more day.

That's what Elizabeth tried to tell her—just get through one day at a time. If you can get through today, you can get through tomorrow. Just one more day. That's good advice from this perspective because we have no clue whatsoever how much one more day is, unless we watch you. "You" being the ones who are left there. So listen to some wisdom: If you can get through one day, you can get through the next day. You may feel like you can't or that it never will happen, but you can. You do. I've seen it with my own two eyes, so to speak. I know that it's true. The human condition can do everything, but the soul's condition can do even more.

So get started now. Learn and grow. Listen to what I tell you from here on out. Not in a demanding way, but in an obedient, loving way. Listen to what is being said, because you are being prepared for an event that is hard to describe. Really listen, put all other thoughts out of your mind and really feel how you feel. I promise you if you get quiet on the inside, it's so much easier to enjoy what's happening on the outside.

I'll tell you more as time moves on......as Chris and Elizabeth write and work. They're fastidious. It's important for people to know—just the general public— what happens ... the nonsense that doesn't ... it's important. It's important because it has to do with the way the soul grows. The more you know about your soul when you're on the Earth, the easier it is to adapt to this world. It's much easier to continue and stay connected with those that you are so deeply in love with, and carry on your soul's purpose. Nobody wants to forget their loved ones, nobody wants to forget their friends, but the reality is you grow into something more. We'll talk about that in future times.

As an onlooker and someone who has poured his heart and soul into this work, literally, I would encourage every person reading this book to read all the readings. It is my hope that reading these would be to every soul's advantage. Contained in each one, my soul's plight was answered. It makes my soul so happy to be able to share with all of you my experiences to help you, perhaps guide you and be with you as you experience yours.

Remember to take care of yourself. Some people drink, some people take drugs, some people eat, some people don't eat at all, some people just want to sleep. Whatever your body tells you to do that's good for you, do it. If you need to sleep, rest. If you're hungry, eat. If you're thirsty, get a drink. But be good to yourself during these days because we watch you and we worry. Take good care of yourself. You'll be glad you did.

Enough said for now. I'll be back to tell you more at another time.

Just know there's always a process. It's never an event. You're never waiting when you're here for the next thing to happen and the next thing that makes you happy. You only "are" happy. You can still, and do, have that same happiness when you're on Earth. Enjoy every moment of your life. Tell the ones you love how much you love them. Make peace with the ones that you don't. Open your mind and heart to what is possible, not just what you've learned, but what you might learn if you listen.

Ladies and gentlemen, make amends now if need be. You never know who the passenger sitting next to you will be on your next flight. So be kind, be open to the circumstances of others and be grateful for your safe arrival.

Until the next time we are in flight,

— Captain Jim Petosa

PART TWO

Reflections of Yesterday and Looking Ahead to Tomorrow

You've read our story and "lived through" our experience with Jim's illness. Our story is a heartbreakingly familiar one which many have lived or will live. We hope Jim's reflections give insight that is important in life whether you are living with terminal illness or not.

As you might guess, someone who lived through the events of this story would think every part is important. Our individual histories, the happiness we knew as a couple, hearing the doctor tell us to get our affairs in order, living with nineteen months of cancer and the end-stage death process; every part is important to us. But the readings with Elizabeth that you are about to read was for me the most healing and therefore most important to me.

I decided to have my first reading with Jim through Elizabeth because I needed to know if he was okay. I needed to know he really did cross over to the other side, that he was happy with what he found there and that I could hear his words one more time. But I also did it because I needed to be okay, too, which I was not. I had watched Jim go through a horrible ordeal with cancer physically, mentally and emotionally. I watched him have to say goodbye to family and friends. I watched him stop flying and have to leave a job he loved. I held Jim in my arms as he breathed his last breath.

Jim had the cancer but I was also suffering. After Jim passed, I was lost. I didn't know where I belonged any more or what I should do next. I didn't know how to be in our house without Jim but I had trouble leaving it for even an hour. I couldn't watch TV shows we had watched together but I had to have the TV on for noise. I had trouble making commitments for anything at all, even lunch or dinner with a friend. I wanted to go out with friends to feel normal but I didn't want to go out because Jim was supposed to be with me. I wanted to be with family but even that was difficult because we were all in so much pain. Truthfully, I didn't want to go on living without Jim. We had no children for me to hold onto, in whom I could see Jim. I wasn't okay.

I chose an unconventional path to help myself. I didn't know Elizabeth well other than having my Reiki sessions with her, but I did have those two experiences of readings with her that were both so helpful and uplifting. We had discussions about my health and well-being and I felt she was genuinely concerned about my progress. I decided to get through the first part of my loss and grief *with* Jim, my partner in life. Conventional counseling didn't do enough for me and I knew I was in trouble if I didn't do something to help myself. I needed to either find the "old Chris" or meet the new one. I had no idea how the current one was going to live without Jim.

What you will read next may shock you, as it did me. I began having conversations with Jim in November 2011, a month after he died. An interesting thing happened two days before my first reading with Jim. I was in meditation class and quite deep in the "zone" when I felt as though I was wrapped in a warm, cozy cocoon. I didn't see Jim's image but I knew without a doubt it had something to do with him. I don't know how I knew but I did. I didn't understand it but I simply enjoyed being in that moment and having that feeling. Two days later I went to have a Reiki session with Elizabeth. When she came to the waiting room to walk me to my session she told me Jim was there and asked me if I wanted to talk to him instead of receiving Reiki that day.

Our conversations began that day. I received answers to my original questions: Jim did cross over to the other side, he was happy with what he found there and I was able to hear his words again. In that first reading he said specific things so I would know it was really him I was talking to. Luckily I took notes because when the TGA started, my short term memory was wiped clean of everything for several hours and those hours of memory never came back. In subsequent readings I learned about his journey in the afterlife and his growth after he no longer had a physical body.

For quite a while Jim was the same Jim I knew in our physical life together. He sounded the same in his comments and used many of our private or personal jokes during readings. We talked of family and friends, our animals, what I was doing around the house; it was conversation that I had always loved and still did. In the beginning I cried most of the way through our sessions, but gradually I was able to listen, talk and laugh for longer periods of time. Before I knew it, I would leave a session with Jim without having cried at all.

As time went on I started noticing a difference in Jim. He was often more serious and eager to tell me information about what his world was like rather than talk about us, family and friends. He still cracked jokes and would discuss anything from my world that I wanted, but he was changing. Jim's transformation had begun. Jim started telling me about what he was learning and how exciting it was for him. He explained his love for me was deeper than ever and because of that, he didn't want me to be alone and lonely. He told me he would be looking for someone for me to meet, enjoy and spend time with.

I began to lose my fear of commitment and was able to leave the house to meet with friends without panicking. I found myself laughing more and stopped thinking about wishing I could join Jim on the other side. I no longer felt that constant pain in my stomach and even looked forward to what the next day would bring. I knew I still loved Jim and always would but was able to accept the fact that he was in his world and I was in mine. I no longer had to talk about him to friends every minute. My transformation had also begun. I was regaining the "old Chris" and developing the new one. I was so relieved to know that "grief-stricken Chris" wasn't the permanent one.

The readings with Jim were obviously the main part of my transformation, but I am and will always be grateful to Elizabeth for her guidance through my difficult grief process. Before each reading, she would "check in" with me, inquiring about my physical, emotional and mental progress. Elizabeth has a reputation of amazing accuracy as a medium. She comes from a place of great integrity and honesty with clients and acts with the highest reverence when communicating with the souls who have passed before us. One of her great strengths is the setting of appropriate boundaries in situations such as mine when it comes to loss. With a caring and soothing demeanor, she will only let a client continue to have readings with loved ones if she sees the client grow and release grief. If the client stays stuck in earthly love for the loved one who has passed, Elizabeth will kindly wean the client from too much contact.

Most people would not choose this unconventional method of working with a medium to deal with their grief. Many don't even know that mediums can help with various life situations other than grief. Inquiring and learning about our health is one example. Another is that mediums are often consulted by law enforcement groups to help solve crimes. Unfortunately, some people believe that mediums are a negative force in the world. I find it hard to believe that anyone could see the progress I've made in my grief process since losing Jim and think that Elizabeth is a negative force in this world.

It is my belief that our loving God can do anything and everything. God gives special gifts to people all over the world, such as working through everyday people to heal others and perform what we would consider miracles. In the Catholic religion those people who become conduits for God's love and energy to perform miracles are called saints. If we do truly believe that God can do anything, why wouldn't God give some people in the world the gift of being able to talk to those in the Heaven realms in order to provide comfort and assistance when needed?

Elizabeth and Maryann encouraged me to continue with Reiki and other means of support that I felt was instrumental to my well-being. I was surrounded by family and friends as well, and through boxes of tissues, tons of tears and many hugs, I slowly started to regain myself—the "real" Chris. I know I never would have taken my own life, although I certainly felt like I wanted to numerous times. But with all the support and all the love, I reached deep within myself and found the old Chris. I have been able to deal with Jim's death in a much healthier way than if I were just out there on my own. I attribute my healthy attitude and acceptance of Jim's death to the support, love and friendship of all those who surrounded me.

As you read through these actual sessions that I had with Elizabeth, realize how grateful I was to know beyond a shadow of a doubt that I was speaking to my husband and other loved ones. Imagine the comfort of knowing this. But most important is the fact that by having these readings, I have been able to work through my grief and know that it is an ongoing process rather than an event. My hope is that you find light beyond moments of despair and ways to move past grief in any healthy manner possible.

Instructions on
How to Interpret
"The Messages"

I want you to have the best experience possible as you delve into these readings. Therefore, let me explain to you how they were transcribed. I hope this helps you feel and experience the way a reading with a medium actually transpires.

After each reading, you will read reflections about the reading from both Jim's and my perspectives. We both feel these reflections are important pieces to include.

When you have a reading with a medium, you might be sitting across from or near the medium, or you might be having the reading over the phone. When Elizabeth starts a session with me, she "checks in" with me, asking how I'm doing, making me feel comfortable and asking what I would like to accomplish during the session. She then says a prayer to start the session.

Sometimes she begins immediately with a prayer and starts right in communicating with souls who have "come in" to talk with me.

Other times, as is often the case with our work on this book, Elizabeth will start speaking with me about information I am meant to understand. If I didn't know better or catch some wording such as "we" or "the ones in the light" or "the Angels," I would think she was just telling me information she thinks would be good for me to know. However, when she does give all of that information, it is "the ones in the light speaking to me through her."

When conversation is taking place, you will see the name or of the soul or person speaking. (See list below.)

Sometimes a soul comes into the reading and Elizabeth tells what they are actually saying. If I am trying to emphasize a word or phrase, the word(s) will be in italics or quotation marks.

If I need to explain something, but am not actually speaking, I use parentheses or asterisks to show an explanation.

Below is a list of people who could be in any of the following readings, along with their coinciding initials or names used to identify them.

Elizabeth: Elizabeth Williams

Chris: Chris Petosa

Jim: Jim Petosa

Bill: Chris's father

Bob: Jim's father

Girlfriend: Nephew's girlfriend

Wanda: Chris's mother

Al: A friend

Messages from the Afterlife

August 18, 2011 · Reading with Elizabeth, Jim & Chris Before Jim's Passing

Elizabeth opens the session, as she always does, with a prayer of gratitude and blessings.

Elizabeth: Jim, your father is hilarious! He says his name is Bob.

Bob: I'm here to set things straight ... how it will take place.

Elizabeth: Chris, your dad, Bill, is here, too. James, Bob's cousin, is here, too, as well as Mary. The "big Catholic family!"

Bob: So ... you can know we're all here. There's nothing to be afraid of. What the hell ... we're waiting right here!

Jim, please talk to your mom for me. She's in a total tizzy. She knows the seriousness of your illness. Thinking negatively will make it worse. Tell her to just be still for a minute. It's hard because she's so upset about you, Jim. You are a lot like me. When something bothers you, you don't say much.

I want to tell you about the way I died; it's significant. It was a time in life when I just let things happen. As much as I didn't want to leave you all, I prayed for it to happen; I just couldn't take any more. It's hard to explain when you have an issue of the mind like I did. It's not something you can touch or feel. I'm more at peace now than ever during my physical life. I am so proud of you and the family. I love my family and will never leave any of you.

Chris, stop it already ... that's enough of watching your wristwatch. There's plenty of time. Where we are, there's no such thing as time. I'm still there with you all now. It's hard to even tell how long I've been on the other side. The only way I know or have any concept of time is by watching all of you. Seeing you age, being a part of your lives and checking in on you ... that's how I know how long I've been away from you; in other words, how long I've been "dead."

Jim, live like young Jimmy. You put his mind to something and you did it.

Nothing ever held you back and this is no exception. If you're worried about money, why not just go rob a bank? Get organized; it's foolish to worry about money.

I was in and out of people's mouths all day long because I was a dentist. At least they can't talk back to you!

I'm still interested in learning just like I was when I was with all of you. We all continue to learn while we're here. I'm going to write a book—I just haven't yet.

When we're told that someone we love, know and remember is leaving their body to come over here, we all gather together and wait. In your world, waiting to die is the hardest part. After you do die, everything gets easier. In our world, we go about our business and we come to get you when the time is right.

Waiting until the next time around is not the right thing to do. We don't just sit around up here. I've gone to Jerusalem to see the Temple. I'm fascinated with travel. The best part about traveling here is that we don't have to pay for it! (Jim laughs out loud at this.) Jimmy, now you can see it all. I'm waiting to show you all the places you've ever dreamed of going. We're busy here, and the best part is that there's plenty of time and always things to do. You can reflect; you learn the truth about life in the physical. One of the reasons I like going to the Temple in Jerusalem is that I find a sense of peace. I was able to contemplate a lot about the life I lived with all of you. Because we're never really separated, it's like you're here through this with me anyway.

When I wondered what it would be like to die, just out of pure curiosity, I wondered if you'd get to eat and enjoy the same things that you do on Earth. In some ways, it's better being here without the trouble of taking care of a body. Our soul is still learning and continues to do so. You learn to enjoy every minute. At first, you're still struggling with leaving behind your family, your friends and your life as a person. I tell you, Jimmy, we enjoy every minute.

Elizabeth: Who's Joanna?

Jim: My mother.

Bob: I see her. I know she wants to spend as much time as possible with you. So do your sisters and brother. I see how tired that makes you. I know you worry about hurting their feelings. In their own way, they are all trying to handle the fact that you're stopping chemo. They know there's nothing else doctors can do.

Elizabeth: Jim, Chris's dad wants you to know how good you are to his daughter. He never was one for being mushy and sappy, but he appreciates what you've done. He was always impressed with you. He doesn't like psychological nonsense, but he's very grateful for everything you are as a man and was very happy with you as a son-in-law. He felt like you were one of his sons.

Bill: We're all just one big, happy family now. We all know each other now and our families have something in common—all of you.

Bob: I don't want to take up the whole time, but whatever you need or want, don't hesitate to call on me and ask for help. I haven't gone far and will stay with both of you. I try to comfort you now.

Chris, I think there are times that you feel something—that "something" is really me and the rest of us here. Don't hesitate to ask for help and support. You have a hard job, young lady. I see how well you take care of my son and I can't thank you enough. Jimmy's used to that from you. We all know how Jimmy likes to take care of everybody; he gets upset that he can't take care of you and that you'll have to take care of yourself soon. He knows you can. It's just hard for him to bear the idea of it. He's so much like me, it's ridiculous. He's worried that you are going to have to work so hard, like Joanna did. There's nothing worse than watching your wife have to struggle to make ends meet because you can't.

Bill: Chris, I always took care of others as much as I could and worked with your mother to do that. Your mom knows how you feel because she's in the same situation that you are going to be in soon. I know I should have taken better care of myself. Learn that from me! Take good care of yourself. I'll be the first to admit—I was scared to death. It scared the hell out of John, too. (John is Chris's uncle.) After it happens ... after you leave your body, it's all okay. You don't really go anywhere but right here. In my case, I'm still a part of your everyday lives.

I am happier now than ever. I've had more rest and fun instead of working so hard. That's one thing I never would wish to have back—working so hard! It's like a permanent vacation here.

Bob: Now, Marianne ... make sure you tell her that I said thank you, and she knows for what. She'll know what I'm talking about.

I'm very pleased with my family. I love my family. I'm fascinated by the power of prayer ... fascinated by it ... energy work and prayer. I was a scientist, but now I'm fascinated by what is beyond. I have been there in the room so many times when you were receiving Reiki, Jim.

Now you can say it, Elizabeth.

Elizabeth: Your dad's been worried about you.

Bob: *You have to rest. (Bob and Elizabeth are laughing.)*

Elizabeth: When I kept telling you that during Reiki sessions, it was your father telling me to tell you that. Resting isn't sitting in your chair doing work or watching TV. He means deep rest like you feel during meditation and Reiki.

Bob: *There were so many patients in and out of my office ... so many lined up. When you run into them, tell them I miss them all and it was a pleasure to have helped them and to get to know them. I am grateful for every day I lived... every day ... and all who were around and willing to help.*

Jim, tell Mom how much I appreciated her. I have a deep sense of gratitude for ALL—especially my family. I wasn't able to always show it. Back then, the doctors tried to diagnose me with a mental illness to explain my behaviors—so many ups and downs—more downs than ups. Joanna had to take over so many responsibilities when I could no longer take care of business and family. Back then, there wasn't much known about depression and the complications of it. Joanna did an amazing job with it all, but still, it was a huge injury to my pride. I wanted to be the one to take care of my family.

The number one rule is to be grateful for everything. That alone makes all the difference.

Elizabeth: Everyone up there seems to agree. They are all smiling with approval.

Bob: *Jim, your grandmother pipes up, as always. I'll let them talk. (Silence.) See what I mean? Give them a chance to talk and no one has anything to say.*

Elizabeth: Bob is shaking his head.

Bob: *Someone has to be in charge so I took charge. There's no going back. We stay together and wait for everyone else. You can't believe how much fun you have here!*

Elizabeth: Bob is emphatic about that.

Bill: *Chris, I try to communicate with you. I have wanted you to pay attention and not to be so worried about enjoying life. You've had a hard time enjoying life* *this past year with everything that's happened with Jim. Remember how much you enjoy life ... your life together, your friends, your family—don't ever lose that. It will come back to you in time. You can learn by watching your mother. Please tell her I always admired her strength and her determination to continue to love life and everyone in it.*

Chris and Jim, both of you need to continue to have fun and enjoy life together, no matter what. I've been trying to tell you that for a while, but it's hard because you're both so caught up in the sickness. Life can be simpler and easier to enjoy, don't just worry all the time. I know you try to hide your worry.

I'm going to hang around you for a while, Chris. Someone has to keep track of you! I'll be with you more. Jim is a very good son-in-law, a good man. Chris, I hope I can bring you some comfort. How much you charge to haunt a house?

Elizabeth: What does he mean?

Chris: When I was a little girl, squirming around in his lap and jabbing my elbows in his stomach, he would ask me how much I charged to haunt a house. I never realized what he meant until a few years later. I used to tell him a nickel!

Elizabeth: Who's Grandma V something?

Jim: Grandma Vanetti.

Elizabeth: She says to tell you, "We don't miss you ... we're all right here!"

(Elizabeth explains that she is beginning to lose contact. She thanks everyone for coming, says a blessing and sends them on their way.)

Elizabeth: What will you both be doing after you leave here?

(Every time a session with Elizabeth ends, she inquires as to what her client(s) will be doing after they leave. She does this out of concern, to make sure they are in a good emotional state before leaving the office and that they have a plan in place in case they need support.)

Chris: We are going to have dinner with family and then attend a healing mass at St. Cecilia's Church tonight.

Elizabeth: I've heard of the priest who celebrates those masses. He reminds me very much of Saint Padre Pio who had stigmata and bled … . Many believe this priest is like Padre Pio and grants intercession and healing. Expect wonderful things.

Chris's Reflections:

As I'm sure you can imagine, having this reading could have been a scary thing to do. Now here we are listening to our family members telling Jim not to be afraid and that they're waiting for him. Clearly Jim wasn't going to beat this disease and stay in this physical world. As devastating as that could have been, it wasn't. We may not have spoken of it much, but we knew at this point that Jim was going to die. Jim would give me instructions for things that needed to be done around the house that only he did.

I would write down the instructions with that familiar gut-wrenching feeling in my stomach and try to stay strong but always sobbed either during the instructions or as soon as I was away from Jim. Intuitively we were ready for this reading. After it was done, we both felt so comfortable about our family members all sounding exactly the same as when they were on this Earth, and it sounded like they were actually having fun! It calmed Jim's mind to know where he was headed and that he would truly be joining our family members. And even though I may have been crying, it calmed my mind, too.

Although there were no more chemotherapy protocols to try, we still hadn't given up hope that Jim would somehow live through this whole ordeal. Now, looking back, I often wonder: if the cancer had left Jim's body and he lived, would the effects from the chemotherapy and other drugs have dissipated, or would Jim's body be permanently damaged? Remember, he was jaundiced, had neuropathy, had lost nearly 80 pounds and his body was weak beyond belief.

From this very first reading (other than my own original one), we were already learning lessons which I was to find out would continue in every single reading to come. One of the huge lessons of this reading was, "The number one rule is to be grateful for everything. That alone makes all the difference." Not only have I realized how important that is, but it has changed my life and enabled me to go on living without Jim yet be grateful for every second that we shared together. I'm still learning and realizing that the more grateful I am, the more I receive in my life. Abundance comes in many forms: love of family and friends, intuition, knowledge and a roof over my head. I am blessed to have each of these in my life.

Jim's Reflections:

As you've read in the words of our story together through life, working and struggling with the loss of children, nothing is more fearful than facing death and leaving behind all you know and love for what "might" be the truth. Sure, we're taught to believe our salvation is Heaven, and that Earth is just a stomping ground for what is to come. It doesn't matter what we're told, what we hear or what we pretend to believe. When a doctor tells you "Get your affairs in order," you hear him or her with your ears but it doesn't sink in. When your friends say they're sorry, when your family says they love you or when your boss says he or she will be there to help you, nothing ... nothing ... really sinks in. It's not that I became ungrateful. I was lucky enough to have a wife like Chris, and if you are a wife, a husband, a companion, even a child or friend, it doesn't sink in until you really know beyond a shadow of a doubt that there's someplace else ... something else.

No matter what you have been taught to believe, sharing what I'm about to say may or will go beyond anything you're ever going to hear.

Hearing that the people you love most in your life are waiting for you in the afterlife is comforting beyond imagination. Better still is knowing that you are able to complete what you left unfinished during your lifetime on Earth. There is still time, there is still an opportunity. When you reach there, you still have the ability to right the wrongs, to change your Self, to transform. We quickly acquire the "knowing" that we, as humans, have the ability and the good fortune to be able to stay connected to the people/souls we love even after we die. We also learn that we live on and on, as well as grow. The ones we love so deeply and cherish the most—our love for them never subsides. Instead, it grows deeper, more compassionate and more real than we could ever imagine.

The reading that my wife, Chris, and I had with Elizabeth Williams was, without a doubt, as human Jim, the most helpful experience of my entire lifetime second only to having Chris as my wife. It confirmed my belief, strengthened my "knowing," and blessed me beyond comparison ... more than any treatment, any food, any job or any adventure I ever had. Other than my marriage to Chris, it was what prepared me for what was to come ... the afterlife, eternity ... the life of the Heavens. Everything I needed to be confirmed happened on August 18, 2011.

Elizabeth did most of the talking. Chris held my hand, prompted me for more questions and helped me to understand what was going to happen next. What Chris didn't know, or at least what I never said out loud, was that I knew ... I knew I was going to leave the Earth. I knew I would never be back in my physical body to hug, kiss and hold Chris ever again. I knew I was going to leave with exactly what I came with ... nothing but love. We made the decision together, Chris and I, that I would stop treatment. Actually, I had already stopped treatment.

We started the reading with cordial hellos, smiles and hugs to each other. We attempted to laugh but we all knew I was leaving and I would not be back, physically, to partake in life as we all knew it. Nonetheless, I would be back one way or another. I didn't want to leave, unlike so many who do. I wanted to stay ... to hold my wife, to tease my siblings, to eat my mother's food and to fly my jets. No matter what I wanted, the reality remained ... I was leaving. What I didn't know for sure is that I would be accompanied by all that I needed in either world. I never felt more fortunate than I did that day.

Chris and I have a friend who calls me FP. It stands for f**k**g pilot. We would laugh and joke about it all the time but, deep in my heart, my CFP wasn't going with me (CFP means co-f**k**g pilot). This was a flight I never dreamed of making alone and now I knew I wouldn't be. When you're young and you think of being old, you don't think of dying, you just think of being old. I was young and I was forced to think of dying. Today was the day I really knew "dying" meant I would live forever.

I spoke to my father first. He was the dad I always knew, the dad everyone loved and revered. The most wondrous part—Dad knew all along I was coming there ... and he was waiting. They all knew. Every single one of them knew. No one stressed more than my grandmother how much they love us all on Earth. When I was physical, I ate lunch with her every day. They were all waiting. All of them spoke of things I had never talked about to Elizabeth—ever.

I cannot stress to you enough, as a reader of this book ... if you believe that communicating with the spirit world is wrong, adapt to a new belief. If you believe some crazy fantasy or nightmare that hell actually exists, open your mind to a new thought, open your heart to a new kind of loving and open your Self to a higher understanding. You'll never be the same.

It is the greatest, most comforting feeling on the planet to know that they are waiting ... with open arms to receive you.

The day I left, I knew I was ready. My body had stopped working, my good-byes were all said, my affairs were in order and my wife was in my arms. The days leading up to this moment were eventful ... . Visitors, "old" friends who entered the room, people, or should I say rather, "souls," I remembered were there. I knew it was close to quitting time.

What astounded me, what was truly profound, were not just the ones who would help me through the tunnel of light, it was those who would stay beside my wife and her brother so they would not be alone. The glorious beings of light,

Angels, and those who never met me but knew my wife. They were there. Chris had friends that I had encountered over the years on Earth and some that I never met that came to bring her comfort while I was leaving. Her father, Big Bill, her friend, Cheeky, from years ago, her grandparents, Podzi and Ek, all of the friends she knew and loved and who so dearly loved her, they came to help her and her brother, Woody, as I would fly away.

To deny that I was afraid would be useless. As that tunnel of while light began to appear, a sense of peace came over me. A peace I would never have known in my physical body. It was a different kind of peace, different from contentment with life from day to day. It was a peace, a grace, an undeniable love.

A sensation in my physical body as my heart began to race was easily soothed by the love of my wife and the blinding white light. They were all there standing, cheering, laughing and celebrating—Dad, Grandma, Grandpa, friends and many others I never even knew. They were all welcoming me, reaching their arms out to hold me, welcome me, encourage me to come to the light. It was amazing. Nothing on Earth but my wife compared to this! I could hear Chris saying, "Go on." I remember Elizabeth's words, "When they come for you, you have to go. You can come back and talk later." My last words that I remember? "I love you, Chris!" My nervous system said other things as I came up out of my body, and then, like flying into the wind, I was up and away. I was gone. Little did I know what was in store for me. The gratitude was unbelievable, the peace unforgettable, the love indescribable. I was going home.

Ladies and gentlemen, we're thanking God for a smooth landing today. The sun is shining. Enjoy it while you can.

— *Captain Jim Petosa*

November 10, 2011 · First Reading After Jim's Death

Elizabeth opens the session, as she always does, with a prayer of gratitude and blessings.

Jim: *It's just us today. I'm good, but still a little weak. I gotta get the hang of this. (Bright smile.) I'm so excited about coming here and doing this—talking to you. It's good to be seen. There is no time here. I've seen you wondering, asking questions. I'll answer questions, Sweetie, I'll answer questions.*

At the end of meditation class, I was trying to get you to see me.

I want to tell you everything. Elements in the environment may have contributed to my cancer, but there was a deeper root to the problem. I haven't figured that out yet. I'll let you know when I do.

I see things differently now. I always loved you, but I wouldn't have worked so much if I knew life would be so short. I see what I would have done differently. We didn't have enough time together.

Sweetie, calm down.

I didn't have pain when I left my body. The comment I made ... "Help me!" ... I wasn't in my right mind. I'm so sorry I scared you.

When I died, John came, and my dad. Mother Mary came, too, and your dad. There were so many to greet me, I couldn't count them. Some I recognized and some I didn't. They were all there to greet me. I had no idea there would be so many. That was so exciting to me. But the most special was the Blessed Mother Mary and St. Francis ... they were both there. I was so happy they were both there! I was so happy to see them! It was all just big light. St. Francis was there! I didn't know for real that they would really be there. I was in such disbelief that I was welcomed in such a way.

Elizabeth: He's wiping his eyes in disbelief.

Jim: *More worthwhile ... they tell me I have to stay with them now for bigger things. This is beyond what I could dream of. I'm still dumbfounded and awestruck. All of my physical experiences are only greater since I've been in Heaven. I'm sure of that. When I got there, I was sure of it, but it's not what I envisioned. I wasn't sure I would make it there, but it was as easy as flying, as everyday work ... so easy! When they came to carry me, I went because I knew I could come back. My body didn't want to keep up with me! (Laughing.)*

Chris: Jim, are you resting?

Jim: No. I can't get enough of what I'm learning. I just can't get enough! I'm taking every opportunity. I told you how many times, Elizabeth, I can rest when I'm dead!

Chris, I'm glad we can have time alone. It's too much when everyone's hovering. I'm sorry that I couldn't stay with you longer ... for a longer life.

I know you have questions.

I love you more than ever before.

Chris: Are you disappointed in anything about me?

Elizabeth: There's a look of disbelief on his face.

Jim: Never! If I knew being married would be this wonderful, I would have met you sooner. I really love you.

Chris: I want to be with you.

Jim: No! You can't be with me.

Elizabeth: His hand is up.

Jim: No! There's a certain timing .... No. There's so much more for you to understand and explore here. You can't go now, and it won't be soon. I was worried that you wouldn't want to live anymore. You have to live. You have to. The Heaven worlds are not meant for someone who has so much .... Not yet.

I know that the way I love you will never change through a long period of time. There's no rush. You can't hurry this. (Laughing.)

I don't want your body to get worse, to have more trouble. You have much to do there.

Chris: Will you guide me?

Jim: Yes, and I'll help you when you're not sure what to do. You can't think about dying when you're living so well. I never thought about dying while living. I thought about living, not dying. I thought about what we could do together. I want you to think about living.

Faith, Chris. Faith. It's all okay. I'm doing okay. I know you're hurting a lot. I can see you haven't stopped crying.

Chris: You were the best.

Jim: I can't be with you all the time yet. Not yet. I'm in your heart, but not in the mortal world all the time yet. I don't have the skills yet. It will take a little while to gain the skills to be able to go back and forth, and when I can, you're the first one I'm coming for.

I'm in no pain whatsoever. It's like I'm sleeping, but I'm awake; it's like a dream. I will not physically be with you ... not yet. Eventually, and I know it seems early, you will grow and expand to where I am. Right now, there is a veil that separates us, yet it is dissolving. All here are growing and expanding—energetically ... in their souls, not in their bodies. Changes really are taking place.

Chris: What do you mean?

Jim: It's the soul that opens up and wakes up. My soul left my body and is reshaping and reforming into a light body ... a resurrected form of me. A body of light. I look like it does when saints appear in pictures on Earth.

As you grow and the grief starts to dissipate, when you feel lighter, you'll be able to be in my world or at least be connected to my world and here. It has nothing to do with religion; it has to do with love and truth. I've learned that so dramatically.

Chris: I love you.

Jim: I'm not that body.

Elizabeth: He's showing his body. It's radiant!

Jim: Energetically, I'm with you always, always in your heart.

Animals ... you have to get a dog. Having animals will keep you busy. The cats know I'm missing. Thelma Lou is whining a lot. I didn't talk with you about this very much, but I hoped that I would get to be around all animals a lot. I loved and had respect for wildlife and nature; that's actually going to be my hobby. I have to stay busy. After a period of rest (laughing), I will be spending time in the forest with animals and in the wild. I will be with you on walks and in nature. I'll be with you in nature. Tell the family I'll be with them on walks and in nature, too.

I'm glad everything in the house got fixed ... repairs ... before I left. It was a pain in the neck. I'm glad things happened before I left.

Elizabeth: He says the kitchen flooded. Is that true?

Chris: Yes, twice.

Elizabeth: He also says water leaked into the basement from the bathroom. He goes on to say he's glad the mold is gone and says something about the laundry room. Does that mean anything to you?

Chris: Yes, it was just redone.

Elizabeth: What is it about two years ago?

Chris: We had it remodeled two years ago, but then we had a leak from the bathroom into the laundry room just recently. It caused mold to grow and the floor joists were soaked. It was a mess and this was while Jim was really, really sick. On top of that, Jim insisted on having almost the whole house repainted so he would know I was taken care of.

Jim: Carry on. Business as usual ... you promised. Holidays and celebrations are coming up. I'll be celebrating with you. Our anniversary. I'll be there for that. That's why I'm resting ... I want to be there for our anniversary.

Elizabeth: He's a younger Jim. What surprises him is that he's a younger Jim than when he left his body. Like about 30 years old.

Jim: Since I was eight years younger than you before, that practically makes me a teenager. You really robbed the cradle now.

Chris: Funny!

Jim: The whole family ... I didn't want anyone to be like this ... crying all the time. No pity party. I can't stand being pitied. It is not okay with me! I never wanted anyone to pity me or themselves.

Everyone here with me in Heaven all went through the same thing ... so much pain, sadness, separation. It's going to get better—I promise. I'll see to it that it does. When you realize what you're capable of, it gets easier. My dad said the same thing.

When I was in the tunnel of light, I turned around to stay with you. Dad said not to worry—that it will get easier. He had the same problem, too ... separating from family.

I didn't want to die, but it's not so bad. Not so bad, Sweetie.

I know how much you miss me. I wish I could do something. We come as a pair. I'm not with you every day because I don't have the strength yet. I will be, but I have to learn how.

I met with the "Council." When it happened, I was shocked to find out there is a Council. They explained to me what parts of my mission and purpose I completed and what would take place again ... what else there is for me to do.

I couldn't believe it, Sweetie! I can't believe it, still. They showed me all my good deeds. What seemed normal to me ... to help others and do for others, like family ... was actually noted by the Council. My faith and spiritual growth were noted at the time of my arrival. It keeps growing.

Chris: How amazing! I had no idea there was even such a council in Heaven. Will you come back in another lifetime?

Jim: *(Smiling.) I will always come back with Christine ... always. It's like we're soul mates. We're together. A union ... long time ... endless ... forever. You won't see me physically again while you're still alive unless I learn while I'm here how to show you it's me in another physical body. I'm still learning. It will be a long period of time.*

I'm not with you yet, but energetically I am. Everything ... our house, work, the truck ... all will have remnants of my energy ... all kinds of things.

But another body—my light body—is being formed and I am learning how to fully form it. To learn how to be here physically in your world will take time ... to be an energy body. The memory of me is there with you now, but my soul body is not ... not yet.

I love you more now than ever before. That's what makes it so hard on me where I am. I'm having a hard time letting go, just like you.

About the vehicles—it's crap. I'm trying to straighten out the mess with the vehicles. I think you have my message about how to rearrange them. You're having a hard time about the lease. Don't let them take advantage of you. I am able to see them trying.

Chris: The hardest part, Jim, is that companies don't seem to care about the fact that you died. The lease just has to be fulfilled.

Jim: Something will be worked out with the lease. Bruce and Rosemary will somehow be involved. You're having a moment of confusion. You just have to wait it out.

Elizabeth: He calls it reality. He says you're just upset.

Chris: I am having confusion right now … that's true. I am really in one.

Jim: I know you did all you could to help me and make me comfortable … everything. The only thing worse than me going first would be that I'd be left there without you. I know how much you love and miss me.

(***I went into a TGA … writing became unintelligible … Elizabeth and Marianne took care of me. Jim knew what was happening before Elizabeth or I did!)

Chris's Reflections:

The second thing Jim says during this reading is, "It's good to be seen." This is such a big deal because after he was diagnosed with stage IV cancer and knew that the probability of dying was very high, he started to say, "It's good to be seen," when others said, "It's good to see you." He was so grateful for being alive for whatever time he had and this was his consistent response. For Jim to say that phrase right away in our very first reading after his death was quite unbelievable. It showed that he remembers his life on Earth, that he still has his sense of humor and it was a quick way to prove to me that it was Jim I was really talking to.

I want to explain to you what happened when Jim said, "At the end of meditation class, I was trying to get you to see me." I was in a meditation class that Elizabeth holds every Tuesday afternoon. Sometimes I would have trouble meditating due to my busy mind and sometimes I would go very deep into the "zone." This particular day that Jim is talking about, I went into the zone and I felt like I was wrapped in a cozy warm cocoon, feeling very safe and comfortable. I felt as though it had something to do with Jim, but I didn't know what and I didn't understand how it could. In this reading, I came to the realization that it was because Jim's spirit really was with me, giving me peace and comfort. I was beginning to understand that my heart was able to tell me more than my mind could.

When my TGA (Transient Global Amnesia) episode was over and I was able to read over my notes from this reading the next day, what really struck me was that Jim was the one who knew first that I was having confusion, not Elizabeth or me. I was actually the second one to realize it, and Elizabeth was the last to know. That would show proof to those who wonder about whether a professional medium "reads" a person, or is actually communicating with those who have passed from this physical life. Clearly, Elizabeth wasn't "reading" me, or she would have been the first to know I was going into a TGA episode.

When a TGA episode begins, I, or anyone else who experiences this, truly need to be taken care of by someone. It involves the memory (short-term recall, not long-term) and without someone to be with me and help me, I don't know what would happen. Elizabeth has many clients and she typically sees them one right after the other. Yet when I had the TGA, she took me to the Urgent Care facility and stayed with me, giving the doctors and nurses all the information she could. She also called my sister-in-law, Marianne, and waited with me until Marianne was able to come to pick me up. I feel blessed that I am working with a professional mediium who is not only extremely accurate in her readings, but also so compassionate that she would take care of me until someone else from my family could arrive.

Jim's Reflection: "The Return"

She was in the chair sobbing. Coming for Reiki but ending with a very different experience. So did I.

It took a long time for Elizabeth to help quiet her. She was sobbing. She wore a red sweater that day, planning to receive Reiki and get some sense of peace. After watching for a full month, I never saw anyone cry so hard, so long, so deeply as I did Chris that day.

I couldn't thank Chris enough for all she had done. I apologized for scaring her—my comment. I'm sorry wouldn't come close to the true sorrow I felt for leaving her. Not to mention "Help me!" when my heart began to race just before I disconnected.

Everything went according to plan. I could give my explanations and make my apologies for the fear that I caused. What we didn't plan on were the events that followed.

Chris slowly began to lose her coordination. Elizabeth, with her eyes closed, deeply entranced in our conversation, didn't visibly see Chris's actions. She was asking the same questions and repeating herself just like the Christmas

Eve before. Chris fidgeted. She cried. She repeated herself. I said very loudly to Elizabeth, "Open your eyes for a minute! Please help her. She's having an episode ... ."

Elizabeth opened her eyes. She watched her actions, she called doctors, she took Chris to the upstairs walk-in clinic. She waited for hours. She called our family. The whole time I was there listening to Chris ask the same question again and again. Did Jimmy come? Did Jimmy come? Looking back now it's silly and funny but when it happened it was not.

Yes, I did come. Yes, we did talk. Yes, I do still love her. The only difference is the love is stronger, deeper, more unbelievable than it ever was on Earth.

I was rapidly growing, changing, transforming, getting prepared for the next steps.

I would be there on Earth in my body if it had lasted. Instead, I'm there/here with her, my wife, sharing my journey in the following pages.

I love you, Chris, Mom, Dad (who is here), Marianne, Roberta, Theresa and Paulie. I love you all so much. The old saying, "Don't ever change"? Nothing could be further from the truth. Don't ever stop growing ... believing ... evolving. I will be there with you every step of the way.

Ladies and gentlemen, it's been a turbulent flight today. Please remain in your seats until the seatbelt light is turned off. Thank God we've arrived safely. We hope to see you again soon.

— Captain Jim Petosa

December 16, 2011

Elizabeth: I need to know how things are going first ... emotionally ... . How are you doing at home? I know you were having trouble sleeping, which is common with the situation that you're in. Sleeping and resting are very important. Many times people try to keep themselves busy instead of listening to their body and resting.

Chris: You telling me about the breathing and the "you're okay" statement ... I have been doing that a lot this week.

Elizabeth: Oh, good. I'm glad you're using the tools we talked about last time and that it's helping. I've been praying for you all week, like I always do. In light of all that's happened, especially the TGA you had during your last visit, I want to make sure you're in a good place before we start this session.

Chris: Thank you. I certainly have my crying and sobbing times, but then I tell myself, "Nope ... you're okay," and I breathe. I do it as many times as I have to, and I'm controlling myself better. So it has been a better week as far as that. I have a lot of emotion right now (crying), but I am okay.

Elizabeth: How are you feeling physically? When I was meditating this morning, I could feel you were limping.

Chris: You could? Well, that's this knee that's been hurting, and receiving Reiki the other day helped. It felt better for a while, but then it went back to hurting. Whatever I did to it last night, made the pain much worse. Luckily, I have an appointment for an MRI tomorrow.

Elizabeth: Did you fall or injure it somehow? How are you managing the pain?

Chris: As far as my knee, I don't know what I originally did. Whatever it was was months ago, but these last few weeks have been very painful. I've been trying to manage the pain but over the counter medication isn't helping.

Elizabeth: Sometimes stressors can cause these physical things, and you're going through a really emotional time with the loss of Jim. If you think there's anything more I can do to help you, please let me know.

Chris: As far as sleeping, my doctor suggested I take a small dose of sleep medication, so my sleeping isn't too bad right now.

Elizabeth: Good. Rest is very important, especially when the body hurts. So what else is going on?

Chris: I have questions for Jim, but I don't remember from last time if I ask him or if you ask him. Actually, I don't remember anything because of the TGA. But I don't feel like I'm going to have one today.

Elizabeth: You seem to be in a pretty good state today. I just needed to hear from you that you're okay.

Chris: I am. Do you think I should take notes while the recorder is on or just listen?

Elizabeth: Whatever is going to keep you more grounded here. Once we "open up" it tends to create a whirlwind, as you know.

Elizabeth opens the session, as she always does, with a prayer of gratitude and blessings.

Elizabeth: Let's start with your full name and your date of birth. Yeah, I know you're already here, Jim.

Chris: Hi Jimmy!

Jim: Why are we going through all this, Elizabeth? I'm already here. You know I'm here. No pun intended, Chris, but I've been dying to tell you everything!

Elizabeth: He wants to keep this as lighthearted and as happy as he possibly can. This is really the way it is for him. He's very lighthearted. He's very happy. He's going to go through this litany of information.

Jim: First of all, Chris, thank you for taking good care of me. I never had a lot of suffering ... physical pain to the point where it was unbearable. I think that had a lot to do with you and how much care you gave me ... made sure I was okay, that I had my medicine and all the things you would do to keep me comfortable and happy. I know that the energy work, Reiki, helped a lot. I also now know that you were doing that for me even when I said I didn't want to, even when I said, "Not now." I want you to know how much I appreciate that.

Remember the day that I fell in church?

Chris: Do you mean at the healing mass?

Jim: That's what it feels like where I am. I'm totally encompassed by, filled with, surrounded by and in total love with the Spirit. Chris, we all feel that way here. It's a state of elation, excitement, joy, spirit. It didn't take long for me to achieve that. I've learned that how you feel after you leave your body seems to be dependent on how you lived your life on Earth.

I know that you've been placed in good hands. Too many people want to help! It was like that when I was going through being sick ... too many people wanted to help. I tried to let them as much as possible but I always felt like I had to help them deal with my dying and I was just too tired. That's why I asked you, Chris, to put limits on how many people came and how long they stayed. I know it hurt my family's feelings the most, but it was so necessary for me. I can't tell you how grateful and how happy that made me.

I'm very shy on the inside, and it was always hard for me to be the one to take from others. I know you are the same way. I've learned that you have to "take"... It's the same as giving. You can't keep giving everybody one hundred percent all the time without taking something back. That's when you get out of whack, you get out of balance. I want you to remember that.

All the care, all the love, all the joy, the goodness that you have brought to people's lives over all this time ... . You've got to learn to take some of that back and really take the help in a way that shows people you're grateful for that help. When you refuse help, you're taking the joy of giving away from others who really want to give. I've learned that people really want to help, not so they can get something back but because they want to help. I now know that. I've really learned a balance.

I've also learned that there's no end to how much I can love, Chris ... no end to how much I can love. This love that I have for you is still romantic love yet goes beyond romantic love. It's beyond intimate love between lovers or spouses. It is a divine, forever love that is God's love. Do you understand that?

Chris: (Crying.) Well, I think so, as well as I can. The hard part is that I still love you as my husband and miss you terribly.

Jim: *I've really gone through a transformation and have made amends. I made amends with my past before I left ... things that I could have done better, relationships that were not as strong as they could have been, forgiving people ... . I made amends with all of those things and I am so glad I did that.*

I didn't want to leave. Elizabeth, you know I didn't want to leave her behind, but I knew she would be in good hands.

Chris: (Crying,) Not as good as with you.

Jim: *I knew we would still be connected. Inside of me, I knew that I wasn't going to leave you. I just couldn't keep my body anymore. My body gave up on me, Chris.*

Elizabeth: It sounds to me like if it was up to him, he would have kept his body and he would have stayed here, physically.

Jim: I learned an awful lot that last year that I was here. How important family is. It was, always, to me, Chris. Family ... nephews, nieces, your family, my family, all one big family. That was so important to me.

   I loved flying, and now I can fly everywhere without a plane.

Elizabeth: He has a big smile. It sounds like he can go anywhere he wants and have a good time. This makes him incredibly happy because he was worried that he was going to be stuck in one place—that he wasn't going to be mobile. He's got to tell you some things that he's been helping you with. He says he sat right next to you ... He's showing me dinner, some kind of special occasion.

Chris: You mean our anniversary dinner?

Elizabeth: Yes, anniversary dinner. He was right there waiting for you to make a toast. He's so sorry he couldn't be there in person, but he was there in spirit. He really was.

Chris: (Crying.) Did the cat jump on his lap?

Elizabeth: He did.

Jim: <u>She</u> did. Most people would think these things were imagination, but I was right there. I wouldn't have missed it for the world.

Chris: (Crying.) Thank you.

Jim: I have found out that I can still stay here. I'm not going to stay until you're okay, because you're always okay. I'm going to stay for as long as I can with you. I'm worried about you not being able to sleep and these confusion migraines. I don't want to dwell on it to get it started. I'm sorry if I seemed kind of perturbed or upset with you at the hospital.

Chris: Do you mean on Christmas Eve when I had the first "episode," as you call them?

Jim: It was really because I felt so badly and knew there was nothing I could do to help. That TGA you had is the strangest thing that ever happened to us, Chris! (Laughing.)

Chris: (Laughing.) It's a story I tell everyone!

Jim: I'm making light of it and laughing about it, but I hope that never happens again. I know it was just because you were upset.

Elizabeth: Who's John?

Chris: Alive or dead?

Elizabeth: Deceased. Your husband says he's actually met up with John. He's laughing about this because he says, "Some people just never change." It's given him peace of mind. Who's William?

Chris: My father.

Elizabeth: Okay. He really goes by Bill, though, doesn't he?

Chris: Yes, he does.

Jim: Bill, your father, was here to get me. Dad … my father, too.

Elizabeth: Who's Robert or Bob?

Chris: That's Jim's father.

Elizabeth: Okay. Both your father, Bill, and Jim's father, Bob are here with him now.

Jim: Give a message to Marianne. I appreciate all that she helped with—going to appointments and helping us cope—and all that she is as a person. I can't thank her enough. Please be sure you thank her.

Tell them all I don't have any favorites—I didn't like any of them! You know I'm only joking!

Chris: Do you know that Marianne's going to Aruba with us?

Jim: No.

Chris: Joe and Marianne are coming to Aruba with us. Will you be there?

Jim: I'm going to make sure of it.

Chris: Oh good!

Jim: She deserves it. (Laughing.) She deserves more than Aruba. Enjoy. We're going to have a great time. I'm so grateful for her. What's strange is Marianne can't hear me and I don't understand why.

A lot of people wanted to come up with an answer to why I had cancer. Sometimes you just have to accept things the way they are ... accept life the way it is. You don't need to come up with an answer. That was one of my greatest life lessons.

I'd ask myself, "Why do I have this disease? Why do I have this cancer?" I assumed it was from my father and the family but now I don't think it was. And it certainly wasn't because I believed I would end up this way, at least not consciously. I think it might be related to the fumes where I worked but I can't be sure. I'm not sure if I should say that because it would stir things up, whatever that means.

Chris: I don't want to sound fearful, but should I warn anyone?

Jim: Even if my problem was caused by fumes I wouldn't have given up flying anyway.

Chris: No, I know you wouldn't do that.

Jim: I never would have changed my life even if I knew beyond a shadow of a doubt that that was how I got sick. My experience with all of you there this time around ... . I never would have changed it—not one thing. I learned so much about myself. There was so much to do, so many places to see, so many things to experience. Even if I had a crystal ball and knew that cancer was coming, I'm not sure I would have done anything differently.

Chris, I want you to know that. I really want you to hear what I'm saying. It's not because I didn't love you enough or want to be with you. I know part of being here on the planet was because I was supposed to learn something. And I did—I learned a lot. I think we both were old souls and that somehow we knew each other long before we met each other. I always had that thought. I knew when I met you I was going to marry you. There was no question in my mind. You were like an old shoe ... something that fit perfectly.

Chris: (Crying.) So did I.

Jim: *(Smiling.) The day we were married was a day I'll never forget throughout eternity. The celebration, the fun, how I felt. I felt that way throughout our whole marriage, throughout our lives.*

Chris: Me, too.

Jim: *We never fought or bickered. We didn't have any trouble. Every time I would see you, it was like it was that time all over again. I'm so glad that you made everything that way for me. Without you being there at home taking care of things I couldn't have lived the life that I lived. There was no one I wanted to see more than you ... to be with more than you ... no one. I never wanted to look or go astray ... ever. No one ever caught my eye like you.*

Chris: I'm not having much fun without him these days.

Jim: *Remember that wherever you're going, I'm right there. You're not without me. Now I really am always with you ... always can be with you. And so if you don't have fun, I don't have any fun. So get out there and have a good time! If you don't have any fun, I don't have any fun.*

Chris: Have you seen our babies?

Elizabeth: He's smiling so brightly! How many pregnancies did you have together?

Chris: We had two.

Jim: *I have met them all three of them. Two are ours.*

Elizabeth: This is so interesting. He says two of them are physical again. It's like their souls decided to inhabit into a different family.

Jim: *I don't know how it all works. We never knew why you couldn't carry a child.*

Chris, I know it was important to both of us but I didn't love you just because I wanted to have children. I hated seeing you so sad about not having kids. I was sad, too, but watching you go through it was the worst. I wanted to be a parent, a dad, but I was able to take other kids under my wing and you were, too.

Jim: *Chris, you would have made a great mom.*

Chris: (Crying.) Thank you.

Jim: *I've been able to reunite with those souls.*

Chris: Does it matter if they're boys or girls, or not?

Jim: *Two boys and a girl.*

Chris: What were our two?

Jim: *A boy and a girl. (Laughing.) We should have had all boys anyway. I would have no idea what to do with a girl. I would have had no idea! Boys I could do, but not girls.*
I want to tell you about some of the things at the house … only because I'm there. Things are slowly getting back to normal. You're putting things back where they belong and getting back to normal. I think that's the best way to go. Home was incredibly important to me. Don't hurry getting things back to normal but I know that will help you feel better. A lot better. If there is anything at all I can do to make it better for you, I will.
The Blessed Mother and St. Francis really do exist. That's a miracle I've experienced just by dying. I want to share that with you as much as I possibly can.

Chris: I share that with everyone.

Jim: *I didn't want to leave you, but now that I'm gone, it's not as bad as you might think. I say this because I no longer have a sick body. Not that I wanted to leave you, but I'm happier than I thought I would be.*

Chris: I'm so glad! Have you been giving me signs? Was the feather at Beaver Lake a sign?

Jim: The geese.

Chris: The geese were a sign?

Jim: I stirred them up.

Chris: Oh, you did! I knew you did!

Jim: I could never be mean to animals but I really needed you to know that I was there.

Chris: Did you show me the single goose on purpose?

Elizabeth: He's going like this, like he's holding it back by the tail.

Jim: That I didn't really do, that was just something that happened. But I did stir them up so that they would all fly out of formation because I wanted you to know I was really there with you. I'm really everywhere with you ... at the grocery store, going to dinner, out with your friends. I just am. You know me, I don't like to rest. I've had enough rest. Since I've been on the other side I've really had enough rest, and now I'm just going to keep track of you!

Chris: Can you do other things and be with me at the same time?

Jim: No. I see that you've been driving my truck.

Chris: Yes. I kept that, not the other vehicle. But you know that.

Jim: (Laughing.) I think you look great driving my truck!

Chris: Do you know I scratched it?

Jim: Yes. Jeez. I can't believe you scratched my truck. Quite a good scratch, too.

Chris: Yes, it is. I'll fix it.

Jim: Jeesh! You know better.

Chris: Do you know I cleaned it and had it detailed, too?

Jim: Yes ... scrubbed it! I'm quite impressed with your efforts!

Chris: I knew you would be.

Jim: Very impressed with your efforts, but ... um ... go gentle and easy on her, please. Just lighten up a little on the truck. (Lots of laughing during this conversation—very lighthearted!) Do you know that song by one of your favorite country singers?

Elizabeth: (starts humming and singing the song)

Chris: Oh ... yes I do.

Elizabeth: I keep hearing that song playing in the background, and he's trying to get you to hear that song. That's a good reminder that he is wherever you go. He was even when he was alive.

Jim: Even when I was alive, I was with you everywhere no matter how far away I was from home. I couldn't wait to get home.

Chris: I knew you always wanted to come home to me.

Jim: We talked about this before I physically left. I stressed that I want you to have a companion.

Chris: Do you mean a dog?

Jim: No, I mean a person. I'm not sure I'm ready for you to be with another person yet though. There's still some time that needs to take place for me to get used to the state I'm in, and you to get used to the state that you're in ... being physical without me. When we have both gotten used to it, then it will be time.

Chris: You talked to me about going on with my life eventually with someone new, but you already know I don't want to.

Jim: I mean somebody else, but getting another pet, like a dog ... that would be great. I know you're not ready, but eventually I do want you to move on with someone else.

Chris: (I'm plugging my ears because I don't want to hear this.)

Jim: Not now. It's almost too much for me to even suggest, but when the time is right, I want you to know that I'm going to try to find someone for you. Nobody should be alone. I was pretty sure of that from the time I was a little guy growing up.

Chris: (Crying.) I can't believe it'll happen, though.

Jim: No one should be alone. It's going to be a long ways away, but it will happen.

Chris: Can I ask what you meant when you told your friend, Joe, to have me write everything down?

Jim: (Laughing.) Because in case you start acting crazy again. I want you to make sure you have your questions written down!

Chris: Oh, is that what you meant? Then you are referring to the two TGAs I had.

Jim: I'm trying to make as light of it as I possibly can. That was a strange, strange thing that happened. That's all behind us now. I don't like all these other aches and pains either ... a lot of aches and pains.

Chris: I always had them; I just didn't tell you.

Jim: Yes. You never complained. I think it's time for you to take good care of "you." It's okay to complain. I didn't think so when I was sick—that complaining about it was the right thing—but it is okay to complain.

Chris: Is it easiest for you to communicate with me when I'm home quietly, like meditating, or outside walking in nature?

Jim: Whatever is easier for you. I can always communicate with you. It's how well you hear me and receive the messages.

Chris: Am I on the right track by thinking I am getting your messages so far?

Jim: So far, so good. You're getting everything that I'm really worried about like repairs on the house, what to do financially, what to write in thank-you cards.

Elizabeth: He never was good about—he's acting kind of embarrassed to say this, but he's saying it, so I'm going to repeat what he's saying—lovemaking, for example. This seemed to be one of your strong points together, and he doesn't want you to go without that for the rest of your life.

Jim: And when the time is right, I'll help you find someone who can take that over for me. I loved that kind of intimacy with you.

Chris: (Crying.) Me, too.

Jim: I don't want you to be without that. It's not normal or not natural. We were lovers, not fighters. We were lovers.

Chris: Did he have anything to do with flashing the lights on my brother's car or the windshield wipers on my car with Marianne?

Jim: Yes. I was just about to get to those topics. Like, um ... Joe. I really wanted to talk to Joe. Joe is such a good guy, and I'm so glad that I could talk to him.

I try to find subtle ways to let you know I'm around. I want it to be like I never left. This will help me and it will help you. I know it can't stay like this forever, but for right now I am there and here.

Chris: Are you here all the time?

Jim: Yeah. All the time.

Chris: (Crying.) So when I was in bed and I got that little message ... like it was a text in my dream, it was really you?

Jim: Yeah, it was definitely me. You can't walk away from a love like we had, and I'm not going to ... . Not now, anyway. I'm going to wait until you get better and until I get better ... until I can reason with it. I have to come to grips with it myself.

Chris: Along with me.

Do you spend a lot of time with my dad and our families?

Jim: Well, as much as I can, but I get more worried about you. As much as I can, I visit them. They've found a great deal of happiness on the other side. Their need to be here isn't like it was when they first left. So they understand, because they've been through it, how much it means to me to just be near you.

People need to know, Chris, that you never really are dead. Never.

Chris: I'm telling everyone. I tell as many people as I can.

Jim: We just leave our bodies behind, but I'm not dead, Chris. I wish I had a better understanding of that when I was physical. I understood it intellectually, but you never really get it until it happens. But I'm not dead.

Please tell Bruce and Rosemary how grateful I am about the way that they've extended their hand and been so good to you and me. I just can't believe it ... the generosity.

Chris: I can't either.

Jim: I'd tell them myself if they could hear me, but they don't always. They are good people walking on the Earth. I just love them so much ... more than bosses. I can't thank them enough for everything they've done.

Chris: I'll be sure and tell them again. They certainly have been good to us.

Do you know that Paul and Leslie are going to have the middle name be James for the baby, even though it's a girl?

Elizabeth: Yes. He gets really soft.

Jim: Jamie would be fine .... It doesn't have to be after me. I'm so honored by that, but give the poor girl a girl's name! What is wrong with people? (Laughing.) I can still hear music playing from Earth. This brought me a lot of gratification ... having music. I can still hear music. I'm so glad about that; I can't describe it to you in words, but music is so important to me—hearing it, feeling it, just listening to music. So the more you play, the better it is. I can even tolerate what you listen to!

Chris: (Laughing.) Wow! I can't believe you would say that!

Elizabeth: Your dad intercedes here. He wants you to know that he's taking really good care not to take attention from Jim. He really loved Jim, too.

Chris: Yes he did, so much.

Elizabeth: It's hard when you get to the other side. That love obviously continues. It's even a different love, though; it's a deeper, stronger love. But your dad says he wants to make sure you know that he doesn't take him away from you, as much as he'd like to because he liked spending time with Jim.

Chris: So my dad understands my talking to Jim more than him now, doesn't he?

Elizabeth: Yes. Jim's father has found ways to occupy himself. Jim's laughing, because this is evidently always the way he was … working, learning, that sort of thing.

He loves traveling … seeing places, going places, but he really loves—perhaps the most—learning, knowledge, the gathering of knowledge, and so he's off at school and he's off doing this and off doing that. He's having a really good time.

Jim is impressed by his enthusiasm to even do that. Really impressed. It's okay for him to say that because when he was alive, there were times when he was down and lacked enthusiasm about anything at all. Do you need to ask Jim anything else?

Chris: Does he have messages for anyone besides Marianne?

Jim: Our nieces and nephews are very important to me.

Elizabeth: Is there a Dan or Danny?

Chris: Yes, Daniel.

Jim: I know that Daniel created something in my honor, and I am really flattered by that.

Chris: A little church that he named St. James?

Jim: Yes. I was impressed by the artwork, but more so impressed by the fact that he did it. It was shocking to me.

Chris: When you were very near death, Jessica came to visit and was very upset. She had written you a letter and I read it to you. Were you aware of everything in the letter?

Jim: I was. It was when my eyes were half-opened .... Yes, I was aware.
    The greatest gift I ever had in this life was to be so loved by so many people. I was so well-loved.

Chris: Yes, and you still are. So well-loved. Can you explain further who John is and talk more about Mother Mary who escorted you with our dads to Heaven?

Jim: Yes. Mary is Mother Mary. She escorted me to Heaven with my dad. John and your dad stayed to comfort you and Woody.

Elizabeth: We always think of Mother Mary as only being in the spirit world. Her loving actions are, in part, to carry souls to the Heaven world. Mother Mary is the one who helps so many get to the other world. She helped Jim get there, as well. This is her grace.

Jim: John was just another wonderful soul that was so helpful. I really know that I left my body and all I could have ever dreamed about can never be summed up as to how good it is, and it's so good because I'm with you, too.

Chris: The best of both worlds? That's wonderful.

Jim: Now the best of both worlds ... that's true. I'm going to give it some time. At this point, that's all that you can do is just give it some time. There's still a lot of the world to see.

Chris: For me?

Jim: Yes. I'll be right with you every step of the way.

Chris: (Crying.) So you know how much I love and miss you still? Do you feel the pain from me or do you just see it? I don't want you to feel it.

Jim: *I know it.*

Chris: Okay. I don't want you to feel it.

Jim: *We just have to give it time ... just got to give it some time.*

Chris: Is there anything I can tell your mother from you? Or any other members of your family? She's very sad and depressed still, of course.

Jim: *Tell her—and you have to be firm and direct about it—she can't come to be here with me; it's not time yet. I don't want anybody walking around, moping around, sad, miserable, upset, all of this. I worry about my mom and you the most. Mom, most of all, has a reason to walk around sad and unhappy. I can't tell her how to feel. I know how hard it is for everyone. We're all so sad. It bothers me so much because I know there's nothing I can really do about it. It breaks my heart.*

Chris: It would make you happier if she could get out of this, wouldn't it?

Jim: *Exactly. Get out of the funk. The whole thing is still pretty recent, though. It's only been a couple of months. I had been on Earth for forty-nine years and now I'm not physically there. We can't expect that we can all get over our losses in just a couple of months. And she's my mother, she had me the longest.*

Chris: She can't help but be in a funk. I can't help but be in a funk either.

Jim: *I didn't believe that last year was going to be my last Christmas. I thought for sure that I had a couple more Christmases to go.*

Elizabeth: He's smiling at me, and he's bringing me back to when we were in the office and he said, "Do you think this is going to be my last Christmas?" I wouldn't answer him. It was kind of like he knew that I knew.

Jim: *Even if Elizabeth had told me, it wouldn't have made a difference. I would still have done everything the way I did. I'm so glad I had last Christmas with everyone, with the family. This Christmas will be a little different. I loved Christmas, I loved the holidays ... getting together with everyone and everything about it. I'll be there.*

Chris: With both families? Because you'll be following me, right?

Jim: Yes. You're going home. I'm going to make sure that I'm there with you. I'll ride with you and be there. I wish I could drive. I can't drive these days, but I can go with you.

Chris: I knew you were riding with me to the flight department party because I knew you wouldn't let me go by myself. I knew you were there.

Jim: It's hard watching you have to do all this on your own. I know nothing else replaces what we had together, but I want you to keep things as normal as you possibly can because I don't want to see you crash.

Chris: Thank you. Somewhere inside, I know that it's you helping me. Have you seen our friend, Al? He just passed recently. I don't know if he's still resting or he's around.

Elizabeth: That's why I keeping yawning, because someone new keeps coming in. The significance of the yawn … it shifts my consciousness, but this deeper yawn means to me that this person is very new to the afterlife. It's very evident. Al is smiling. Who is Donna? No, not Donna. Dor … Doreen maybe?

Chris: His wife.

Al: Would you tell her it was easy? It was like the time I passed out. It was very easy to die. She just needs to hang in there. I'm so worried about Doreen. She's a mess.

Chris: Yes, but she doesn't act it.

Al: That's what I'm worried about—that she's so internally struggling that she's not expressing how she really feels. I'm worried that she's going to have a meltdown. She's trying to be strong for everyone.

Chris: Should she come for a reading?

Al: If she's interested. We never really talked about stuff like this. I always figured there was something beyond life as we know it. I just didn't know what. Doreen *is strong. I know she'll get through this. It's hard on her as it is, not to mention that the holidays are here. There are some private things that I want to talk to her about. I never was good at it—communicating. We didn't always do that so well.*

I'm not going to stay and take up all your time, but I want her to know that I saw all the arrangements that were made and the way she carried everything through. I'm really grateful for that. It was never easy for me to say thank-you in a way that sounded sincere but I was so glad the way that she did everything.

Elizabeth: It appears he was involved in some kind of sports. He has a tough demeanor, but I don't feel as though he's as tough on the inside as he was on the outside.

Chris: He was a football coach for many years so he was a bit of a tough guy.

Al: I tried to be as good as I could be at telling her I loved her, but I didn't always see the need for it. Now that I'm on the other side, I have a different perspective. There were many things that I wish I had said and done but didn't. I want her to know that.

Jim: It tires me out getting used to both places—the physical world and the other side. So there are times when all I do is rest. I'm not quite used to it all.

I don't have any regrets about our life, about you as a wife, me as a husband ... we were like one person. I would do it all over again in a second.

Chris: Me, too.

Jim: These communications help me to grow because I know you're trying to be happy. It makes me happy and it seems to be helping you, too. I actually have to go through a similar process of grieving, of losing my body. It takes a while to get used to being here. It isn't like you see on TV—that all of a sudden you're this enlightened, amazing being. It takes a while to get used to it. I'm having the same kind of trouble that you are in terms of grief and sadness and feeling like we're separated.

Elizabeth: I hope Jim knows I won't allow people to get too attached to communication with loved ones because everyone needs to take responsibility for how they feel.

Chris: Jim knows I worry about everyone. I'm especially worried about his family. Can he tell me, from his view, how he thinks they're doing?

Jim: Everyone seems to be holding their own under the circumstances. I get a little worried about Theresa. We had the same birthday. It's hard to watch everyone suffer. It's especially difficult with Theresa and Mom, only because everyone else has more support. I've been working through my own feelings of suffering and separation from all of you. I never was one to like to see anybody cry. I feel especially helpless because I'm not there to provide comfort.

Chris: And you know how sad they all are?

Jim: Yes, I know, but I don't know what to do about it or how to help. I'll be there with all of you as much as I can. I guess you have to feel what you feel at the moment. I have to go rest. (Laughing.) It takes a lot out of me to be here.

Chris: I love that you came today and that you could spend this time with me.

Jim: (Laughing.) I try to make the most of every moment, and I didn't think that resting was going to be something I would really do over here.

Chris: You always used to say, "I can rest when I'm dead."

Jim: I really know I have to. It takes a lot of energy and I need to take the time to rest, so I am actually going to go home and rest.

Chris: Okay. Bye, Sweetie.

Jim: I love you so much.

Chris: I love you so much.

Jim: It doesn't go away—none of that goes away. You really take it with you.

Elizabeth: Everyone who visited today has to go back now. They all have work to do. Jim's work right now is to go find a place to rest. They have to go back to work, doing what they are assigned to do.

Chris's Reflections:

This was my first full reading since Jim's passing because of the TGA during the very first reading. As time went on and readings for this book continued, I almost felt like Elizabeth wasn't in the room and I was simply having a discussion with Jim or whomever I was speaking with at the time. Although even a first reading with a medium is very easy to understand, you should know that from the very beginning, you can speak directly to the person with whom you are communicating. It is a very clear and smooth process as you move through the reading.

Giving versus receiving is such an important concept and I never realized we had to have this balance in our lives. What we give out to the universe really does come back to us. For example, if we only think about what we don't have, that is what will come back to us. To be healthy human beings mentally, physically, spiritually and emotionally, we must be in balance. There needs to be an exchange—that you allow what you give to come back to you. This keeps life in balance.

We've all seen or experienced times that we work so hard for so long that we come down with an illness; that's because we're out of balance. I grew up believing that it's good to be a giver and do for others as much as I possibly can ... and that's true. However, the necessity of allowing ourselves to receive was never explained. If someone offers to do something for us or give us a gift, and we constantly say no to their offers, two things will happen.

First, we take away the joy of giving from the person who is doing the offering. Is it ever fair to take joy away from anyone? Of course not. By accepting an offer, we actually contribute to that person's joy and spreading of joy to others. Second, if we continue to endlessly refuse to accept from others, those offers will end, we will continue to do for others, and we will be totally out of balance. We sometimes hear people say, "I give and give to everyone around me and the life is being sucked out of me."

I learned it is necessary to let people who offer me help to give me help. It also came to my awareness that sometimes the actual cause of "life being sucked out of someone" is that they don't accept what others try to give. We must do both: give to others but also accept or receive with grace and gratitude.

I was so thrilled to hear from Jim in this reading that he was not only mobile on the other side, but that he could now do what he loved the most—fly—without an airplane. He can go anywhere he wants, however he wants, and he's not stuck in one spot. I think many or most of us believe in life after death, but when you don't know what that really means, it can be a little scary.

Will I be someone with a little harp sitting blissfully forever on a cloud in the sky? This may sound silly, but that is what I used to picture when I thought about everlasting life. From all the souls I spoke with for this book, I learned that everything is the same as on Earth, but usually better. They travel, learn, have jobs and entertainment; this list goes on and on. They just don't have the dense physical bodies that we do, so it's all much easier for them than for us.

So many people talk about our loved ones who have passed still being with us and that now we have an "angel" to guide us in our life. First, as I learned from my readings, people don't become angels just because they physically die. What I also learned, however, and it's clear in this reading and most, if not all of them, is that we are simply energy ... energy that transforms.

Remember learning in science class that "energy is neither created nor destroyed; it just changes form"? That's what we all are—energy in the physical form. Those who have passed from the physical to the spirit world are also energy, but have simply changed form. So our loved ones aren't seen by most of us, but yes, they are around us. They are in their "light bodies" or spirit form.

Jim was truly with me at the dining room table when I sat there by myself celebrating our anniversary after he died. I did put out two place-settings, a candle, his picture, and two wine glasses filled with wine. I did make a toast to him. Jim is the one who brought this up in this reading, not me. Elizabeth didn't know I did all of that for our anniversary, so she certainly couldn't have brought it up. Jim did. He was literally right there at the table with me. I just couldn't see him in the form of energy that he's in. When I asked about the cat jumping up on his lap, Elizabeth said "he" and Jim is the one who corrected her and said "she" did.

Exciting stuff, isn't it? That's the reason it's so important for us to do our best to get out there and have a good time after we've lost a loved one. They are with us, and if we're having a good time, so are they. In a way, they are living vicariously through us. Jim can no longer have his chianti or merlot wine and all the great food he loved, but he can still enjoy it through witnessing me and my enjoyment of it. How wonderful is that?

Jim talks about how difficult it is getting used to not having a body, that he didn't want to leave me or this physical life and that it's hard watching me or others do things without being able to help. What amazes me is the fact that at the same time, he is very happy and in awe of how wonderful it is to be on the other side. That has helped me so much, because selfishly I wanted Jim to still love and miss me, but even more, I wanted him to be happy where he is now. What could be better than knowing that you still have to grieve and learn to heal the grief, but at the same time be what I feel is blissfully happy? That applies to those on the other side and to us human beings as well.

Jim's Reflections:

These reflections were dictated by me more than three years after I left my body, but I remember everything about this visit.

I knew I was two months out of the body only from the perspective and view of watching you, Chris, and all that you had done as well as what you were preparing for. I knew that something was brewing. I knew that life was still continuing. I watched life through my siblings, you and everyone around you. I was so apprehensive this day because I didn't want another episode (TGA) to happen. I didn't want one more thing to put you into a setback. I knew at this point you had already started having trouble with your knee and that it was painful. Not that you complained to anyone, but I witnessed how hard it was for you to get around.

I saw that you wore my crucifix and wedding ring around your neck. At first, I thought there was a sweetness to this. I witnessed this as a great gesture—a kind, loving one. I missed touching you so much and being physical. I missed being with you laughing, joking and doing the everyday chores that we used to do together as much as we possibly could.

When it was time for this reading, and I knew it was time when I came in, I thought you would be okay but I just wanted to make sure that all things were in place and in order. I wondered if you had an emergency bracelet, if you knew who to call, where your papers were ... all the things to do with having another episode. So I watched, listened and observed to make sure that when Elizabeth's eyes were closed, that your eyes were open, you were paying attention and you weren't "fuzzy." I was very concerned about this.

I have been moving to and into much higher realms, and have gone through exercises and assessments. They were preparing me for the next step in the other world ... something I would do that would change the way you and I interact with one another just for a short period of time. They tell us here in this world that we must prepare to appear in front of the Divine Council. Little did I know that steps in the human world were closer than what most people would realize. In other words, preparation occurs even while people are physical. Still, preparation needed to take place. I was ready to do so.

After I left my body, I named all the people that I encountered one by one ... people who had come, people who continued to leave and people who still were calling and checking on you. I was of great appreciation for the ones who kept calling even after a couple of months, because usually people go away. You see them for a short time and then they go on with their lives. I was happy that people had stuck by you. That was one of my greatest prayers. By the way, I did still pray at that time of being out of my body. I prayed fiercely that you would be okay.

I watched you go through the hardest times that anyone would ever have to go through. I watched you and contributed to trying to help you through those hard times. I was there for our wedding anniversary and for the first Thanksgiving. Everybody tried to laugh and make fun but it never was really quite the same. I kept yelling to you, "I'm right here! Can't you see me? Can't you hear me? I'm right here!" And I was. I was right there. Right there in our house listening, laughing and doing the best I could.

Most people think that when you go through the death or the dying experience, that it's easy as one-two-three. You leave the body, you go with the light beings and you go higher and higher. But that's not true. I left my body and went with the light beings, but I still had great attachments to the physical world ... my family, you, my sisters and brother, brothers and sisters-in-law, nieces and nephews ... I had huge attachments to all of them. Of course, this was holiday time and I loved Christmas. I loved time together with the family. I liked buying presents, laughing and joking ... and getting presents. People say giving is better than receiving, but I liked getting presents just the same! It was fun.

I watched the animals always looking for me, putting their heads around the corner. I would move through the house quietly so as not to disturb anyone, but just to observe you. I saw your sadness but knew your perseverance.

It seemed something had changed almost every day that month, in those weeks before this reading. Al came to visit. Al left his body and came right to the spirit world. He didn't look for me directly, but he was here. We reunited. He saw the pain in his wife's eyes. Thank God for her faith because she was a mess. In front of people she showed she was happy. Most people do when they're in front of everyone else.

I saw that you were putting things back together a little at a time, back in order in the house, back in order in your life. You were taking care of business as usual because that's what you did—made sure everything was in perfect order. This bill was paid, that present was bought, everything was done in Sergeant Chris's way. That's what I knew you to do.

I wanted so badly for you to be able to feel me, to touch me, to hug me, to hold me and for me to do the same for you. I wanted it so badly, so deeply. But I knew that was never going to happen again, at least during this lifetime. I wanted to encourage you to have someone else, someone to care about, someone to care about you. I knew there would be no way in this short period of time you would even consider such a thing and yet I had to say it anyway. I had to say that more than anything, I wanted your happiness. If that entailed having someone else, then that was happiness for me.

Just know I would like it to be different for you. I wanted it to be different for you, of all people in the world. I wanted you to be happy. I wanted to hear you laugh again ... really laugh like you used to when we both were together telling jokes or saying stupid things. That laughter was gone, and I was so worried about the laughter being gone. I wanted it back for you, no matter what. If being with someone else meant more laughter for you, I was all for it. I loved you that much. When the time is right, I'm hoping you'll find another. Someone to laugh, someone to joke, someone to be goofy just like we both were when we were here together.

I went to church with you every week, not to see how much attention you would get, but because I loved going to church. I loved that quiet time, that solemn peace, that very, very deep quiet that I would achieve when I was there. Most people laugh about going to church but it was important to me. So much was still important ... so many activities that I was used to. They were all still meaningful to me.

I would do them over and over again, as much as they would allow, "they" being the ones in the Heavens that opened up and closed the doors. There's no curfew, really, there's no such thing as time where I am. You just know you have to go back. One way or another, you do. I spent the majority of time around you. I was given that privilege almost immediately because I was obedient. I would go back when I was told to, but I knew we still needed one another's companionship. We made a great team and I was having as difficult a time separating as you were.

As I look back now and observe ... I witnessed, I watched, I learned, I grew ... I realized the love for you never got any different, but better. It never grew less; it was stronger. But it was a different kind of love, a different kind of love altogether. It was the kind of love that you hope for, that you wish for, that you dream of. It was the kind of love that everyone and anyone would want. It's that deep love of the soul ... a time you remembered each other from waaay before the time you spent together in this life. It was a love that was endless. That, I am sure of.

When I saw how you were always still helping to take care of everyone, I assumed at first that was you being your natural self—doing what you needed to do, needing to do what you were doing just to stay busy, just to stay active, just to stay involved. I was worried because you became thinner. You became more tired. I worried about you because you weren't exactly like I remembered you always were. It's odd that you still worry when you're where I am. People think those feelings go away, but you do worry, you do wonder, you are curious.

More than anything, I wanted you to keep on learning, to keep on growing. It was then, when you were quiet, that I was able to make some contact with you, to have "you and me" time. It taught me an incredible amount. It gave me useful tools to function in the other world. It was important.

To go on and on about being a great wife and a best friend and all that you are would just be redundant. You know what you were to me and I certainly know what I was to you. I was rejoined with so many, but the one person I missed the most was you. The laughter. I would quietly encourage you all the time to laugh ... to watch TV and laugh, hear music on the radio, go to one of the kids' games ... anything and everything that would bring you some state of laughter. It seemed it had been so long since I really heard you laugh. That part I remember so clearly.

It was so good to talk to you that day. I'd been there so many times and "listened in" ... all your sessions, all the things you would do and say. I was around you so frequently and yet you still could not hear me. That's why there's nothing like the interaction we share together during a reading with a medium. We were actually able to converse because of the medium. I'm so grateful ... so grateful that there's an available person in the world to allow that to happen.

To bring a little light to the situation, pun intended, that's what I have been trying to do ... learn more about how I can bring light to the situation, how I can be light to the situation. So to all those who remain after someone departs, learn how to laugh and still keep that state of joy. Nothing makes us happier than watching how happy you are. So do not mourn when I go away. Like with anyone else, don't be sad that I'm gone or they're gone or we're gone. We're just an earful away. It's not that hard.

I didn't really miss working as much as I thought I would. I didn't miss being away on long trips. I didn't miss it. I missed being with my wife. To physically be able to touch her and feel her touching me ... I missed it. To say I didn't would be a lie. To say I still don't would be even more of a lie. Going to the other side has taught me many lessons, but one in particular is that there "is" another side. There are two sides to every story, as they say, whoever "they" are. Two sides to a coin. Two halves that make a whole. You were my half that made a whole. I thought I would stop missing you very quickly, that I would forget about you and everyone else on Earth, but I didn't, and quite frankly, I'm glad I didn't. I didn't want to.

So read on in the pages ahead. We never really die—that's for sure. But it doesn't happen all at once ... that you die and suddenly you go to the greatest of the higher worlds. It's a process. There's always a process involved. The key is learning the process.

Until next time, ladies and gentlemen, when you decide to take another trip or go to a foreign land, remember those who are right where you left them. No matter how far away you go, the memory of where you once were stays with you. Especially if it was real.

The plane has landed. This journey has stopped. Until the next time we fly the friendly skies, thank our flight crew, thank all those involved, be happy with the one you sat next to. Hopefully you talked and learned a little about each other. That's the beauty of human beings; we're all so complex. An even deeper beauty is the soul. Uncharted territory for now.

Please gather your belongings, what little you have here—your faith, your hope, your love—and take them with you as you go. Thank you, once again, for flying the friendly skies. Until next time.

— Captain Jim Petosa

January 20, 2012

Elizabeth: This is a year where logic and reason (science) and spirituality become one and the same for people like you who have a very active mind. This will be a very easy year for your transformation. It will be so wonderful. The reason is that the conflict that often exists when people who are really spiritual and on a spiritual path is that they don't realize that science is just a way to prove spirituality and spirituality is proven by science. They're the same thing. So this year, taking a logical, reasonable approach to the way that your life is right now without your husband is going to be incredibly effective for you to heal.

I'm going to give you an exercise to help you get into that state. What they say in the higher realms is to look at your emotional situation from a logical, reasonable viewpoint. We're going to start with the first lesson, which is fear. Very simple … . Let's say one hundred days out of the year, it snows. Let's say someone has a fear of driving in the snow. Out of these hundred days, ninety-nine times this person drives in the snow and nothing happens. One time out of those hundred days, the person slips and goes off the road. Logic and reason say the odds are still in their favor that nothing will happen because ninety-nine times, the person drove and nothing happened.

It's the same thing with you and grief. Look at it in a really practical way. What day did Jim die?

Chris: October, 11, 2011.

Elizabeth: So, 102 days ago, Jim died and went to the afterlife. This is not to minimize what's going on with you. Out of those 102 days, how many days are you still here, healthy and well?

Chris: 102.

Elizabeth: That would mean that out of all the days Jim's been gone, you haven't died. The odds are in your favor, logically and reasonably, that you're going to stay here and that grief or sadness hasn't completely done you in.

Now look from Jim's point of view. For 102 days, he's been on the other side. He's had 102 days to get acclimated, comfortable, used to being on the other side and being without you, physically. He hasn't come back physically, so what are the odds that he's going to?

Chris: Zero.

Elizabeth: All we're trying to do is get your unconscious mind to resolve the conflict. The conflict is, "I'm so sad I feel like I'm going to die. I want him to come back, he has to come back, he's going to come back." We can use logic and reason here and say that for 102 days he hasn't and for 102 days, you've lived, which means that for 102 more days you can live in this way and feel better. Doesn't it?

Chris: Yes.

Elizabeth: For 102 days, Jim can be more in the afterlife and he can live and feel better. Let's just let that thought absorb into your unconscious. We're going to take this process in steps. That's all we can do … correct?

Chris: Correct.

Elizabeth: Because they are viewing this at a cellular level as well, remember these beings have a higher view. Every day, say to yourself, "I've lived 102 days without Jim. I can live 102 more, happily." Jim will do the same thing. For 102 days, he's been in the spirit world and he can go 102 more days … and then 102 more days. Why is this important? It's not because I want you both to separate. What's more important is the healing aspect of your body. Your body cannot take that amount of grief every day without doing something with it, or in other words, without creating an ache or a pain or a problem. Grief is so dense and so heavy that your body has to do something with it and it usually translates grief to pain.

We want you to be out of your physical pain but still in your body, or grounded, as we say in spirituality—connected to your body. Many people tell me they have a high tolerance for pain. The reality is pain is not a natural state of the body. Nobody is meant to have pain. I'd like you to do this exercise. When you wake up in the morning and you feel a little gloomy, say, "Okay, 102 days I've spent so far doing well and I can do 102 more." Because it's not 102 more days until you die, it's 102 more days of living well. Let's start doing that tomorrow and adding the days. Do you understand what to do?

Chris: I do understand and I'll do this exercise. I want to be free of this grief, but I want to remember Jim.

Elizabeth: Now, with your permission, I want to ask them what it is that you can do this year that answers to your life's mission. It's not the answer that's as important as how you ask the question. I think, based on my experiences of working with people in your situation, it might be time to ask, "What are some things that you can do as a human being to answer to your life's mission?" How do you feel about that?

Chris: I would love that. That's what I really wanted, coming here today.

Elizabeth: How do you want to feel about yourself in the absence of Jim?

Chris: I don't want to stop loving him and missing him, but I do want to stop feeling sad. I want to feel happy again. I want to feel alive again.

Elizabeth: Was there ever a time in your life where you felt alive before you knew Jim?

Chris: Certainly.

Elizabeth: When?

Chris: Most of my life, except during a divorce before Jim and when I miscarried several pregnancies. But you're asking for specifics about when I felt alive?

Elizabeth: So you, as a separate entity from your former husband, from having a baby, you in your life experience … when did you just feel good, happy and healthy?

Chris: Riding my horse.

Elizabeth: Good. How old were you?

Chris: We got him as a family when I was 5, and he died when I was 15, so I had him in my life for ten years. I loved having him.

Elizabeth: What was your horse's name?

Chris: Ike.

Elizabeth: What else?

Chris: Growing up in the country. We lived in the middle of nowhere and we would ride our horses all day, wherever we wanted, and as long as we were home by suppertime, it was all good. Growing up, we always had dogs. I loved that, loved being with my family on vacations.

Elizabeth: Good.

Chris: Picnics. My dad would take two weeks of vacation a year. Once we rented somewhere, but usually we never went anywhere. We just went on picnics and had wonderful times. I loved family gatherings, going to college, and I loved teaching.

Elizabeth: Then it's safe to say there was something inside of you that was loving. Otherwise you couldn't have done those things, right?

Chris: Absolutely.

Elizabeth: Something inside of you was loving before Jim came along, and that part of you that is so loving is what attracted Jim.

Chris: Yes, I think so.

Elizabeth: So what we want to do is get you back to that state of just loving life because you know you can love life without him being there.

Chris: Logically, yes.

Elizabeth: Logically, you know you can love life without him being there. Logic and reason serve on a conscious level. If logic and reason and spirituality are the same thing, that means your state of consciousness can adapt to Jim not being here and you will still be happy.

Chris: I do believe that, logically.

Elizabeth: It's just going to take some time for transformation to take place. What else would you like to ask?

Chris: My thoughts were—and I think that's why I had a setback after going on vacation—I do want to get this knee back in order and it's not yet. This would take physical means and right now that hurts, but I do want to volunteer with rescue horses. I also think I'll get a dog, but I might wait until spring. I really want to write a book, and I want to ask if that's something I should be thinking about or not.

Elizabeth: Okay. So let's just ask what activities in your daily life could help bring your spirit back into your body.

Chris: Yes. I also want to help my mom. She's 88 and I want to be able to spend time with her. She may come to live with me at some point. I'm not sure yet. Those are the main things I've been thinking about doing.

Elizabeth: What is your mom's name?

Chris: Wanda.

Elizabeth: Wanda. What a cool name!

Chris: She's a cool person.

Elizabeth: What is Wanda's last name?

Chris: Her maiden name was Mazurowski, and her married name is Frank. My dad has passed. He's Bill.

Elizabeth: Bill, are you the one who was here earlier?

Chris: Was he?

Elizabeth: (Laughing.) He was. I kept asking the people that were here before you if they knew who William was. They said no. Now I know who Bill is. Alright, Bill, you can talk to us if you'd like to. Jim, where are you? Okay. Are you telling me that he's not going to come in today? I guess we're going to hold off. The ones in the higher light … it's not that Jim isn't there, certainly; it's more like he's letting other things unfold before he comes in. That's good, Jim. Thank you.

Chris: Will he come in later?

Elizabeth: Yes. He's going to stand on the outside. He's laughing.

Jim: I don't want to dominate the whole thing, Elizabeth.

Elizabeth: He likes his quiet presence to be known. He wants to tell you something before we even get started, though, and he's smiling.

Jim: I never really died, Chris. I never really died. I just don't have my body. The darn thing didn't work very well anyway!

Chris: He says that in every reading.

Jim: I never really died.

Elizabeth opens the session, as she always does, with a prayer of gratitude and blessings.

Elizabeth: Dad, you can come in. Of course you can.

Chris: Hi, Dad!

Elizabeth: He's peeking in and says, "Can I come in? Can I come in? Can I come in?"

Chris: I'm so glad he's here. I wanted some guidance from him today.

Elizabeth: Bill, you can come in. Do you want to start, Bill?

Bill: I don't have all the answers, but I think I've got some things I can tell you that might put you in the right direction. The first thing is that sometimes I ask too much of you kids. If it's too much, I don't want you to go overboard with what I'm asking. If it's too much, it's okay to say it's too much.

Chris: I'm not sure if you know this or not, Elizabeth, but it takes two hours to drive to my mother's house and he must see me going back and forth regularly.

Elizabeth: He obviously knows that something is going on with your knee because he's pointing at your knee and he's pointing at different parts of your body.

Bill: You can't let your body go to pot. You've got to be able to take good care of yourself. I don't want you to worry so much about taking care of Mom right now. Just let her be there for you and you be there for her until this knee thing gets better.

Elizabeth: Now, I'll tell you, the "Higher Ups"—the ones in the higher light—are saying family, this year, is everything. Your family includes your immediate family but also your friends and loved ones, church family and other people that are around you. Family is everything. The planet, the consciousness of the planet, is moving very quickly into everyone being a part of the same family ... humanity. You're going to find that any and all activities that relate to family this year ... sharing with friends ... it may be hard for you to want to go out and be away from home.

Chris: They're probably telling me that because now that Jim's gone, it is so hard for me to make any kind of a commitment, even simply going to lunch with a friend —it isn't easy for me to do.

Elizabeth: Keep it in your mind that it's only been three months since Jim died. He knows you're having a hard time because he is still having a hard time separating from you. You have to remember, when many people die, especially if they had the kind of love that you both shared, they, too, have a very difficult time detaching from their loved ones.

No matter where you go, Jim will be there. You don't have to be at home or in your bedroom or in the bathroom or anything like that. No matter where you go, he's there. So make visiting your family a priority this year. Not only for you to help them, but for them to comfort you. The love that you experience from family will help you heal. That's what this whole year is going to be about for you—letting people help you!

Jim: Please listen to what she's saying. She's right; you don't let enough people help you.

Elizabeth: Now, let's get back to talking to the ones in the light. That's what this whole entire year is about for you — transformation. Transformation — the concept that you are a spirit having a physical experience. Jim, your father, all of your loved ones now … all are spirits who were having a physical experience. They've now realized they weren't physical beings having a spiritual experience. You are becoming keenly and acutely aware this year that you truly are a spirit that's having a physical experience. The spirit of life, of light, of love flows through your body and your being, healing it, transforming it and healing the unconscious parts of you that are in conflict, especially healing grief.

Chris: Would you say that again? Give me a different explanation? I don't understand.

Elizabeth: Your spirit is having a physical experience. That's really what's happening. We're really spiritual beings, spirit beings, having a physical experience. Your husband was the same way. Your father was the same way. They were all, and we are all, spirits having a physical experience. When their spirits leave the body, it goes back to the spirit world.

Since you are a spirit having a physical experience, now what's happening is, with this expansion of consciousness, you come to a realization. That's the transformation they are talking about. The first step to transformation is coming to the realization that you are a spirit having a physical experience.

Jim, your dad and some of your friends are in the spirit world. It will be very easy, by year's end, to heal your body from these physical ailments … it will be much easier to do that. As you meditate, as you do energy work like Reiki and allow the universal spirit to move through your being, you heal on all levels of consciousness—physical, subconscious and unconscious. The times it's easier to be aware of your spirit are during times of meditation, during times when you are connecting with nature, times when you are engaging in loving activities. Spending time with your family, spending time with your friends, spending time alone connecting with yourself, spending time with children, teaching, laughing, celebrating, being engaged in sport activities. These are all times to be aware of your spirit.

Nothing you do this year will be done on a personal or small scale, and while others will tell you being busy is avoiding how you feel, it's rather nurturing the need that exists within all humans … to love and be loved. An innate need of the spirit is to love and to be loved.

Reading and writing make you solid, grounded. Make your thoughts into words and your words into things on paper. The process pulls these thoughts, these things, out of your field that exists around you, out of your body and gives you greater room for healing. As we scan your mental and emotional bodies we can see that both are quite full. Writing, allowing your thoughts to flow through you and putting them on paper takes these thoughts out of your field. It clears your energy field. Writing can be very healing for you. The strong suggestion is to write. Put it all down on paper: what you're thinking, what you're feeling, even if it's negative, if it's angry, if there's doubt, if there's struggle, whatever the feelings are, all of them matter. Whether they're negative or positive, all your feelings and thoughts matter, not just one. Write, write, write. Write them all down!

A compilation of these thoughts and feelings, at a later time, will be used as healing for others.

People who are working through their grief process and at a deeper spiritual level will be healed without you physically touching them or being close to them. Words—feelings in words—carry a vibration, a frequency. When you're writing, and the time comes for others to be reading this writing, the energy of the words will flow through them the same as they flow through you while you are writing. This will be very healing. You are meant, in time to come, to help others heal the grief.

Physical health. You're going to find that your immune system begins to strengthen in ways that it never knew strength before—biofeedback, nutritional status, changing diet and supplements. You're someone who will fare much better with earthly guidance in this way rather than modern technology, and you'll find this irritable bowel and these troubles with your digestive system will all simply diminish to the point where you can at least live with it, if not completely heal it altogether. Supplements and foods ... any and all that boost or increase your immune system ... this will be helpful through the year to come.

Romance is well on the scene for you. We don't mean romance in a companionship kind of way, but romantic idealism—loving, music, art, beauty—all that is romantic in flavor. This is where you want to put your attention—languages, anything that is related to romanticism. This will be very much on the scene for you this year. You won't have to worry about companionship and meeting someone new and this sort of thing, but rather just completely indulging and being a part of this romanticism that's taking place on the planet, where everyone is romancing one another and helping to bring more light and love to the planet than ever before. Be aware and be awake to the ideas of romance, putting your interest in art, music, writing, literature, communication ... communication of all forms.

The more time Jim can spend with family and with you, the better he'll be able to go through his healing process. Therefore, help will be received by all from both sides.

Jim's biggest goal is to help people who have had the same kind of problem—cancer.

Jim: *I was never one to whine much or complain, but it was a merciless disease in that it just kept taking over. No matter what I did or didn't do, it just kept taking over.*

I'm now trying to help people on Earth from the spirit world and I'm going to get more involved in this. So there are going to be times when you're going to feel like I'm not there ... because I'm not.

What I want to do more than anything is to help people who are in the situation I was. I'm still on the fence whether the chemo and the medicines I was given actually helped me or hurt me. I realize now that it was both. I'm still on the fence with that, though.

Chris: I wondered about the ablation of the tumors ... whether that was a good or a bad thing.

Jim: I think that was a bad thing. I think it was bad because of the way I felt. At least with the other things I had done—chemo and the other treatments—I didn't feel as badly as I did after I had the ablation.

Chris: And I pushed you to have that.

Jim: I didn't do it for you. I was so grateful to you for trying to find anything that would work to keep me alive. So don't feel guilty or feel badly about this. I did it because I wanted to live. I don't regret anything I did to try to stay alive. All the things that I did, I did because I thought they could make me live.

Some people get involved in cancer studies and research projects to help the doctors figure out better methods of treatment of cancer. After we went out west and I was turned down for any treatment because our insurance wouldn't cover it, I lost all interest whatsoever in helping doctors and research projects that lost interest in helping me and others with the same problem.

I'm going to be working in the afterlife. I'm actually going to go through some proficiencies, some skills. There are laboratories and places where I can go and learn. Now that may sound outrageous to you, but it's true.

Chris: Really?

Jim: So I'm going to learn more, experience more, and get in tune or in touch with more as it relates to helping people heal this terrible disease. Not just from an aspect of medicine but from an emotional and mental standpoint, too. I realize that was a component that either lessened or worsened my condition.

Chris: That's fabulous!

Jim: No matter what anyone would tell me, there's nothing that can make me believe I created this problem—cancer. Nobody here, not one soul that I've encountered, would say that on a conscious level, they created the problem. I want to learn more about what people meant on Earth when they insisted all diseases— not just cancer—we create ourselves.

I promise you if I consciously knew that I was creating my cancer, there's no way possible I would do that. No one, except smokers, who has ever gone through treatment for cancer would have done something so awful to themselves. You just wouldn't. In my case, the cure was worse than the problem.

So I am going to study hard and work hard to find different ways to help people who have cancer. I want to find out as much as possible how one gets cancer, why someone has cancer and as many different ways as possible on how to fix it. I am convinced there is going to be a breakthrough. I'm sure of it.

If there are times when you feel I'm away from you, or you feel like I'm gone in some way, it's simply because I'm off trying to find the right answers.

Chris: And it doesn't mean you've forgotten about me?

Jim: *Absolutely not.*

Chris: You just won't be there right then.

Jim: *I'll be in my man cave, studying. I just want you to know where I'll be.*

Chris: Okay. Thank you, Sweetie.

Jim: *It will be just like when I was away flying. It's the same principle, the same concept.*

Chris: I'm so proud of you!

Jim: *I'm so proud of you because I know most people would have jumped by now. (Laughing.) I told you you were going to have to stay here for a long time without me and I'm just a phone call away.*

Elizabeth: He keeps referring to plugging in your phone.

Chris: Oh, he is? How cute!

Elizabeth: He's just a phone call away. He's going to make sure that he stays in contact with you.

Chris: And you help me find things when I ask you to, don't you?

Jim: *You're absentminded, Sweetie! You forget where you put things.*

Chris: You helped me find the checkbook the other day, right?

Jim: *Yup, I sure did. I love to be able to interact in this way, but if I'm taking all this time to help you find things, I can't be studying and doing the things I want to do to help other people. Please put things where they belong!*

I am trying to get used to life on the other side the way you're trying to get used to life here without me physical any longer. It's still taking me time to get used to this transition. I won't lie to you, Chris, it's been very hard to get used to this. I'm still unclear on how to be in both worlds at once. I'm learning more ways to be in both worlds.

What I loved doing the most I want you to continue, and that was being with family, being in nature and enjoying life because as you're doing that, I can join you in these activities.

Chris: So does that mean you didn't enjoy Aruba because I was so sad?

Jim: *Actually, it's the opposite. I loved being with you and I kept trying to comfort you by being around you. And I love it there. I never cared what kind of mood you were in, as long as I was with you. That part hasn't changed. So no matter what kind of mood you were in, it was fine with me. It was just what was meant to be at the moment.*

I've caught up on some reading. One of the jokes that I used to make was that I needed some time to catch up on reading and learning. I've taken the opportunity because I still need to rest and recuperate to regain my strength.

Chris: Are you just reading aviation material or are you reading about medicine and cancer now?

Elizabeth: It's so funny you would say that because he's thumbing through these books about old airplanes and flight schedules. He keeps turning pages.

Chris: That's all he ever read before!

Jim: *I've shifted my ideas and I'm looking more at cells and what happens at a cellular level when dealing with cancer. Something I always found complicated was that the doctors would use medical lingo that they understood. There was so much information I didn't really understand. I found it very difficult to listen to the doctors explain information I knew nothing about. That frustrated me. Now I have a lot of time on my hands. I read books as well as any and all other information that I can about cancer. I should have taken more responsibility to* *learn about cancer when I was there. I should have known more about a body—my own, since I had one. I especially should have known more about how to stay healthy to fight the cancer. I kept trying, not to ignore it, but to put my attention other places.*

Now I'm going to continue to take the time to learn how cancer really affected me on all levels ... physically, mentally and emotionally. If I were more knowledgeable and knew at the level I'm learning from now that chemo was doing so much damage to my body, I would have stopped what I was doing. I would have sought after different ways to stay healthy and reverse the damage done to my physical body. I wouldn't necessarily have stopped looking for a way to stop the cancer, but I would have looked at different ways to stay healthy.

There's a way, Chris, that we both can heal from being separated from one another and at the same time not feel so badly about the separation. We in the spirit world are getting used to being separated from you, physically, and learning ways to heal our own grief of being without you. It's a great exchange that takes place. In our society, we don't necessarily learn how to separate from one another in a healthy way. We tend to stay fixed on the problem and the sadness and blame, rather than cure or change the problems that we have. Separation from one another, whether it is the separation between you and me or someone else in a similar situation—both parties have to learn a healthy way to separate and move on with their lives.

Please remind our nieces and nephews how special they were and are to both of us. They were almost like our children because we didn't have children of our own. Never for a second let them forget how much I love them and how much they helped me.

I just wanted to fill you in on everything that's been happening in my world and let you know I'm still involved in yours. Not for a second have I stopped loving you. The love just gets stronger.

Elizabeth: Jim is pointing to the door to the other side. He's telling me it's time to exit.

He's so proud of you for not having another one of those "spells." He knows you've seen past all that. As always, Jim says thank you. You're so welcome, Jim. Jim has one foot out the door.

Chris: Is Jim still here? Can I tell him something first before he goes?

Jim: Sure. Hurry up. I've gotta go.

Chris: You wanted me to thank Rosemary and Bruce for everything they've done. I did that and Rosemary asked if there was any chance you were at Walter Reed Army Hospital when they were there with the wounded soldiers.

Jim: This is the luxury that I have now. That I can travel without cost and without the trouble. Yes, I was there, and I was trying to get their attention. I wasn't sure how to do it. Tell them I can't thank them enough. I will show up whenever I can to help my friends and family.

Bruce is a natural at helping people. The same way with Rosemary. It's the way that she is, she's such a good person. I've been trying to leave, but as long as I'm still here I want to say one last thing.

Elizabeth: He winks at me and says he has to get the last word in.

Jim: Keep your phone charged all the time.

Chris: Why ... don't you want to beep me?

Jim: If your phone's charged all the time, I'm there with you.

Chris: Oh, I see.

Elizabeth: He shakes his head at you like, "Oh geez! Just keep your phone charged all the time," he says. He's so funny.

Chris: Believe me, I can't even wait until the charge goes down anymore, because then I can charge it and you can beep me. But you've done it even when I'm not charging it, correct?

Jim: I have. I do try and communicate with you this way. I make the TV flicker and do some things to the radio. I did something with the speaker in Aruba.

Elizabeth: He's laughing. He's such a jokester.

Chris: Did you have anything to do with the rainbows that were in Aruba?

Jim: No, I just loved watching them with you and seeing them.

Chris: Woody and Martha have never seen rainbows in Aruba since they started going there in 2001 and there were three in a row. They were on the tenth, eleventh and twelfth, my point being that you died on the eleventh of October.

Jim: I can't take the credit for that, but they sure were beautiful.

Chris: Can I ask one more question? This is a practical one. Can you tell me the password to your iPad?

Elizabeth: Airplanes. It's the name of the airplane. Do you know the name of the airplane?

Chris: Yes, it's Falcon.

Elizabeth: Try it with a capital F. It's the name of the airplane with a number. Nine hundred. Falcon 900. It's the name of the airplane.

Chris: Okay. Thank you, Sweetie. I can't use it otherwise.

Jim: I know. I got nothin' to hide!

Chris: Of course you don't, but I want to be able to use it. Sweetie, I love you more than anything in the world.

Elizabeth: We'll see you soon, Jim. You're right … you've got to take off.

Jim: I've got to take off now.

Chris: Okay. Bye, Sweetie.

Elizabeth: He's showing me it's time for take-off, like he's going in an airplane. It looks like the ones in the higher light are pretty clear. Let's get you in motion here. A little at a time we'll see how this energy begins to change and reshape your unconscious. Thank you, Angels.

Chris: May I ask about one more person, or not?

Elizabeth: Sure. Go ahead.

Chris: My nephew's girlfriend who passed away. Do you know if she's around?

Elizabeth: Did she drown?

Chris: Well, I don't ... .

Elizabeth: She keeps telling me she drowned.

Chris: Oh, really? She had a seizure in the bathtub. Is she okay? Would she have a message for my nephew? Or is she not settled enough on the other side yet?

Elizabeth: She wants to talk to him.

Girlfriend: Everyone is a mess.

Elizabeth: The problem relates to ... she had a seizure and then got water, aspirated or something. It scared her. Not because she had a seizure, but everybody's response to her death. This isn't something that she had planned on, not even a little. She's still in some kind of shock and she knows Michael is still in shock ... really in shock.

Girlfriend: Tell him not to worry. That's not going to solve anything.

Elizabeth: Who is Judy to you?

Chris: Judy is my best friend from college.

Elizabeth: I hear a woman's voice and it keeps repeating Judy, Judy, Judy.

Chris: Well, both of her parents are on the other side.

Elizabeth: I believe this woman is probably her mother. Somebody's trying to get a message to Judy. I'll leave it up to you as to whether you want to tell her or not.

Let's go back to the girlfriend for a minute. She says she is not resting because it's not time to rest. First of all, she wants her family and your nephew to know she's very sorry for putting them through such trauma. She says it scared the person who found her this way. She's so concerned and worried that she created a lot of trauma for this person and for all of them. She knows there's going to be an opportunity for your nephew and her to reconnect. She thanks you for even inquiring about her.

Chris: We had a long talk on Christmas Eve about her, you (Elizabeth), my nephew coming for a reading, everything. We talked a lot.

Elizabeth: Michael's so scared to death.

Girlfriend: Tell him I don't want him to be scared or worried. I want to reassure him that I'm really okay, and that I need them all ... him ... as much as they need me. I promise that I won't do anything to make him afraid.

Chris: Do you mean if he comes to talk to you?

Elizabeth: Yes. She feels so badly. She's sobbing because she can't be with him and her family. She's practically yelling.

Chris: Yes. They loved each other, but they had broken up.

Girlfriend: This was a total shocker to me and everyone else. Please tell him, and he'll understand this if you don't ... I didn't do anything to bring this on.

Elizabeth: In other words, she didn't stop taking her medicine or she didn't take too much of something out of spite. This was something very "flukey" and just goes to show how much you have to tell people how you really feel
    She says she never made amends with your nephew. She's not going to stay today—she can't. It's clearly not that she doesn't want to. She repeats several times, "I *can't* stay."

Girlfriend: Tell him how much I really love him ... love him ... even when we weren't together.

Chris: I think he knows that, but I'll tell him. Thank you.

Elizabeth: She gives this big smile and says, "Thank you!" She says this is the first time she's smiled since she's been there. She heard all of you talking about her. It's been very hard on her to adjust to the afterlife. She thanks me and she's leaving. You're welcome.

So we have to close down. Thank you for all your help.

Chris: Thank you, Elizabeth.

Chris's Reflections:

An important fact to mention about having readings with Elizabeth is that she always began each session asking about me in order to get a sense of how I was dealing with the grief of losing Jim and life on a day-to-day basis. To me, Elizabeth wasn't simply a medium; she used her skills as a grief counselor to guide me through the grief process. Much of her information on using certain exercises to help me came from the sixteen years of having her own practice.

Sometimes, I didn't know if suggestions were coming from Elizabeth, the person, or Elizabeth, the medium—in other words, from the souls on the other side. It didn't matter. I've told Elizabeth so many times that she made such a difference in my life, because when Jim first died, I really did want to go with him. I know that many people who lose their loved ones feel that way. Elizabeth helped me gradually move away from that desire. When I would tell her she helped me so much, her response was always, "It doesn't come from me, it comes from God. God has given me these gifts, and then you work through it." That may be true, but I still say she helped me so much!

As I write these reflections after all the readings for the book have been completed, I can now look back and see what was happening from the very beginning. This was the first reading in which the divine beings in the Heaven realms spoke to me directly about how important it is that I use writing as a form of releasing my grief, and in turn, help people with that writing. I had always loved to write, but I never knew in what direction it would take me.

What I did know is that during Jim's illness, there was a time period when he appeared to be cancer-free. No tumors were lighting up on the PET scans, and there seemed to be no evidence of disease. During that time, I asked Jim what he thought about the two of us writing a book that would discuss various aspects of cancer from the perspective of both the patient and the caregiver. Jim was willing, but then the cancer came back and that plan could not be carried out. After Jim died, I still had a great urge to write a book about our experience that could help others in the same situation.

When I heard in this reading that I should be writing, and that this writing would help others, I was thrilled. It confirmed for me that writing was truly what I was meant to do in the next part of my life, something that I now realize my intuition had been telling me all along.

This was the very first reading where Jim started to talk about the "bigger picture" of life and Earth in general. He now had begun to read about the disease he had, and made plans to help others who were going through the same horrible ordeal that he did. The first three readings you read were simply telling me information about where he is or talking about family and friends still here on Earth … items important for him to tell me and that I wanted to hear.

In the beginning of these readings, I desperately needed to hear the basic information from Jim so I could cope with his loss and know he was okay. As the readings continued, however, I realized these readings were a form of counseling for me … the type of counseling I needed to move on with my own life. I had been through hard times before, as you know from our story, but Jim's death was the hardest thing I ever dealt with. By talking with Jim and other family members and friends who had passed to the other side, I gradually regained the strength I knew I had.

The holidays had been difficult, vacation without Jim was difficult, and yet I was beginning to feel just a bit more like my old self. My family and friends were not only supportive of my self-help through these readings, but they were interested for their own purposes as well. As you might guess, there are always the naysayers, and some of my friends even verbally expressed that they felt I was "going down the wrong path."

It didn't matter to me what others thought or said; my main goal was to feel better and that is exactly what was happening. Can I call that transformation? Probably not yet, but at least I could get through a session with Elizabeth without sobbing through the whole thing. Although seemingly slow, transformation was occurring.

Jim's family, my family, our friends, me … we all struggled in our own way to adapt to living life without Jim. Some carried on as usual and firmly stated they tried not to think about him being gone. It seemed at times that when I wanted to talk about Jim, some were annoyed or even angry. Clearly, some were happy to talk about Jim. They missed him and easily expressed it through conversation. I was one who needed to talk about Jim to help myself, but often sensed discomfort in those around me when I did.

I think you'll be amazed, as I was, at the transformation Jim goes through as you read each reading, as well as my transformation of learning to detach from him, my process seemingly being so much slower. Over two and a half years, a compilation of readings have been collected. The readings that are in this book allow you to get a glimpse of what souls go through once they pass to the spirit world. Keep this reading in mind as the beginning of the real transformation … my own and Jim's. Yet as Jim's transformation happens, he is still able to have the same personality that he had in his physical life.

Although you will see some transformation of Jim in this book, there will be readings in subsequent books where you will realize the amazing transformation he goes through as an ascending soul. Hopefully, you will see my transformation as well.

In many readings, other souls come to the sessions to communicate. Members of our families come in quite often, my nephew's former girlfriend being a case in point. I think it's tremendously important that you see and hear each soul as they come through, because just like all of us here in our physical lives on Earth, everyone is different. It's important to see that each soul in the afterlife responds differently to their situation, just as we do on Earth.

My nephew's former girlfriend is a perfect example. She passed five days before Jim but had a much more harsh and shocking death than Jim. The fact that she told us this is the first day she smiled since she had been there shows the difference between souls on the other side. Jim had nineteen months to think about the idea that he could and eventually would die, unlike the girlfriend who died quickly and unexpectedly of a seizure. This may be why the girlfriend had a more difficult time than Jim making the adjustment to living on the other side.

As Elizabeth instructs, it's important not to be agenda-driven so that the souls that want to come into a reading are able to communicate as well. Being contacted by souls I never expected to hear from made me realize how important we all are to all souls on the other side. You'll learn so much more about this type of thing as the readings continue.

And now we come to my needing the password to Jim's iPad. I had tried every password I could think of to get into that iPad so I could start using it. I knew it had to involve the jets he flew but I just couldn't figure it out. When I left this reading with the information Jim gave through Elizabeth, I immediately tried again to get into his iPad, and this time it worked. Jim had given me the password to his iPad!

This is the type of everyday living experience that most people can relate to. Elizabeth certainly didn't know his password. Nobody knew the password except for Jim. There may be many people who believe that mediums are "scam artists" but Elizabeth's accuracy in this example cannot be denied. While I'm not writing this book to convince anyone to believe in the work of mediums, it's pretty tough to explain how this could happen if Elizabeth didn't have a true gift from God.

Jim's Reflections:

This was a time frame when I was beginning to learn that detachment was so necessary. Not detachment from the memories, not detachment from the good times, the bad times or all that was learned, but detachment from the feeling that kept me so stuck, so glued to one space. So absolutely frozen. Frozen to a point of existence where I couldn't move, and I didn't want that for myself, nor did I want it for Chris.

Because of this, I made a commitment to myself that I would move higher and see things in a greater light. That's exactly what I began to do. Before I even went to the reading that day, I knew that more than anything, I needed to detach from how I felt about wanting to stay in my physical body. I knew there would be so much more that was necessary for me to grow and for me to still be of service, because service is still a part of that growth. As situations began to unfold from the Heaven worlds and I was introduced to many of the teachers and masters, little did I know that there was something beginning to form. Something that, in later times, we will talk about a great deal.

We call it the Entourage. It's a group of very humble, very wise, very learned beings who wish to help humankind. I was so glad to hear that I would be a part of this, but I needed to go through a process. Part of the process was, in fact, learning, growing and separating more and more. As you have learned by reading my words, I was still greatly attached to my wife, Chris. In human time, in her world, it had only been three months or so. It seemed like eternity for me, no pun intended.

So off I went to learn ... to grow. They taught me that I, too, could continue to evolve in my soul body. I chose to do it in this form.

I was so proud of Chris and so willing to be of any kind of help and service to her, to share with her any information that I knew. When this book began to form ... when the Angels told us that Chris would be writing and that would help to dispel her grief, I was so glad to hear, although she had so many family and friends who were willing to help. Many, at times, would even share with her their grief of missing me. But mostly, she had some sort of mission; she had a reason for wanting to stay. It was clear to me that she wanted the old Chris back, and I was determined to help her.

Many people must learn there has to be a reason and purpose for being on the planet. You find that purpose deep within your heart. Perhaps it's being a parent, perhaps it's helping with children, perhaps it's learning to fly or make scientific discoveries; there is a whole host of reasons. But you still have to find it. Let me give you a little clue; you don't look outside yourself for the answer. You look deep within the soul. That's what I saw Chris begin to do.

That's the whole point. I was learning to do that. When I was sick, there were times when I would think about being sick and wonder, "How can I fix this?" Everyone outside of me seemed to have the answer: chemotherapy, eating well, drinking right, receiving Reiki, doing energy work, doing this, doing that. There were a whole bunch of different ways to help the problem, but really, I knew the answer had to come from me. I was determined to find the answer.

Now that I'm here in the Heaven worlds, the higher realms of the astral world, I'm able to begin to look deeper. The only way we can look deeper is if we detach completely and fully from others. That does not mean that you don't love one another. It means you love them more deeply because you're willing to let go of how they feel, what they think and you're willing to look deep within to know what's right and best for you. I knew one thing was for sure. I still had a soul. How did I know? Because I carried that soul with me wherever I went.

You know I loved flying—that's a no-brainer at this point. I loved all the things of the earthly world—we've talked about that before. However, I realized one day during time of contemplation that we have failed to mention how much we all are placed together in each other's lives for some certain reason. I especially realized this when we talked that day: my family, Chris's family, our friends ... all the people who were so heavily and deeply involved with one another.

When you learn to really listen to one another, listen from a soul's perspective, a deep perspective ... rather than just listen to what someone says, "hear" what they say and apply it to your life. Listen to those who are older and wiser. Sometimes they do it through humor. Sometimes it's done simply by talking. But the idea is that it's not just listening that's important—it's "hearing" what's said. Hearing means you can apply what you listen to.

One of the things I realized with our nephew's former girlfriend when I saw her wandering and wondering what to do, where to go and how to get there, was that she needed a familiar face. She needed someone familiar around her, so off I went *to see if I could help. I wasn't demanding, I only suggested. She knew I wanted to help her. That's why she came when she did. She never thought about dying. She was young and if she did, she certainly never voiced it. Our nephew was so in love with her, so wanting to be with her. She took what she knew and she tried to make a change. That's what everyone should learn to do. Take what you know and try to make a change for the better. It all starts from within yourself.*

Michael's girlfriend and I were so happy to see each other. She was happy that she finally recognized someone who could explain to her where she was and where she had to go. She didn't have time to prepare like I did. There were many reasons for Michael to love her and many reasons for all of us to like her, but perhaps the biggest reason when we found one another was that we could help each other. She, in some ways, was a mirrored reflection of me when I first arrived. I wanted to show her what is capable of happening in the world in which she now was living without her body.

We try to leave signs from the spirit world to let you know that we're around. The signs come in all forms. Beeps on a cell phone, stereo equipment not working properly, some of us drop coins, some play songs on the radio. We all have our own little ways of letting you know we're around.

One of the better qualities of Elizabeth—and she uses that quality—she never believed for one second that she couldn't communicate with others. Maybe it's because she was born that way. Maybe it's because she developed that. Who knows, but she never doubted that she could.

When I gave her that password to my iPad that Chris needed, everyone except Elizabeth was astonished. The lesson here is that it's not what you can do, it's what you tell yourself you can't that's important. The more you tell yourself you can't, the less you'll be able to do. So when you make a choice, choose wisely. Use your wisdom, not just your intelligence. I know all about intelligence. Everyone does. I was a scientist, for God's sake. I knew how to fly a jet airplane. I knew how to do all kinds of things on the Earth, all the things that come from logic and reason.

I went to church, I said my prayers, I was grateful. I did all the right things and listened to all the right people. But the one person I left out was me. That's one of the good parts of watching Chris with Elizabeth. Elizabeth doesn't let Chris leave out "Chris." She keeps reminding her how important it is that she includes herself first.

So when I say to you that I'm learning to detach, the less I know about how I feel about something, the more I know the truth about what is, the better kind of soul I can be.

So, Chris, before I go, if you have a question, now would be the time to ask it.

Chris: Would you talk about the fact that when you lose someone, whether it's to death or something else, that you need to still take care of yourself without wanting to stop living, without abusing substances, using good nutrition and those kinds of things?

Jim: I'll say a little bit about it. God knows you nagged me enough about eating those stupid, disgusting muffins! I tried everything! I would have eaten bark if you told me to. Yes, I know—you do try everything. The key point here is you don't wait until it's bad to try and fix it. If you take good care of yourself all the time, when something happens it's much easier to handle it.

I could see Michael's point of view ... losing the love of his life, having very little to rely on financially but having a mother who loved him so dearly and still does, family. It doesn't matter how much you love another person to get them to change. What matters is that person has to love him- or herself.

I can't stress enough to the reader that although you feel like you want to die, yourself, when you lose someone for whatever reason, don't stop taking good care of "you"—it just makes you feel worse, not better. You have importance, you have value. Every human being does, otherwise you wouldn't be there. The first person to know that is me. I knew if I didn't do something, I thought of what it would be like the other way around. If it were Chris who had this problem, what would I do? I'd probably go into a funk just like anybody else does. The point is you can't.

I used to think it was selfish when people would say, "Take care of yourself first. Then you can take care of everyone else." But really, that's selfless. If you take good care of yourself, you're able to handle things a lot better, a lot easier. Don't fall prey to things that make you feel worse just to numb how you feel. Talk to somebody about how you feel. Talk to a friend, a therapist, a counselor, a spiritual communicator or talk to God directly, right to His own ears from your mouth. But do discuss it. I learned that by keeping it all inside, it made everything worse. If I had talked more, would I have lived longer? Who knows? I sure wish I had said more. They call it strong confidence, a quiet confidence. Yes, I had that. But I also believed that I could do what I wanted. I put my mind to it. More important, now I know, and just like I would tell all of you, you can accomplish more when your heart is in it, and when you are in your heart.

As you read on, you'll see ... your mind has to be in the right place but your heart has to be one hundred percent behind your mind. Otherwise it's just a thought that floats around out there, and we want our thoughts to become things so those things can help others.

So thank you, Chris and Elizabeth, for doing this work. It's hard. The long hours away from family and friends. The reality is it takes devotion. Be devoted to yourself and take care of you so if it ever happens that you have to care for someone else, you can do it with finesse and grace.

For today, we're coming in for a nice smooth landing. As you know, take your objects with you that are stowed ... your heart, your mind and your body. Check the aisles for anything that might be remaining. Thank the flight crew and your friends and family. Thank you for flying the friendly skies today.

— *Captain Jim Petosa*

March 1, 2012

Chris: My intended session was for Reiki, but Elizabeth could tell I was in despair and offered to do some communication to get answers to questions and put my mind at ease. She spent some time giving me Reiki and then did a reading for me. Elizabeth didn't know what had occurred. She offered to speak to someone who could provide insight and guidance from a different perspective.

Elizabeth opens the session, as she always does, with a prayer of gratitude and blessings.

Jim: I know our family is trying to get a grip on what has just happened with Michael.

Chris: (We were very connected to our nieces and nephews. Jim was very protective of this nephew.)

Jim: I was there trying to get him to come out of the bathroom. I heard his cries of desperation. I see the situation from a completely different perspective. I don't think he really wants to kill himself. He just needs attention and his life has been full of despair. He's so upset and from my perspective, justly so. He had just lost the love of his life the week before I died and it appears he wasn't getting much attention because of my death. I see your fragile state and I worry that you are getting overly involved. I hope the establishment Michael is in won't let him out until he has the necessary assistance set up.

Just look at the past year alone ... what the poor guy has been through. We both know he's a survivor. He will find a way within himself to make a change.

I see him as trying to find something to live for, especially now that the one woman he loved has died.

But, Chris, I'm worried about you right now. Michael is in a safe place. You'll know better when the time is right to help.

Elizabeth: Because your own grief is so fresh, limit your exposure to any situations that are draining. Love and support family and friends, but you need to get rest and not absorb the emotional pain of others around you. When one family member changes, the whole family changes. If you pray, meditate, et cetera, this can help them. Be the best kind of person you can be without over-helping. You know your limitations.

Your nephew wants to regain his spirit. He wants to feel young and important. Reiki would help. When someone isn't meant to enter the spirit world, there's always a way for it to be prevented. He doesn't really want to come to the other side. There are still lessons for him to learn on Earth. He would like his family to heal, given their history. That would really make him feel better. He is tired of being afraid.

You have nothing to do with the decisions he has made. He has to take responsibility for his actions.

Your nephew's mind is on overload. He would benefit from someone listening to him express his feelings of grief of losing someone so close just like you have. She's around him frequently, giving support and messages that he is not consciously aware of.

This woman that I have here doesn't want her name mentioned. I believe it's his girlfriend. She saw how much pain she put everyone through by leaving. "Tell him there's nothing worse than watching your mother cry about something she couldn't help you with. Trust me, you don't want to do that." She always carries that with her. Instead of worrying about the afterlife, he has to worry about living. He has a lot to look forward to.

Chris's Reflections:

This reading is about a very serious matter that happened to someone in our family. He and this woman were very much in love but broke up because of their addiction issues. They were planning to get married, but she decided that taking a break from the relationship would benefit both of them. During their time apart, the young woman died while having a seizure in the bathtub. She was alone at the time. About four months after she died, he attempted suicide. This is what Jim was referring to when he spoke of hearing his cries of desperation and trying to get him to come out of the bathroom.

This is an extraordinarily important reading for several reasons. First, by Jim telling about the exact time he was attempting suicide, it shows that our loved ones are truly around us trying to guide and help us.

A common myth that I've heard is that when people die unexpectedly, they may get "stuck" and have difficulty fully crossing over into the light. Although it's unclear as to what state she's in, it was comforting to hear from her and for her to offer advice to our nephew.

This woman speaks a bit toward the end and gives insight that could help any of us about living our lives. We can all learn from her heart-wrenching words, "Tell him there's nothing worse than watching your mother cry about something she couldn't help you with. Trust me, you don't want to do that." The woman is trying to get the word to him that from where she is, she can see her mother in tremendous pain. It's so endearing that she gives the advice to our nephew that he has to worry about living instead of thinking about the afterlife, and that he has lots to look forward to in our world. That is true love. She doesn't want him to be in the same spot she is … worrying about the pain of those who are left behind.

If someone is not meant to enter the spirit world, it will be prevented. That must mean that if someone is meant to go to the spirit world, nothing can stop it. We can't control God. No matter what we do, we must know there is something greater that is in control. Example: Sometimes sick people have so many praying for them and they die anyway, while some have just as many or fewer praying and they live. When it's our time, it's our time. We are not the deciding factor.

Jim's Reflections:

Although the reading itself was not very lengthy, much needs to be said as the project continues. It is far more than what we first imagined it to be. It is a great privilege and pleasure to work and do this project with the group that I am now surrounded with and by. It may seem impossible to you on the Earth that many from the Heaven worlds are so willing to help all of you who exist in the physical form. However, it is possible.

What I'd like to share with you is incredibly important for you to understand. It's not just the matter that life and the soul go on and on and on. It's more than that. It's that we can be a part of your life and stay a part of your life and you be part of ours. That was something most profound for me to learn. I learned that before I left my own body. Before that, I assumed that when you leave the physical Earth, when you leave the body, all contact would be broken. I never had any clue whatsoever that communication would actually be possible ... that there's a bridge, a way to close the gap between this world and that world. We'd like you to understand ... we being this group, the Entourage, with which I am so closely connected by this time ... there's a reason beyond a total comprehension and understanding at this moment that we are all born together at certain times, at certain ages, in certain groups so that we might help one another grow to become stronger, better people.

This is something most people figure out when they're on the Earth to begin with, but there are times when many people fail to figure it out. They look and see the world around them and they expect they can do everything themselves—that they work alone, so to speak. The self-made man or the self-made woman. The reality is nothing could be further from the truth. Many people think that being married or having that companion, having that person to share with is the only way to live, but that isn't the only way. There is a part of us that has to be in complete attunement with our own self. That's where it all begins. So learn to know yourself well and learn to know what exists. Don't just take the words of others for the truth. Learn. Learn and grow.

I know Michael doesn't mind me talking about this. When I saw him in the bathroom ... that he was drinking heavily and taking pills on top of that ... I did everything in my power from the other world to let that be known. I knew beyond a shadow of a doubt it wasn't his time. I knew and he knew in some way that it wasn't his time. What was so important was that he really needed to know that.

The group that I am working with ... they're the ones that first gave me the information of when the time would be for Michael to exit the body and what he expected would happen. It was impossible for that to happen; it wasn't his time. The ones that I'm working with—we've called them the Entourage —they know because they are wise and knowing, they are helpful and useful. They "know."

As this all took place in the physical world, we were watching, ever so studious. We watch not just because we learn from what you do, but we learn from what you don't do on the Earth. We learn when people fail to communicate with themselves, to know themselves well, to learn about their souls, and we're right there to help. We're right there to help as things begin to fall apart.

So as odd as it may seem, as strange as it may appear, we were there that night and so was Michael's former girlfriend. She was there waiting and watching, waiting for the perfect opportunity to tell Michael to clean up his act, to turn around... that it wasn't his time... because some people believe they can do whatever they want.

To desecrate the body is not the biggest sin that we can commit. To desecrate someone else's body ... that definitely is something that God doesn't like. We have to listen to God. We have to listen to the Angels, the learned ones that are here. The only punishment is the punishment we give ourselves. Michael was not ready. His ego told him he was. He felt as though he had nothing to live for. Most people don't fully realize the soul and the body are one until they no longer can stay connected to each other. That's what happened to me when I left the world. My soul and my body were one body. One body. There is a body, mind and spirit connection all in alignment, all in perfect order with the higher worlds. Michael learned the hard way that night. We were fortunate to witness not the destruction but the saving. We were fortunate to watch and to be able to interfere and to help. That's what makes this process so amazing. We're still able to learn. We're able to learn about the human condition and see it from a different view.

For those of you who may be reading this, many people have different ideas about what's right and what's wrong about leaving the body as you choose. Many people take matters into their own hands and they leave as they wish. When they do so, they slow down their path. They slow down the action of the soul. In other words, they stagnate.

We did not want to see this happen to Michael. What we wanted him to see is that he had so much to live for as do so many who are hopeless, so many who are without joy in their hearts. Sometimes it's chemicals, sometimes it's a lack of knowledge, sometimes it's abuse of drugs and alcohol. There can be a million reasons why. The reality is it's your job to find out why. It is your job to feel and understand why you cannot feel God within you. It is your job to do just that.

My suggestion to you, and from the Entourage, is to find those who can help you change if you cannot do it on your own. Find those who are connected to their faith. Not that God is outside of them, but that you and God are one. That you are one being. One in being with the Father. If you have troubles, pray to those who are helpful. Find ways to feel grateful. Pray to the saints and ask them to pray on your behalf. Saint Jude, help for the hopeless. Mother Mary. Pray to your loved ones and ask them to help you.

The one thing that's important here is to pray. Pray not prayers of want and "give me" but prayers of thanks for having me and giving me this body to love. Don't judge others who won't do it, rather, teach others what can happen if they do. Help them. Help others as you would help yourself. A wise man once told me, "The person that will treat you best is the one who takes good care of himself." If *they find value and worth within themselves, they'll find value and worth in you. They'll see you for your soul as God does. God does not see the outside of you, as one might believe. Being born with good looks, a perfect body, being born with all the things related to being human ... those are genetic factors. But being born with a soul ... that's a God factor. That's something that God gave you. Respect it. And since it's inside of you, what better place to begin than inside. Self-respect. Really learning to know yourself as one thing with God. One in being with the Father. You'll be glad that you did.*

There are many of us here in the higher realms of the afterlife in the other world. We know we are one with God. That's the one very interesting thing about leaving your body. One might think that you feel more disconnected from God without a body. The reality is you feel closer to God than ever.

Michael, I hope you do well on your journey. Get addicted to God. I know you say, "You have a lot of room to talk" ... all the things that I loved about the Earthly world. There's no doubt. But the one thing I never forgot was the gratitude for being there, being where all of you are now. And for all those who I knew I would encounter ... not just family. I wasn't quite sure what would happen ... but I knew in the space above, around or however you want to say it, I knew there must be some "one," some "thing" that could help us. That someone or something is God.

On your journey, on your next flight, fly within. Stop looking outside of yourself for answers that you know to be right within you. Look for the value that you have as a soul, that all people have as souls. When you see one another as a soul being, you treat them much differently. When you see yourself as a soul being, you treat yourself much differently. I knew I must have a soul. From the time I was very young, I knew there must be something more to all this than just me as a person, just me as a good man, as my wife, Chris, will tell you. I knew there was more to it than just that. Some people find it in church, some find it through meditation, sometimes it just shows up magically in your life somehow, through some terrible event. But it doesn't have to be terrible for you to learn, to know and to grow.

So if you haven't started loving, open your heart to love. If you haven't given God another thought, start a few minutes a day and wonder what it's all about. Wonder ... if you can be the best kind of person, the best kind of soul ... what would that be? It isn't someone who eats themselves to death, smokes a couple of packs of cigarettes a day, gets into the booze, is drug-addicted ... there are so many examples of how people numb their pain. Yes, we can feel sorry for them, but we can redirect them, as well, if they so choose to be redirected. I mean to offend no one when I say these things, only to open your eyes to more, to help you to really see that every human being has value ... every single person, no matter who they are.

There are no prejudices here, no discrepancies of color, no discrepancies of male versus female—none whatsoever. We're all only one thing here and that one thing is one giant soul connected together. Even some of the souls in the lower realms of the afterworld listen, still, and refuse to seek to connect with God. They interact and involve themselves in your daily practices, your daily life because they become so familiar with the Earth, this is what they know to do. Everyone continues to learn, each in their own way. Every single soul does. So remember, someone is always watching. Someone is always looking out for you. Sometimes they learn from you; sometimes, if you're quiet, you can learn from them.

The goal of this project is to help many just learn. Take from this whatever you possibly can. You won't bring any belongings with you. You won't bring anything with you into the afterworld. You'll only bring your soul. Let it be your greatest hope that yours is a soul filled with love, filled with God, so that you will no longer continue to make the same mistakes. Break the cycle. If you think that your job in this lifetime is to break your own cycle or a family cycle, then do it. It's that simple because one way or another you're going to anyway.

Some people refuse. Many people get stuck in what they want—they want what they want when they want it. Some people get what they want and then want it no longer. There are all different walks of life but one thing is for sure: every "body" is walking around with a soul and it's the body's job to find the soul.

So let your eyes be awakened, wipe the sleep out of them, take a look at yourself and look very deeply at yourself in the mirror, for it is within the eyes that you'll see exactly what you're looking for. You'll see "you"—the real you. You don't have to wait until you're here. You don't have to wait at all. If you do, that's your choice, too, but it's helpful to start looking now while you're still on the Earth.

To my copilot, Chris, my wife ... I'm glad you've been looking. Even when I wouldn't go, even when I thought it was silly or crazy, even when people would get wrapped up in the phenomena, you saw it for something greater than it seemed. Many around you believe that communicating with the spirit world is hocus-pocus or nonsense, but it's not at all. It's the one thing that helped.

We in the Heaven worlds want to help you all. First, look at yourself. Look within. As you look within, your soul will shine like light just as it's meant to do.

Until the next time you fly the friendly skies, this is Captain Jim Petosa signing off.

— Captain Jim Petosa

April 12, 2012

Elizabeth: Could I tell you something that I've noticed from observing you since Jim's passing? Slowly, you're beginning to laugh and smile more and have the disposition back that you had before Jim got sick. It appears as though you are more upbeat these days.

After meditating, I thought it might be a good idea to do something called an akashic record reading. This kind of reading gives information about what you can do to contribute to your well-being and the well-being of others. An akashic record, by definition, is a record of your soul, the knowledge you received in other lifetimes and in this one and how a combination of the two would be helpful to you. This type of reading tells not only where you have been but also what you have learned and accrued in your spiritual journey throughout time, as well as how you could affect others now and in the future. Yours is lengthy in nature because you are a busy girl. How do you feel about doing something like this today?

Chris: Thank you for noticing the change in me. Other people have made comments, too. Innately, I have always felt upbeat and positive. When I was teaching, a couple of friends called me Miss Mary Sunshine. I do feel like I'm getting back to that point. I attribute some of it to both my Dad and Jim wanting me to, but most of all, I'm beginning to remember when I naturally felt well and slowly that feeling is coming back.

I love the idea of doing that kind of reading so I can find out how I can be helpful to other people.

Elizabeth does her usual ritual of prayers of gratitude and blessings to begin the session. In addition, she asks permission to enter into my akashic record.

Elizabeth: I could feel this must be a sacred place although I can't describe my feelings to you.

Elizabeth: Sure, come on in, Jim. (Elizabeth is laughing.) He always thinks it's so funny that I say a prayer and go through the formalities. The masters of the akashic records are here today so it is that much more special.

Chris: Does he laugh because I have to say my full name and date of birth? It's probably my date of birth he's laughing at, right?

Elizabeth: He's laughing because I'm being so formal and he says it's unnecessary; it's only him. He's trying to be his usual humble self. I just do that because we need to give thanks that the light is around us. I say a prayer because we always want to show reverence to those in the spirit world not to mention everyone who is still here on Earth. It's easy to tell that Jim has gone through some kind of transformation. He's beaming with light.

We do have special guests today. That's why I'm being even more respectful than usual.

Jim: Hi Sweetie, hi Sweetie, hi Sweetie, hi Sweetie, hi Sweetie. I am especially excited because before you arrived, Elizabeth told me what's going to happen today.

Chris: I am so excited, too!

Jim: I've been hearing you talk to me all morning long.

Chris: I have been. To make sure you got here on time. I said, "Please come, please come, please come."

Jim: I am really excited about this, too, because I know that learning about your progression may somehow help me in my evolution. I'm always looking for ways to learn how I can further progress or grow, and how I can also help with what your goals are.

I lived out what I wanted to do on Earth. I always wanted to be married to you, I loved being with my family and, of course, I always wanted to fly.

Since I got here, I've learned that having children wasn't such a big deal after all. Chris, it was better that we didn't have children because they would have had to go through all this, too. It's bad enough what we went through together, let alone having children watch their father die. I know firsthand what that was like.

When I look at our family as a whole—all of the kids—it's a tough world to grow up in. I was away a lot and you were so busy with your teaching career. At times, it seemed too much. It certainly would have been a lot for both of us if we had children. You having to take care of them while I was away so often and then I got sick. They would have had to watch me die. I certainly didn't want to leave you behind, let alone children.

From my viewpoint it's as if I am twenty feet above you. Really, it's not even that far. It's just another state of existence, a higher state of existence. I now have the capability of being around everyone there. I now have a "hawk-eye" view. I'm able to witness what goes on in the entire family. Don't worry—I still spend a lot of time with you, too, because you have always been part of the family. I definitely don't want you to get so drained.

I know you. I know how you can be. You go overboard with wanting to help. We both were like that. That's what you do but we had each other for support. You go overboard when it's someone you love, when it's family. But sometimes with the smaller concerns we have to let them go. You have to learn to say no in order to help them figure out the smaller problems on their own instead of running to their rescue.

I want Michael to know I've met up with his former girlfriend. When I saw her I wanted to help her. She just had that look like she needed help.

Elizabeth: Now he's not being egotistical about this; there's no ego involved here at all. It looks like she died after Jim and it's so odd because the time frame that it took for them to meet up with one another in the afterlife is almost as if she left later. Some of it has to do with her fear of leaving. I don't know if she actually died before him ... .

Chris: Yes, five days before Jim.

Elizabeth: ... but it has a lot to do with her fear.

Jim: Tell Michael that although I didn't know her well enough to tell her what to do I did my best to help her even though I didn't really know what to do. She's in a much better situation now. I can't give you all the details about what's happening with her. She's right here. You can talk to her yourself.

Girlfriend: There's only so much I can do here in the afterlife—how much inter- action I can have in your world. I'll do my best to watch over Michael and to keep him on the right track. I want to make that promise to you and to your family as well. Please tell Kathy, if you would, that I'll do the best I can for him.

Chris: I will do that. Thank you.

Elizabeth: She seems so likeable. She really seems concerned about Michael's well-being. She keeps extending thank-yous to me. You're very welcome. Thank you for coming by.

Jim: Chris! (Emphatically.) Let's get on with it. We don't have to talk about problems the whole time. We want to talk about good things!

Chris: Oh, my Jimmy!

Jim: We don't have time to talk about all the problems. I'm excited to find out about the real you as a soul. I do want to know more about the history. The lifetime I just completed triggered my curiosity about dying. I was very devoted to the church and spiritual development. That's the reason I joined the men's group at church.

The concept of reincarnation was an idea I never thought about before. I didn't sit around thinking about the fact that I could have lived before or what had happened before now to bring it into this lifetime. This type of reading about your soul is a first-time experience for me other than my own visit with the Council when I entered the afterlife. Even then, they only discussed what occurred during this lifetime with me. I believed it was possible; I just never pursued what it meant.

(Smiling.) You know what I'm talking about, Elizabeth, because we had that conversation before.

Chris, there's something I think you should know before we go on. I want to bring up a topic that Elizabeth and I talked about a lot. From my new viewpoint I can see that jet fuel seemed to have a different impact on me than it did on others, contributing to my cancer. Some people fly all the time and never get it and some people never fly and do. I can't say jet fuel was the cause. There were other factors. I'm learning that I already had a propensity for cancer and that maybe the environment weakened my system more so. It is yet to be determined what the actual cause was. I always felt healthy and happy but looking back, just like you said to me, my diet wasn't always the best.

I believe you now, Elizabeth. My work certainly could have had an impact on my physical health. In the beginning I wanted it so badly it wouldn't have mattered, I would have flown anyway.

In a perfect world I would have picked to stay with you, Chris, and still have flown. That's just not the way it happened.

I'm just learning. I'm just getting enough ... courage. When I was raised and went to church we were taught not to question anything. I'm just now mustering up enough courage to ask questions and learn more.

I didn't have any trouble going to the other side. I remain in the afterlife ready to move into the higher levels of Heaven as I learn more and grow. I'm learning to ask questions about the next steps of my existence and keep the same humility while doing so.

The afterworld is so easy to access. I know that some people have a natural gift to be able to communicate in this way. I'm really happy that's the case; otherwise it certainly would limit my communication with the people I want to stay connected with.

Chris, you were always so smart and always so loving to everyone. You shined. I'm not sure but based on what I'm learning, I believe this "shine" or this light could be part of the reason it's easier to access the other world. I think this has something to do with being able to reach all of us.

We are all right here, you just have to be quiet in your mind and be a good listener. That's what I think is going to help you the most ... to just sit and listen and stop thinking and doubting yourself. Stop doubting yourself, Chris. You listen differently. You listen with your intuition. That's the way it is here. In the higher realms we have a lot less thought and it's easier to communicate with one another.

I'm close to you and want very much to be close to you. The reason I'm near you is not because I'm lonely or sad or stuck or anything. I'm near you simply because I love you.

Chris: I love you, too.

Jim: *I'm giving this explanation because I know many people are questioning whether communicating with me is the right thing to do. When you love someone, it's always the right thing to do.*

I know that there's going to come a time ... and they, in this realm, have already informed me of this. ("They" being the "helpers," so to speak, on the other side.) They've already informed me that being in the middle ... there's going to be a time when I'm going to make a choice. It's not going to be right away but there will be a time when I will make a choice and the choice to be made is whether I will want to remain here or want to move into another realm of existence. That's exactly what it is—another realm of existence. Currently I've decided I'm going to stay where I am as long as I possibly can because I can still learn. I can learn from church as well as from reading and studying. I learn from you and what you're doing to learn. I can still learn. That's the important piece to this.

Chris: Wow. I know how much you loved learning. It's amazing that you can still learn things from Earth.

Jim: Knowledge is everywhere. Wisdom is everywhere. Understanding ... all these facets ... they're everywhere, in your world and in mine. Knowledge is in any universe that you travel through. Case in point for me, there's a lot I can still get from being where I am right now. It's fascinating!

What I love doing and what I'm going to continue to do ... the ways of Jesus, the ways of the saints, the ways of healing, compassion and love ... I aspire to be this way. In my heart I aspire to be that way and I'm doing whatever I can to learn more from those teachers on how to do it ... wisdom of the universe, if you will. The more you start trusting, the more you know yourself to be worthy and have humility, the more you are able to learn. I had to learn so much about this when I was taken to the other side.

They tell us to be in awe of the universe. Where I am, I still have a sense of myself as Jim.

Chris: Can I develop here or do I have to develop on the other side?

Jim: I've developed on the other side, but you are developing here.

I've said all my thank-yous. I hope everyone knows how much I appreciated their being with us through all of this—our friends and so on. I still see you cry. I come to put my arms around you.

Chris: Thank you.

Jim: I still see you crying. I know you're having a tough time. It's bittersweet watching you make these decisions about our home, our house. I knew you had it in you! (Laughing.)

Chris: I just don't like to do it myself. I want you with me to do it.

Jim: I would like to make a suggestion.

Elizabeth: He's being a smart-aleck!

Chris: He is? Oh great!

Elizabeth: His suggestion is ... he makes this motion as if he's testing dust.

Chris: Clean up the house and get the house in order.

Jim: (*Laughing.*) *If I could just make that suggestion! I realize that just before my departure everything went into boxes and bags so all the walls could be painted. I can't help you with doing that but I'm noticing that it's getting a little dusty.*

Chris: Did you see the curio cabinet I just bought?

Jim: Yes.

Chris: That is going to make me able to start to put things back.

Jim: Reorganize. I think this is a good idea ... the reorganization. I know that the hard part is over and now it's just learning how you're going to live and put things together. I don't want you to do it in accordance to me. I want you to think about what it will be like for you to have everything in order to make it easier to live on your own.

Chris: Alright.

Jim: I'd like to tell you something. The experiences that I had at church, prayer, masses, receiving Reiki and energy work with Maryann and with other people helped me more than I could possibly have known when I was alive. I realized that more when I reached the other side. Having these treatments set the stage for me. It's very much like being out of your body when you're receiving a Reiki treatment ... . That's the way I feel now.

    Chris, you can understand what I mean because I know the same thing happens to you. Being the way I am is like being out of your body during a Reiki treatment.

    I have no pain, I feel very peaceful and I still have somewhat of a consciousness so I can still feel what's going on. When I received Reiki treatments I would go off into another world and not feel my body and it's the same way now. I'm off into this other dimension, this higher space and I can't feel my body. I only can feel peace and comfort and no pain. I feel a great sense of peace. I have a lot of light. I want you to know what it's like for me. That's the best way I can describe it.

    The one good thing is that I don't have people looking at me and being scared or feeling sorry for me. I hated that.

Chris: Yes, I know you did.

Jim: Where I am, everybody is just like me and it's a much more normal way of being now. It has taken me a little while to get acclimated to the other side. I was so used to having a body for so long.

Chris: Do you make new friends there?

Jim: I am definitely making new friends. I'm involved with service to humanity. I learn every day how to be of greater service to humanity. I love Jesus and the saints.

Chris: Have you seen Jesus?

Elizabeth: Yes! He goes, "Uh, yeah!" He was in awe, just total awe. (I just want to add, Jim's not being irreverent here … just excited.)

Jim: The love that comes from Him—it's unbelievable, Chris.

Chris: I can't wait to find that out!

Jim: You can feel it now even. The love that comes from Him is so good and so profound. You don't even have to go to church although I still do.

Chris: Do you go with me?

Jim: I do go with you. I don't want you to stop going either, just because I'm not physically with you.

Chris: No, I won't. And do you still put your hand on my hand on the pew?

Jim: Every time, on the pew when you have to stand. I am right there. I know you miss me. There's no doubt; I know that. The priest … I love to hear the sermons he gives. I still learn. I love the fellowship.

Chris: Do you go to the men's group on those Saturdays?

Jim: I like to sit in. I don't offer much, as you can imagine!

Chris: You're funny.

Jim: This planet is still a place of learning, and I'm interested in learning as much as I can.

Elizabeth: Jim, is there anything else you want to ask us or tell us?

Jim: Do you mind if I stay during this reading? I'm very interested in what is going to be said.

Chris: Of course I want you to be here. I'm interested in how we knew each other before.

Jim: I haven't inquired much about where I ever was or what I ever did so I'd like to know what kind of information I can find out about that. I do know for sure just because you die doesn't mean that you become an enlightened soul. I'm learning more and more about becoming an enlightened soul but I'm not quite there yet. Any information I can learn will help me grow.

I was fortunate that I had so much guidance and direction from my mother taking me to church. I liked going to church and the lessons I learned there. From an early age I learned to listen to myself, an inner knowing, I guess you would call it. And you supported that.

I do want to ask a question. I love this. I want to know if we were ever together in other lifetimes. We must have been because we loved each other so deeply in this lifetime. Did we live lifetimes together when we were not in love?

Chris: (****Elizabeth explained something called automatic writing. This allows a medium to produce written words without consciously writing. The words come to her from a spiritual source. She explains that it will take several minutes to decipher what has been written. I couldn't believe what I saw! As I watched Elizabeth do the automatic writing, her pen seemed to glide along the paper with no effort and her eyes were closed. It was evident that she was not the one doing the writing. When it was completed, it looked illegible. Frankly, it looked like scribbling. I didn't think she would be able to read it back to me. It looked like one long run-on sentence that needed punctuation. When she showed me the writing after she deciphered it, I could see that there were real words and sentences. It was one of the most amazing things I've ever seen.

Elizabeth did the automatic writing. She received answers to questions I asked that did not pertain to Jim, but fully answered Jim's questions as well.

In future books, we will further reference many other sessions and readings such as these when messages were delivered but not shared in this book.)

Elizabeth: Based on what I can decipher from the writing, it's very interesting that you asked the question the other day about why it feels so different to meditate at the nearby facility as opposed to where we are now. They give the answer clearly in the writing.

Chris: (Elizabeth shows me in the automatic writing how that question of mine was answered.)

Elizabeth: What they're saying is to continue being the best human being you can be. Seek out ways to do that. Your human mission, what you want to put forth to society, is writing and putting out information, literally publishing and offering information.

Chris: And I plan to, so I love hearing that again.

Elizabeth: Good. I do think it will help relieve some energy in your body, too. Just as they directed, writing on paper will help take the pain of what you're feeling out of your body.

Can I ask you a question? This may seem very strange to ask but did you ever think that Jim had a secret of something that he held onto? Like maybe he shared it with you but the person he needed to share it with, he never told?

Chris: Well, I felt like there was an old girlfriend who he never had closure with. I don't know if it's a secret, exactly. He did contact her—at least on the premise, from my viewpoint —to see if she knew of any doctors where she lived that could help him, but I really think that what he wanted was closure with her. He wrote her a letter and she did get back to him. He sent her an email to which she never responded. I firmly believe she didn't get it or she would have responded. I think he thought sending this email was the closure he needed but I'm not sure it was. He didn't keep a secret from me but I believe he was afraid I would be hurt if I thought he needed the closure with her. Of course I did know he needed the closure with her.

Elizabeth: He definitely did. He's saying something about this. Some of this wrenching feeling that I felt in his belly, and just now, is related to holding onto a secret. Maybe that he didn't have closure but wanted it or needed it. I don't think he was ever, even in his thoughts, unfaithful to you or wanted to be. I do feel there was a lot of unfinished business—mostly that he just didn't want to leave you.

Jim: Since we're on the topic of emotion, I think some of the emotions that ate at me were related to my father. Not that it was my father's fault, but more in regard to those emotions around his sickness not being fully dealt with or healed.

Chris: His father was sick for a long time with what the family called depression. From what I understood from Jim, in Jim's early life his father did not have that depression. I do know that Jim's father was sick when Jim was in high school and then when Jim went into the Navy. There may have been unfinished business there.

I know Jim always wondered why his father died and what caused it. That was the reason why Jim didn't ever want to take pills, and then ironically he had to take so much medicine during his illness. One of the reasons Jim never wanted to take medicine was because he thought his father's death may have been caused by taking too many medications. From what I understand the family never really knew.

Elizabeth: Did his father overdose?

Chris: No. In a reading with Jim's sister their father made it sound like there was something in his brain—maybe an aneurysm—something to do with his brain. I believe Jim, and maybe the family, thought it was to do with the medication that he was taking for his depression.

Elizabeth: Did you ask someone with an "M" name to come in today?

Chris: My friend, Midge. I thought she might show up today because I did ask her before I came.

Elizabeth: Well, we have quite a few in the room now. We'll see if we can get to Midge. Let's give thanks to all those in the Heaven world for helping us today. Jim's telling me he's going to step aside so he can let them all come in and be a part of the day. He'll just wait while they do that.

There seem to be quite a few. He says he loves you and he'll be right here. He knows you are worried about him leaving. Jim is saying he was so honored to be a part of this conversation.

Do you know who Cheeky is? He's saying, "Cheeky! Cheek, Cheek, Cheek, Cheeky." He wants me to tell you that when Jim was ready to leave the Earth he was there in the room and saw you suffering. He came to comfort you while Jim was passing.

Chris: Yes, he was a good friend who died of a massive heart attack. Tell him I thank him for comforting me when Jim died.

Elizabeth: Your dad is here and says you've got to get better. The horses are waiting for you. The horses await. The chariots await, my dear.

Chris: Oh, my dad's here?

Elizabeth: Yes. He smiles and puts his head to the side. It's like Mr. Romance came here.

Bill: I think that you should be riding in these chariots, being with the horses and grooming them. I think your mother would enjoy a trip to do so. This is something that would be great for all of you. Don't hold back when it comes to getting better so that you can get on one of the horses and get riding. I always loved horses and I know you do, too.

Chris: Yes, and you got us our first horses. I'll always be grateful for that.

Bill: It'll be just like the old days. You kids were never sick or had any kind of problems when you were little. I think it was all the fresh air, good healthy food, the outdoors and these animals that were so much a part of your lives. (Smiling.)

Bill: You've got to get riding. Get back up on the horse.

Chris: Have you seen my horse, Ike, in Heaven?

Bill: (Laughing.) In Heaven.....yes! I used to joke and say that Ike was going to turn into one of those flying horses like Pegasus. He had a majestic way about him. A proud way, but gentle. I've definitely had the opportunity to ride Ike. My activities are very much the same as they were when I was physical although I don't spend as much time with the family because Jim is so involved with them right now.

Jim left very early. I had more time to really enjoy life and I appreciated life more and more every day, especially as I got older.

That's one of the reasons you can't "check out" or leave just yet. There's a lot more fun to be had. There is a level of appreciation of just being alive that matters, along with having fairly decent health.

I watch my grandson, Michael. He has to develop or come up with an appreciation for life. It's one thing to just get through life and daily survival. It's another to appreciate life and being alive on the Earth. I am concerned it may take him a little while to do that.

Jim: *You have to realize that not everybody had it peachy and roses. We all know your sister and especially her older children haven't had it very easy. I wanted to make sure your life was as happy as it could possibly be.*

Chris: You made it that way.

Jim: *I'm going to have to go soon.*

Chris: I wish you didn't have to go. Is there anybody else here?

Elizabeth: Your dad has got a couple more things on his list before he will take off. He's agenda-driven today. He pretends to look at his watch and makes a joke. "I'm pressed for time." He's got a great sense of humor.

Chris: He does. He always did.

Bill: *I want you to know that Heaven is a better place because Jim's here with me now.*

Chris: What a sweet thing to say.

Bill: *I've definitely learned that it really does make a difference ... family, people that you care about, people that you love, friends, whoever ... when they're with you. Jim and I spend some time together as well. I know you made the right decision by marrying Jim. I'm concerned about you being alone. I know you don't like* *to be alone but you did the right thing by having Jim for as long as you did. The value that Mom places on life ... I'm so proud of her. Most people would have given up. Most people would have just thrown in the towel, lied down and died. She can barely see or hear and she has no sense of smell or taste. I want her to know that I see that this quality, especially her perseverance, is so admirable.*

Elizabeth: Dad appears to be incredibly wise.

Chris: And he's a wise-guy as well.

Elizabeth: He has good humor and he puts things in perspective in a wise way.

Bill: You should watch for me when you're going to buy a horse. I'll direct you to the right one. I believe you actually should buy one, own one, have one ... somebody to ride, a companion ... and Jim agrees.

Chris: It would mean moving.

Bill: In time to come, way down the road. You and Jim talked about it, that when you retired you would get horses and maybe some kind of farm somewhere. I think getting involved now might be a good thing. There's a horse out there waiting for you. Forget the dog; there's a horse.

Elizabeth: He wants you to get back on the horse. He's saying figuratively and literally to get back on the horse.

I don't know why he wants me to see this but what is this big preference for strawberry jam and desserts? (I'm laughing.) What is this about?

Chris: He used to tease my mother all the time about making strawberry pies. We'd all say, yeah, he never gets strawberry pie, but she would make him strawberry pie regularly. We just mentioned it at Easter time. We all just talked about this!

Bill: Well, would you please remind her that I'm waiting?

Chris: (Laughing.) You're waiting for your strawberry pie!

Bill: I don't care if she's blind, can't hear and has no sense of taste—I want my strawberry pie!

Elizabeth: That's funny. That is very funny.

Chris: He's so funny and always was.

Bill: Please give her that message. Then she'll know it's me for sure.

Chris: Yes, she will. Do you have anything else to say, Dad? Do you have anything to say about Woody? Woody would love a message from you, I think.

Elizabeth: (Laughing.) Is Woody your brother?

Chris: Yes.

Elizabeth: Your father started laughing.

Chris: Woody misses my father so much.

Elizabeth: How did he get the name Woody?

Chris: I think my cousin couldn't say Willie, and Dad was a William.

Elizabeth: I see. So you called him Woody.

Bill: Because my name ... I didn't want to be Woody! So I had to call somebody Woody and that was my son. Tell Woody—oh, what the hell—don't tell him anything. You can see I haven't lost my sense of humor at all. That's the good part.

Chris: No, you haven't.

Bill: I see Woody driving down the road, and he's in some kind of truck. Sometimes I see Woody chuckle or bust right out laughing thinking of the funny things we would say together and having good memories of these things. I miss him a lot, too. I loved having a son. There's something special about having daughters but there's something so masculine and good about having a son. I was really grateful for that. How would I have lived in that house with just girls?

Elizabeth: How do you say your sister's name … Cassie?

Chris: Kathy is her name. Kasie is her nickname.

Bill: Kathy is my oldest daughter. She was a wonderful daughter and a really great mother. You two are very different. I love to see how she is connected to animals and sensitive to everyone's needs. Tell her I wish I paid more attention to what she was really like. We always seemed to point out what Kathy could have done better instead of just saying how great she was to begin with. She's a really good girl and she gets taken for granted way too much.

Woody has become a good man in spite of the fact that he grew up in a house of girls. They really whipped him into shape! You can't help but like him, he's just so darn likeable.

I love seeing that you've all stayed so connected or maybe even become closer. I always knew that even though there was some distance when you guys were younger, that when you got older you'd find a lot more comfort in being together.

Jim: I have to go. Just for now, I'm going to go recuperate and get some rest. I'm happy that you're doing so much better and keeping yourself occupied.

Chris: I love you, Sweetie.

Jim: I love you like crazy.

Elizabeth: He has tears in his eyes; he loves you. He will never be far away. Jim, do you want to go through the door? Thank you, Jim.

Chris: Bye, Sweetie. Thank you so much. That was tremendous!

Elizabeth: There was a lot of company.

Chris: There sure was!

Elizabeth: Many times you'll have so much company to show you have a lot of support.

Chris's Reflections:

Notice that in this reading, Jim mentions the concept of past lives and reincarnation. At a later time, in a compilation of other readings, Jim will speak frequently about this. Having an akashic record reading enhanced my desire to write a book as Jim and I had spoken of during the time his cancer had improved. You read previously that Jim wants readers to know that enlightenment doesn't happen simply because you die. Some people become enlightened while they're in their physical bodies and some reach enlightenment in the afterlife. This reading was done almost six months to the day after Jim died, or left his body. He's still learning so much and it all takes time. Six months later and he still hadn't learned very much about the fact that he or anyone had lived lives other than the one they're in now. Watch throughout these readings how Jim transforms and learns so much about the truths of our existence.

It's amazing to me how Jim and other souls learn so much about their existence here on Earth after their soul leaves the body and they cross to the other side. For instance, Jim finds out what contributed to his cancer and will continue to learn more about that as time goes on. He sees from the other side how prayer, Reiki (energy work) and healing masses helped him live longer when he was ill. Even though he knew it was doing something when he was physical, he didn't know what. Now he does and can tell us.

We began some discussion about Jim's father and, more important, Jim's feelings about how his dad's illness of depression affected him during this lifetime. There is more to come in future readings.

Jim's Reflections:

I want to start by saying that the process that I have been through is much like what you keep going through on the Earth. So many people have questions as to what we do up here or out here ... around here. I'd like to make it known that we don't just sit around and do nothing. We really do have obligations and assignments that are not just suggested but obligatory to our growth and evolution much like service is on the planet.

This particular reading was important to me because I was never offered the concept of reincarnation when I was on Earth. I always believed that until the age of 2 or 3 years old many of us have vivid memories of what happened before we came to Earth and are able to see the world for what it truly is. Then we become conditioned by our surroundings and those memories fade. The reading that was done this particular day was about what I always believed was true, or expected was true ... that the soul really does live forever. The experiences of déjà vu, having been to a place and being familiar with it ... it's not just your imagination or circumstances or something that someone tells you. It is actually your soul having memories of where you once were.

The moment I learned that everything is for God's will and really knew it from a soul's perspective, I almost cried. In a human world, sometimes our ego gets the better of us and we believe we're greater than God. At that very moment when I knew beyond a shadow of a doubt everything is in God's hands, it made me trust more in a loving God. There are many teachings on the Earth that would lend to the idea that God is some kind of punisher. Why would we have to put our faith in a God that would punish us for wrongdoing rather than love us and give us the intuition to right the wrongs in our lives? That concept alone strengthened my faith as a soul.

In time to come, I am eager to share with you what I've learned regarding a soul's record—an actual recording that takes place for each and every soul on the planet. During this session with Elizabeth and Chris, when Elizabeth did automatic writing and showed Chris information she could have never known, it was astonishing. Elizabeth actually accessed this record and shared vital information that was meant for Chris's evolution. The process is so lengthy and far deeper than where we are to delve now in the readings of this book. The future writings will reference the records and many other mystical topics that are undeniable and will help to strengthen your faith.

I began remembering having cancer. I couldn't help but wonder ... if I had learned to quiet myself while on Earth to a state of peace, could I have found a solution to cure my problem? I don't regret what happened to me because now I can share with all of you a possible solution to the problem. Perhaps what amazed me most was not that I had cancer and that maybe it could have been cured, but that we live so many lifetimes and we don't consciously remember them.

I can't stress this enough to all readers: what you do not take care of, focus on and draw your attention to in your physical life, there is always hope and knowledge available to correct that when you leave your physical body. I chose to seek enlightenment in the non-physical world that you refer to as the Heavens. Some souls seek to do the same thing on Earth.

Chris seeks a path to enlightenment while she's still in her physical body. She's looking for a way to rise above the pain, the sadness and the grief that she feels and has felt since my death. She doesn't fear her own death any longer nor does she plan it or hope for it. The opposite seems to be true; she looks forward now to the day ahead rather than dreading one more day there on the planet without me.

It's funny; when you get here and you're shown information as well as how to access it ... if people really knew the knowledge, the wisdom and the information that is available to them ... if the lay person knew it the world would be an incredible place! There would be no more destruction, pollution or struggle. Everyone would get along instead of competing with each other. That's the best part about being where I am—there's no competition. We all get along. Just like so many who are on Earth, there are that many more who are here in the Heaven worlds trying to figure out how we can help those who are still on Earth.

When I left my body and saw all the people waiting, how excited they were to see me and how excited I was to see them, it was amazing. I never knew a more peaceful moment than that time. Because I'm still learning, I don't know whether I felt that peace because I believed in it before I left or because I still seek that peace now.

It's interesting to think that you encounter people over here that you knew in the physical world. It's interesting for so many reasons and it's also a blessing. It helps you get settled here, acclimated, used to it. It makes it a lot easier on the soul—not that you need somebody else but it's nice to have if you want somebody else.

When I saw our nephew and how much trouble he was having, how Chris, the family—everyone—was trying so hard to help him, I wanted so much to be able to intercede. In some cases you can, but not in every case. Sometimes being an innocent bystander is harder than jumping in and helping to fix everything but you know it's a lesson the person needs to fix for themselves. His girlfriend seemed aimless, not because she lacked intelligence or any other judgmental reason why, but simply because she didn't remember one thing about Heaven. She didn't care to be thinking about it, much like I didn't. You never think about dying even when you're doing it. It's a great feeling to help another soul. Her other family members and friends also gathered around her to help put her in the right direction. Sometimes we think we know everything. We can't even begin to describe ... we can't even "begin" to describe the information and knowledge of what really happens when our souls leave the bodies that we are so familiar with.

It was nice to see old friends and it was good for me to see that my wife was being watched and cared for. Not like a Peeping Tom watched but a good close eye kept on her so she didn't have to be so sad, so worried and feel so terrible every second. The fact that her friend, Cheeky, and her loved ones came to help her when I was leaving my body made me feel so peaceful in my heart. So many people were there to help. You can never be grateful enough, ever.

When I was a child growing up we never gave a thought about hard times. We only saw things for the way they were. When you're a child, you see your parents struggle and work hard. You just learn to accept that's the way it is. Once you get here you realize there are souls who had it much worse than you did while they were on the Earth. That's why the gratitude is so profound. It's not just something that you say or that you mimic because you read it in a book or in the daily quotes. It's something you feel almost like it's a part of you. It's a deep, deep part of you.

You learn that you never want to waste one minute. Once you get here, you think about everything you would have done differently. The thing that I thought about the most, the biggest thing that my heart felt, was to be grateful for everything because in everything there is a lesson. In everything that we do, there's a lesson somewhere. Somewhere along the way—good, bad or indifferent—there's a lesson. So pay attention even when it's hard. Now don't misunderstand. Like Elizabeth says, "Sometimes a glass of water is just a glass of water." We read too much into the circumstances that go on in our lives. As long as we get the gist of it, as long as we understand that for everything that we do something else takes place—it is an effect of that thing. It's so important that we keep that in mind.

Seeing the little ones run around laughing and joking—that's the way we always want to live our lives. We forget that children are the perfect example of what we are supposed to be like our whole lives. Instead, we put a hammer in somebody's hand, or a book, or a "something" that says, "Work, do this, do that, work, work, work," and you never really interact with the people that you love the most. So if I could give you a good piece of knowledge it would be to take the time to interact. Take the moment, leave the dirty dishes in the sink, the dirty laundry for another day, eat the food you want, dance, sing, laugh and enjoy life.

Enjoy life like you've never lived before. Because the funny thing is you have lived before and one of the reasons you're back there is because you haven't enjoyed anything! You haven't learned. So take the time to learn about your soul. Take the time to realize that you don't have to be serious every second. There are things on Earth that are fun and funny. Places to go, people to meet. Yes, you have to carry out your everyday tasks but, at the same time, don't let those everyday tasks carry you away.

I can guarantee you not one soul here ever said, "I wish I worked harder. I wish I spent more time away from home. I wish I was away from my niece or my nephew or my daughter or my son, my husband, my wife." Nobody here ever thinks like that.

Before you know it your time is up. For whatever reason, your time is up. Stop trying to find the reason and start looking for the reasons to live. Even the smallest thing has meaning when it comes from the heart. If you never read another page in this book, remember: it's the little things in life, the ones that are heartfelt, that truly matter. It doesn't matter what life you do them in, one way or another you have to keep doing it, being it and living it until you do it right. You may as well get it right the first time like women do. I'm saying that as a compliment. When I don't know something, I ask a woman. They usually have the answer as to how to get the job done.

Right now, that's all I have to say. This was a long reading—fun in some parts, not so much fun in others.

Until the next chapter, this is James Petosa signing off. All planes are landed. Please take your belongings as you exit.

— Captain Jim Petosa

May 11, 2012

Elizabeth: It's good to see you. I woke up early this morning, as always, and did my daily meditation. As you know, before every reading, I always do a meditation about the person with whom I'm going to meet. This morning I felt like there was an issue with your knee. How are you feeling, physically?

Chris: Physically, my knee is having some positive changes. It still hurts a lot going downstairs, though.

Elizabeth: How's your digestion? I know that's been a problem in the past.

Chris: I'm trying to follow suggestions from last month's reading, but sometimes a good old cup of coffee is what works the best.

Elizabeth opens the session, as she always does, with a prayer of gratitude and blessings.

Elizabeth: For the record, let's start with full name and date of birth.

Chris: (I gave my full name and date of birth as Elizabeth always requests.) Jim's laughing, right?

Elizabeth: Yes, he is.

Chris: He always laughs at that, doesn't he?

Elizabeth: Yes. He makes a joke constantly about the fact that you robbed the cradle, so when you say your birthdate he always laughs. I have to ask you … what are you going to do later today?

Chris: I have to do some things for my neighbor because he's been in the hospital, but then I'm going to leave for Pennsylvania to go to a wedding.

Elizabeth: Oh, okay … you're traveling. Jim kept talking about you traveling.

Jim: *We have to go easy on her. I don't want her to have another episode today, especially while she's driving.*

Chris: He said that?

Jim: *I don't want anything to happen to you.*

Chris: Because of my episodes. But, you know what? If I was going to have a head thing—one of those TGAs—it would have happened in the last couple of days, because our neighbor really has needed care the full two days. I know my family was worried about me, but I'm okay. But thank you, Jim, for worrying about me traveling.

Elizabeth: In my opinion, I don't think we can ever take too good of care of someone. Chuck. Who is Chuck?

Chris: Chuck is the neighbor I'm helping. He's been our neighbor for over twenty years. Chuck is in the hospital, hopefully for a minor problem, but his concern is really more for his wife.

Jim: *Tell Chuck I said hello. He's a really good guy. When he's ready, because he's been so good to me, I'll be there to help him and his wife, too, whenever she decides to go.*

Chris: They love each other. They're more than good friends—they're more like uncle and nephew. Chuck is worried and concerned because his wife has dementia. Therefore, when he's not able to be home, his concern is magnified. I've been trying to visit Chuck in the hospital but also take care of his wife at home.

Elizabeth: I know that. That's why I'm concerned. Jim was very specific about wanting to be here today. It's related to growth and your elevation. You are experiencing, as a person, growth and elevation; he can partake in this growth as well.

There's still a part of his personality that is focused on the planet. Earth and all the people on it are still here.

Chris: I asked him to come today. I told him I'd love it if he stayed the whole time if he wanted to. I also wondered if he could tell me what he knows that we don't about some family situations.

Elizabeth: I see that you're overwhelmed; we're going from topic to topic.

Jim: Let's take one thing at a time.

Elizabeth: Jim, do you want to discuss this or do you have a different agenda? Yes, Jim seems to have his own agenda, but he's open to answering questions from his point of view. I get a sense that there's something going on. Jim, you can speak at any time.

Chris: My mind is all over the place. I'm sure it's because Jim passed seven months ago today. I've missed him for seven months. We toasted to him at breakfast this morning.

Elizabeth: Yes, he knows. (Elizabeth is laughing.) He's going like this: Cheers!

Chris: Yes, exactly!

Elizabeth: That's very funny. Who toasted with you?

Chris: My Friday breakfast group—teachers I've worked with. But one of them, Karen ... she and Jim always had a fun relationship. We went on vacation together a couple of times. We were swimming with stingrays once and he scared her to death, acting like he was a stingray swimming up and touching her in the back. When we toasted to him, I told Karen Jim was probably right next to her trying to scare her.

Elizabeth: That's funny. Jim, you are a character. He loved that aspect of his life. He wants you to know something … a whole bunch of stuff here. There are two ideas he would really like to get across to you. Number one (he knows how I like to be to the point), he says the first thing that is necessary or important for you to know is that he still enjoys doing earthly things, and the more that you do this, the more that you're around other people, the more that you are celebrating with other people, the more that you're enjoying life, the more he is enjoying watching you. So there's a participation aspect going on here and it's very, very dear. In other words continue on as you used to. Enjoy life.

The second thing he didn't know how to verbalize when he was here physically and it is about enlightenment. He has learned by watching you that there is this other aspect of everyone. He calls his the "perfect Jim self." He wants to become the "enlightened Jim." The way he describes it would be as if all of the good qualities of Jim were amplified times one hundred. He's not being boastful. He's trying to convey that he has connected to this part of himself that he always knew existed, yet couldn't quite explain.

Jim: I'm not a saint, I can't perform miracles, I can't do all of that, but I am connected into the light worlds. I'm in Heaven. I'm in Heaven. I'm in Heaven. If we looked at it a different way, like we were flying … Chris, we can fly!

Elizabeth: He's way up in this higher vibration, I guess you would say. He's looking down, watching and experiencing everything that's taking place here with you, your friends and families. He keeps going on and on with this big long list of people, and how he still enjoys all of this and is still able to witness it. The only thing that's different is that he's watching it happen instead of actually physically being a participant. Jim gets overly concerned because you are an active participant. He knows all you want to do is help. He's just concerned, as always, that you overdo when people can do for themselves.

Who is the man that is his friend that flies the planes? Jim keeps showing me he's a pilot. He's also showing me that this man comes behind him, whatever that means.

Chris: Well, he worked with a lot of men who were pilots.

Elizabeth: He shows me a cockpit and the part of the plane where the pilot is. He's still showing me that he goes after Jim.

Jim: *I fly with him sometimes.*

Chris: Is it the man who took Jim's pilot position when Jim stopped flying for the company?

Jim: *That is who I mean. He had a different background, so I'm able to learn from him. I like to learn how to fly the big jets. I can fly just about anything and now there's new technology, new machines, newer airplanes. I love learning about them.*
Being here in the afterlife is not all just spiritual growth. It really is learning more about technology and advancements as well. I enjoy it a great deal. I do my best to keep my spirits up for you. I know that nights are the hardest.

Chris: Yes, they are.

Jim: *I wish I could say I'm with you every second, however, I'm not. The tasks you are doing a lot of the time—this is something you are choosing to do on your own. It's not because I want it this way or because I like it this way, it's just the way it is. I'm still trying to overcome the aspect of missing you. I'm not sure I'm ever going to get over that, but I'm learning how to adapt to it.*

Elizabeth: He's showing me the remote control, flipping through the channels on the TV, hearing music and other aspects of being physical that people do to occupy their minds.

Jim: *Maybe you just need to sit down and watch the TV. Turn the damn TV on for a minute.*

Chris: I don't do it that much.

Jim: *Would you do something normal like that for a change! I know you don't like just sitting there because it's too lonely and it's too hard for you to forget me or too hard for you to get me out of your mind.*
There's one thing I want to thank you for, and I mean this sincerely. I want to thank you for remembering the times that I wasn't sick ... that we had a life, that we had fun, that we could go on vacation. All the things that we did when I wasn't sick. Those are the things I remember.

Chris: That is more of what I remember.

Elizabeth: When he says it, he's all choked up about it.

Jim: *Those are the things that I want you to remember. I don't want you to remember the times that I was sick and just dwell on that.*

In the future, what I want to do ... what I really want to do ... is help people who had and have cancer. There's no regulation as to what is being put into the atmosphere. As a population, we think there is because we're told to think so, but there really isn't. There are not enough regulations.

I know this contributed to my problem. It was not just jet fuel. I believe the amount of pollution I actually witnessed was part of the problem as well. I've become very interested in matters of pollution. Although I never said much about it, I could see it while flying above it. I could see all the pollution coming up from factories and manufacturers. They'd like to tell you that it doesn't matter, but it does.

I flew internationally numerous times ... overseas ... and it seemed obvious to me, based on the amount of pollution I could see in the air, it was easy to tell the areas where more regulations were enforced than others. Ironically, the thing that I loved most is one of the things I think contributed to the problem. I like to do a lot of "rescue work"—going to help people, to rescue people. I love doing this.

Elizabeth: He's showing me pilots that fly into rough waters. He's not being symbolic here ... like diver pilots and Coast Guard and these kinds of people. He would have liked an opportunity to do that more. He's showing me helicopters and other flying devices and different types of machines.

Jim: *I had a cushy job.*

Elizabeth: This is something that would be kind of a piece of his rescue nature, but also that daring kind of male side of him, if you will. He has a lot of this kind of work to do; if he can do it, he's going to do it.

Jim: *I'm going to take the opportunity if it comes to me.*

Chris: I know how important these kinds of things are to you. You were always that way.

Jim: One of the reasons I'm not with you every second is because I'm finding things to do.

I know that in a year from now, it's going to be so different for both of us. I don't know how, but it's going to be different. I already see how much you've changed and how much you have learned, but also how much you let go of. I'm so happy about that.

Chris: (Crying.) But I haven't let go of you. I'm trying to learn to live with it.

Jim: I know you're doing what you can to get through it and to get used to me being gone, physically. That's the worst thing for me. The only thing that could be worse would be you going first and me being stuck on Earth without you.

Chris: Yeah … thanks, Jim. Thanks a lot! I agree, because this is hell.

Elizabeth: He says you've got to … he goes like this … he pushes your chin up.

Jim: Keep your chin up. I know you're sick of hearing that. F**k … I know you're sick of hearing that! I know, I know, I know, I know. There's nothing else to do, though.

Chris: But you do know that if I can toast in the morning with coffee without crying at the time you died seven months ago, that I am getting better?

Jim: What's important here is that you express how you feel, not necessarily the feeling itself. I don't want you to work "harder" at feeling better; I just want you to do what you feel like. That's all you can do, Chris. That's all you can do.

Marianne. I want you to tell her I miss our long talks and our time together … being able to talk about deeper things. And I'm saying this in the most loving way … it takes her a long time to get to the point! I loved that about her. I liked to just listen to her rattle things off.

Elizabeth: Who's Mark?

Chris: Her husband.

Jim: Now that we don't have each other to talk to, she'll have to talk to Mark a lot more. (He's laughing.) Mark knows I'm just kidding. This is a good thing. I'm *so worried about my family. They're all still in mourning and going through the grieving process a little differently than you.*

Elizabeth: He's showing me a priest.

Chris: That must be the priest from our church.

Jim: The priest at our church is great at dealing with the parishioners, but he feels their sadness, pain and troubles just like we do. I watch him and see how busy he is. We all know how busy priests can be, having a whole parish or more to care for. We have to remember that priests are human.

I see Father listening to the woes and troubles of people in their daily lives. Sometimes we're harder on them than we realize and unnecessarily so. Being a priest is truly a labor of love and sometimes the rest of us take that for granted.

The church doesn't approve of some of the healing methods we chose, but true wisdom always shows itself. The establishment simply named it something different—"the union of saints."

I think Father knows intellectually that it's okay, and he's very intellectual. Just like all those seeking answers in the church ... if the answer cannot be found by faith alone, it can be proven by science. Even though Father and I didn't get to know each other on a deeply personal level while I was physical, Father does have memories of me. For that, I am very grateful.

Chris: Do you know that the men's group is singing in church on Mothers' Day? I think some part of it has to do with you or others who have passed this year.

Elizabeth: They're doing some kind of memorial. Jim puts his head down in a humble manner. It's a wonderful gesture and gratitude just radiates from him.

Jim: I wish I could be there physically to honor all mothers. They have a hard job.

I notice that especially during the services, there is a very clear, brilliant, beautiful white light that descends over all churches, but I especially notice our church because that's where I spend my time.

Elizabeth: He's showing, literally, this very spiritual light that he sees from the Heavens.

Jim: *It's not a light of your world; it's a light that descends from the Heavens. I'm not separate from it, but in order to describe it to you, that's the only way I can say it. There's this light that descends over the church and the people in it. The light gets brighter somehow when people are praising. I'm not really sure why, I just know that it happens and it's amazing to see.*

I know from my own experience that Reiki and energy work come from that light, or appear to, to me. I can tell the difference when prayers are said from the heart. I can see a glow around people's hearts when they're praying. That's what we want to remember. I don't understand why they're doing away with things like Reiki and energy work.

It's all the same light. It's all the same God.

I was so grateful for the healing that I received from the healing priest and the healing masses. This really touched my heart ... the number of people that came to express their love, but also the healing that I experienced. This was at a deep spiritual level for me while I was still on Earth. The healing that I experienced was immense. I can't put it into words.

I wanted to live a life that was led by the Holy Spirit and guided by the Holy Spirit. It's a lot easier to do that where I am now because I am a spirit, and always was, but it's harder to realize in the flesh.

(He's laughing.) Being physical comes with its own set of complications. Being physical feels good, but in the spirit world we don't have the flesh to distract us. There are certainly pros and cons to that. I know I didn't talk this way when I was physical, but no one really knows what another person is thinking. I joked and goofed a lot; that's just part of being. In reality, though, my prayer was always to live a life like Jesus and be guided by the Holy Spirit. I wanted to live my live with compassion and help others to do the same. I was fascinated by technology and travel but knew a compassionate heart was needed. I knew there were both sides to life and I tried to find a way to make them mesh.

I never understood what it meant to "change your vibration" or to "raise your vibration" but now I know it means to raise your vibration to the light ... to raise your soul and let your soul fill with light. Intellectually, I understood that when I was physical, but never really comprehended what it meant until I was in the spirit world. Now I "know" it. And this "light body," I guess we would call it, that I travel in ... .

Elizabeth: He's looking down and he gives a look of astonishment.

Jim: It's so amazing to me ... this whole concept ... everything about it is just so amazing! You can be that light while you're on Earth, Chris. You are that light.

Chris: While I'm here, physically?

Jim: Yes.

Chris: Do you know I'm working at it a lot?

Jim: I do know. I see it every day—that you're being prayerful and contemplative and becoming even more spiritual than you already were. I didn't see you as this healing presence that you are in the way that I do now. I can't believe I missed that! I know how loving and wonderful you are, but there's this other part of you that is so ... "brilliant!"

Elizabeth: He's showing me *light* ... that it's all light and happy and brilliance.

Chris: Aww ... thanks, Jim! But, isn't that true about everyone?

Jim: Yes, but your light seems to shine a little brighter.

Chris: In me?

Jim: Yes. You're more uplifted. You don't have to be like that every second, but I definitely see the difference. Especially with different people that are around you—they take it for granted. It takes work, it takes diligence, it takes perseverance, all of which you have!

I need to tell you something else. We were fortunate to be connected to one another. We knew it ... being connected to church, being connected to family and our friends ... we were fortunate that we knew it.

Chris: Definitely, we were. We had a great relationship.

Jim: I don't want to change the subject, but I want you to know this. When Michael starts having a deep connection with Jesus or God—pick one—it's more likely that he will get better than he is now.

Chris: I keep praying that he'll realize some kind of guidance.

Jim: In a lot of ways, I feel like he's our son, so when something bad happens, I'm right there. Remind him of how important it is, and was to me, to know Jesus and to know the good works of Jesus and the Holy Spirit. I don't want to sound like a preacher, but this is what got me through everything when I was on the Earth. If I had woes or troubles or hard times, I would remember and be so grateful for the connection that I had to Jesus and the Holy Spirit ... the Heavens.

Chris: Michael told me he isn't feeling suicidal. Do you agree with that?

Jim: I don't think he is. I know that Michael's trouble is something at the core, at the deep part of his core, like a sense of value.

Elizabeth: When he says it, he has this really pensive way about it, and he's trying to find the right words to convey that this problem with drinking isn't just about drinking. There's more to it than that.

Jim: It must feel terrible to Michael to desperately want more in his life, but to feel so unworthy that drinking is what he turns to. Once you get here, you find out there's so much more, but Michael can do the same thing on Earth.

That is something Michael has to realize. This isn't something he can fix at an intellectual level as much as he tries, because he does try to think his way through it. This is something I know is hard for him. It's hard because this problem isn't solved by thinking. Finding a new hobby would be a great thing for him.

Chris: Is there anything else I need to know about this?

Jim: I know that sometimes you want more for people than they want for themselves.

Elizabeth: He's very quiet. I'm not sure what this means exactly, but he says, "Show her. Tell her what I have." He has roses. They're not rich, red roses like you might imagine. They're all different colors—pink, yellow, white, a couple of red—there's a whole big bushel. It's a bouquet, much bigger than a normal size bouquet. Jim wishes he could give that to your mother and his mother for Mothers' Day coming up.

Who's Jeannie or Jannie? Do you know who that is?

Chris: Ginnie?

Elizabeth: There we go. Who's that?

Chris: She's a neighbor and mother of a dear friend of Jim's.

Elizabeth: Jim is bringing up her name. The big bouquet would be his gift to all women and mothers. He loves women—just the company of women—not in any other way. He keeps offering this big bouquet of flowers for his mother, for your mom, Marianne and the rest of his sisters, for Ginny, for you, for all the women who are celebrating Mothers' Day. He wants you to get some roses—different colors—to take to your mom. Jim is so sincere about this.

Jim: Tell her they're from us. She can't see, but she knows everything! She knows what's going on. (He's smiling.)

Chris: That would be Jim. He always took the time to acknowledge mothers—our own mothers as well as others.
   Do you know that Marianne and I are going to Atlanta in June to take care of the girls while Paul and Leslie go away?

Jim: Yes! I'm so excited about that! I can't wait to get my hands on the baby! When's the last time you held a baby? Can you believe my brother had another baby? And Marianne can't wait to get her hands on the baby either.

Chris: Her name is Ava James.

Jim: I can't believe it. (He's laughing.) They shouldn't have named a girl a boy's name!

Chris: I think it's beautiful. What do you think, Jim?

Jim: I'm very touched and honored by the whole thing. Call her Ava Jimmy for short!

Chris: Okay, I'll tell Paul and Leslie. They'll just love that! Were you at the barn with us when Eric and I did the community service with the horses for his confirmation?

Jim: *I wasn't. It was too hard to watch. I knew you were going and I knew what you were doing. It was just too hard to watch.*

Chris: For what reason?

Jim: *For you. I know you're trying to make the best of it, but it would be better if I was there. It's a milestone for Eric and a memorable one for me. I always thought of these occasions as being important.*

Chris: So, you'll be at Eric's confirmation in a couple of weeks, won't you?

Jim: *I sure will. I know Eric asked you to sponsor him because his Uncle Jimmy isn't there in person. I'm really honored by that.*
   I see the problems and the pain that you continue to have with your knee and the other health issues you have. I know you still have to take quite a few medicines, but I'm glad that at least you're taking fewer than you used to. I know how I hated taking pills and I don't like to see you have to do that.

Chris: Yes, I know you hated taking pills. It was hard to get you to take an aspirin if you had a headache.

Jim: *I believe that there's going to come a day when you're not going to have all the problems and ailments that you do now.*

Chris: Oh, I hope you're right, Jim.

Jim: *(Laughing.) I never could meditate, Elizabeth.*

Elizabeth: I asked him if there's anything he would like to share about what would help you grow and develop more, spiritually.

Chris: (Sometimes Elizabeth communicates telepathically with the souls we're speaking with. When having a reading, I am sometimes so involved in what's happening that I don't realize Elizabeth is already having a telepathic conversation. That's why she's quiet. Sometimes, because I'm so excited about talking to my loved ones, I become too agenda-driven. I learned over time that it's most helpful not to come with a preconceived notion of what I hope to get from the reading. It's helpful to keep an open mind because what the souls want to say and what I came to hear may not be the same thing.)

Jim: *I know you're going to tell her meditation. I never could meditate.*

Elizabeth: Sitting still and trying to quiet his thoughts was difficult. He's impressed with your ability to meditate and to get quiet. He's so impressed by this that he says he's going to learn a few pointers from you! It wasn't something that he could do very well. That part he's sure of. He is glad that you're learning in this way.

He never understood Reiki and energy work. He just knew that it worked. When he sees you meditating, sees how much growth you've gone through and how it has helped you get rid of some of this grief and heaviness, it makes him happy.

Jim: *I think I've talked enough; I've said enough today.*

Elizabeth: He wasn't always one much for words.

Chris: May I ask one more thing? Have I finally thanked everyone I needed to thank for him?

Jim: *I don't think you've left anybody out. (Laughing.)*

Elizabeth: When he says it, he kind of leans over and emphasizes …

Jim: *I don't think you've left anyone out! You even thanked people that didn't need to be thanked! And then some.*

Chris: Oh Jim, that's funny!

Jim: *Seriously, though, I appreciate what you have done about that. I'll see you very soon.*

Elizabeth: He's still learning "how" and how to describe it. He's laughing.

Jim: *It's so funny. Our whole lives we spend trying to figure out what we don't understand about spirit, and then when you come here you spend a lot of time wondering how you become a human being again.*

Chris: Really? Is that why people reincarnate?

Jim: That's why I want to.

Chris: You really do? Can you wait for me and give me a break and let me be there for a while? Please? Because this is hard!

Jim: (Laughing.) Yes, I definitely can and I will.

Chris: Okay, because this life is hard right now.

Jim: It's too much. If it's any consolation, I think all the time, wonder all the time, how do I get back to being physical. It's no different than what you think about. I know that's only because I miss you, our families and our friends so much. One thing's for sure—it ain't easy! (Laughing.) It sure ain't easy. I've found out that acceptance is the answer. We just have to accept.

Elizabeth: You'll be fine, Jim.

Jim: Thank you. I love you so much, Chris.

Chris: I love you, Jim.

Jim: That part I know.

Chris: Because I tell you all the time.

Jim: And because I know what it feels like. I just know. I feel it.

Chris: (My father came in to the reading next and we discussed an immensely serious personal family matter. It is very comforting to know that I can talk about family issues through a medium and can often get help with how to cope. At the very least, I receive great comfort from it.)

Chris: Is the sister that he brought in my sister-in-law's sister? Nona? Because I requested that she come.

Elizabeth: Bill, who is it? He says, *"When I'm done...."* (laughing). Very funny.

Chris: Oh, okay! Sorry, Dad!

Bill: *Have you seen any dragonflies lately?*

Chris: Is it you who sends them to be around us? You started with Kathy, didn't you?

Bill: *Yes … big ones, small ones, some on your coat, on your dresses and shirts. I did start sending them to your sister first.*

Chris: For any particular reason?

Bill: *To try and get her to pay attention. I try to put them everywhere, stir them up over the pond, even on clothes so she'll see them places that she goes. I try to give her that symbol, not that she's on the right track, but to pay attention.*

Chris: She does totally believe you're sending them.

Bill: *I use hummingbirds, too. I had a special connection to both dragonflies and hummingbirds, so I send them to all of you. I use coins, too, but you seem to notice them the most.*

Chris: (Dad and I carried on another personal family conversation. I am always amazed at how involved our loved ones in the afterlife are in our daily lives.)

Elizabeth: Boy, your dad must have had a busy mind. From the way he comes across, it takes me a minute to put everything in order. It's fun for both of us because he can be who he is and I get to witness what that might have been like for you. Your dad's thoughts keep moving very quickly from one thing to another. It's not necessary for me as a medium to make sure their thoughts are quiet, but as you can imagine, if someone has an active mind when they're in the afterlife, they often jump from topic to topic and sometimes the conversation can even come across as being disjointed. So if four or five people show up and they're all talking or all trying to communicate at once, it does come across just as it's happening. All I do is repeat what I'm hearing.

You may not know this, but when souls are at different levels of evolution, the information comes through just as they relay it and will show their state of consciousness in the afterlife. So if we put all of what I just explained together, if a soul has not grown or is still feeling heavy emotions, those feelings will come through as well. My job is simply to relay to you what is being said or telepathically communicated to me.

When we consider a mind that has been calmed through meditation in this world, the calmed mind allows easier communication and a peaceful inner existence. When Jim said he couldn't meditate, much of the reason was because he had such an active mind that disrupted his inner peace. That would make sense since he was sick with cancer for so long and his body was filled with drugs. That would influence his mind as well. You witnessed the effects of the chemo drugs firsthand, Chris, so you know what I'm talking about.

Alright, sure, you can come in. I'm not sure who you are, but you can. This woman has very little energy to expend. It appears that she's not accustomed to this world yet. I can't really get a clear image of her. I'm not quite sure what she's trying to convey. I wish the message were more clear.

Chris: Can I say a name?

Elizabeth: Is there Nina, Nina?

Chris: Nona? I asked her if she would come in.

Elizabeth: Who does this lady belong to?

Chris: She is my brother's wife's sister. She died of cancer.

Elizabeth: Recently?

Chris: A few years ago.

Elizabeth: This woman has not regained a lot of momentum. It's like her spirit is still very heavy. There's a sense of mourning to her and a real sense of loss. I'm sorry, but I can't get a real clear view of her. One thing that's very clear to me is the fact that she's very dense still. Often when people have a difficult death experience, recuperation is needed in order to have the energy to communicate within the mortal world. We can assume that the chemo drugs she was taking might have affected the way she presents today. There's one more person here. Who are you, please? Do you know who Jill is? Jill is physical.

Chris: I have a very good friend, Jill.

Elizabeth: I see. This woman is looking for Jill.

Chris: Grandmother?

Elizabeth: It is definitely an older, wiser spirit … definitely an older soul. Wandering.

Chris: Jill's grandmother died of Alzheimer's.

Elizabeth: Jill apparently has an active mind or an active wonder about this, like "How could this happen to such a good person, to such a nice person, to such a dear person?"

Chris: That makes sense.

Elizabeth: Jill seems to be searching or doing a lot of soul-searching these days on why and how this could happen to someone so sweet. The grandmother wants her to know she's very much at rest and very much at peace—much more than before. The way she is presenting is indicative of her condition or ailment at the time of her death. She wants me to see this so I understand and can share with you. It appears that she has been busy ridding herself of the human nature. She's doing much better. Much better. So tell Jill that, please. Grandma says, "I know she spends a lot of time thinking about me."

Chris: I thank her for coming. I will tell Jill.

Elizabeth: I don't have anyone else here. Let's make sure they all go back to their respective places. Thank you for coming.

Chris's Reflections:

I might talk about this particular reflection over and over again, because I think it is amazing, and it has affected my life tremendously. What amazes me is that not only our loved ones on the other side, but also saints and Angels can and do know what our thoughts and actions are at all times. I know that many of us are brought up knowing or believing that God is all-knowing. Of course I have always believed that and knew that, but I tended to take that for granted, or "got used to" that idea. Now that I have conversations with my loved ones on the other side, I truly "get it." They don't interfere with our private lives and daily goings on, but they can know exactly what's going on in our lives. They are telepathic so they know what we're thinking, they see how we act, they hear what we say ... the list goes on and on.

For example, in the very first reading I ever had, my father, who had died ten years before, knew all sorts of events and family situations that had gone on during those years. When I speak to Jim in a reading, he will often talk to me about a concern I've had before I even bring it up. How has this changed my life? It doesn't scare me, because I know they love us no matter what, but it does make me more careful about my thoughts, words or actions that aren't as kind or well-meaning as they should be. I think twice now before I do many things, asking myself what Jim or my mom or dad would think of this if I did it. If I know in my heart it's the right thing to do, then I go ahead, but if thinking twice makes me realize I could make a better choice, then I do.

This has changed my life in a good way. Some may be thinking, "This is where I stop reading this book; I don't want to change the fun I'm having, and if I make my decisions based on my parents and what they would think, I won't have any more fun." That's not at all what I mean. Fun, joy, laughter, music—anything that gives us enjoyment—is what we're expected to do. But sometimes we get carried away and do or say things that hurt others or cause us to hurt ourselves. For me, knowing that our thoughts and actions are open to the universe just keeps me in check. I look at it as having a whole lot of "helpers" out there in the universe!

I love knowing that in "real life" on the other side, we can do even more than we can here on Earth. When Jim says, "Chris, we can fly!" he means it! They create what they want with their thoughts. Can you imagine? Can you imagine being able to travel to other countries, to other galaxies and to other universes? I'm in no hurry to leave this Earth, but when I do, I sure plan on having fun seeing and experiencing everything available on the other side.

I also love that Jim now instinctively knows at his heart center that some therapies, practices and medicines worked and some didn't, even though he doesn't yet understand why. Healing masses and Reiki are two examples of what did work even though Jim can't explain why. Although Jim was extremely spiritual during his physical life, he was quiet about it. Jim didn't go around preaching his thoughts and beliefs, but they were deeply rooted and he means it when he says he wanted to live like Jesus.

On the other hand, Jim was very skeptical of many things while physically alive, whether they were alternative therapies, drugs that were supposed to help him, some religious rituals and practices or someone selling something to him that sounded like a miracle item. So when Jim says he doesn't understand how it works, but that healing masses and Reiki helped him during his illness, it shows us that we can't prove everything in the scientific world that can help us or are good for us. Some things help us whether we understand them or not.

Healing masses performed by a priest and Reiki or any energy work is healing from God and the universe coming through the hands of the healer. That person is not the healer … God is. Once again, if we really truly believe God can do anything, it seems, then, that that same God can send healing through the hands of those around us who make it their life's work to help heal others.

Most people I've met leave a reading with a medium saying, "I can't believe what he/she knew about me and things in my life. Did you tell them about me?" Well, no, of course I didn't … they were given a gift from God to help us understand as many things as possible that we don't understand by what we see, read or hear.

I would like to note that, personally, I would only have a reading with a medium that I knew of from others … word of mouth is always the best way for me.

Along a similar vein, can you imagine, just for a minute, being Jim on the other side looking down at churches and seeing a beautiful light around them? Without even talking about it further, that says so much to me.

Last reflection for this reading: This, again, shows how those on the other side are telepathic. I had never met Jill's grandmother. But Jill adored her, and I heard so many stories about her from Jill. Jill was always distressed by the fact that her dear grandmother had Alzheimer's disease. Therefore, it didn't really surprise me to have Jill's grandmother come in to my reading to give Jill a message. Telepathy allows them to know who is a friend of whom and how they can reach them. Jill's grandmother did just that. A message, short and quick, that when delivered to Jill, made her happy knowing her sweet grandmother was now doing much better and was at peace. Could that be made up by a medium when I didn't even know the person on the other side?

Jim's Reflections:

As we've said before, "we" being me and others who are here with us, we keep a close eye on the ones we love. That's something that's just a given ... you do it whether you were physical, not physical, however you want. But when that close eye consists of doing everything for everyone and not letting others do on their own, that close eye becomes wrongly used for helping others. In other words, we must learn to let people help themselves to some degree.

I would watch Chris go from here to there, running here and running there, working hard on this book, keeping up with friendships and helping this person and that person. Yes, that's a very noble effort, but she would get fatigued and at times ... she would never be resentful ... but when others would do what she knew was not right, it was sometimes hard for her to accept.

That's the message for the first part of this reflection. We must let others learn from doing and helping in order to develop their own growth. We must let others do on their own first until they come and ask for help. We're always so quick to offer, to offer, to offer and some of it is based on being given so much in the physical world. That's wonderful. However, at the same time, the lesson for many people is about pride and having to lose their sense of pride, not in a sense of humiliation, but rather a sense of vanity. Many people have to lose their pride so that they can learn how to ask for help.

One of the things that is noteworthy to mention here is that many people fail to ask for help. They don't ask for help because they believe they can fix whatever the problem is. How much are they willing to listen to those who can help them and give good advice? Are they willing to listen to suggestions? It's a proud man who will not accept help from another.

However, it's a fool who will accept help from those who want to give and yet not do anything for themselves. So the next time you want to help someone, the next time you want to extend your hand, ask yourself how much this person is helping themselves. How much are they able to help themselves?

I mean no disregard to anyone—none whatsoever. Just realize that there is a time and place when you have to decide whether you are too proud to accept help from others. There is also a time and place when you have to decide if someone is doing enough for themselves before you extend your hand to them. Both types of character in people present lessons to be learned during their lifetime.

When I watched Chris, all the work that she does in the family ... all the things she does for this person and that person ... it was hard for me even when I was physical to keep up with what she was doing. I wanted to help. I wanted to give. But sometimes I would just sit back, watch and notice. Notice her reaction and disappointment when she would give so much and others gave back so little or tried even less. So the message here today is to let people do for themselves. If they truly want help, they'll ask. If they truly want to seek, they will. Maybe you can be the type of person to direct people, to send them in the right direction. Remember, when you're doing more for the person than they will do for themselves, you're doing too much.

In this reading, I asked Chris countless times to sit and be quiet, watch TV, listen to music ... just sit and rest. Sometimes one of the biggest mistakes that people make when they go through grief is that they have to find something to do. Many people are like this. They have to have something to do. The trouble is, or perhaps not the trouble for me was that I didn't always need something to do. Sometimes I could just sit on the couch and watch the TV or read a book. Sometimes I could just do nothing. Because sometimes that's what we're meant to do ... nothing. So take no offense.

The next point I would like to make is the point about religion. I would in no way ever want to offend or try to change the beliefs of other people. From what I've learned, the best way to know if a religion is meant for you, for your family and how you want to teach them is to ask yourself if it's based in love. Is it grounded in love ... the love of one Creator that loves all people, all things, the Earth, animals, plants, humans, everyone the same?

That's the real message. Is the love for all people and things the same? Many people practice in different ways. Most religions are based on love but many people get carried away and believe that human beings are responsible for creating the universe. I used to chuckle to myself, as I would never make fun of another, when people would say that we have power on the planet. We have such little power. It's the fear of having such little power that is ironic.

We have very little power if any at all. You see, I wanted to live. I wanted to stay on the planet. I wanted to stay in my body, and I had the power and freedom to make a choice as to what I would do to heal my problem. That's true. I lacked knowledge. Perhaps I lacked what I needed to know in order to be able to do that. Many people do. There's a big difference between those who will seek out ways and those who expect others will do it for them. So if you ever have a problem such as mine, don't expect others will take care of you. Expect that they will take care of you as you participate actively in your own care.

The same is true for religion. Expect that religion, expect that spirituality can work for you if you allow it to. If it's grounded, if it's rooted in love, if it's meant to be used to show love and to love, for loving is so natural, then you most likely have found the religion or spirituality that is right for you. Many of the churches *that we hear about on the Earth nowadays don't allow for Reiki and other energy work and treatments, believing that this energy work is of some form other than God. Nothing could be further from the truth. God gives many people the ability to bring His light through to help others fill their souls with light, to help others heal. That's true healing when you help another bring light to their soul. Religions often are based in control, wanting so much to control people who are involved in them, wanting so much to use power, money and other examples like these for what is best for everyone involved.*

The reality is what is best is love. If you know someone who is being helped with Reiki, if you know someone who is being helped with what's known as "energy work," know that the energy does not come from the practitioner; it comes through them from the greater source of light. It comes from God. So when you choose a practitioner, when you choose someone who can best help you, choose one who is connected with God and knows that and realizes that Reiki comes through them, not from them, and that they are just the channel or the conduit for this to take place.

I really urge each and every one of you, whether you are ill, not ill or somewhere in between ... try it and see what happens. Notice how still the soul becomes. Notice how still you become in the physical way. Notice how still it makes you. Why? Because that's what the soul is: it's stillness, it's quiet, it's light. At least this was my experience. I never understood the whole aspect of vibration. "Raising your vibration." That's the big lingo on the scene these days. What you're doing is raising your vibration, your soul's vibration, to the vibration of light. Think of how much light is in the universe. Think about the spiritual light that you see beaming from the hearts of saints, teachers, loved ones or even people you simply know of on the planet. That's light. That's truth. Think about those people.

Interaction with loved ones continues after you leave your physical body. Sometimes you have difficulty hearing us. When I say "us" I mean those of us who are in this world. It is hard to hear us word for word. That's where a medium comes in. Sometimes we send little notes, little tidbits, little blessings here and there and everywhere just to let you know that we're around, that we're watching, that we care, that we want you to find peace ... peace that exists within all people. It really does exist in each and every soul. You just simply need find it. So when I tell you to look, I ask you to look for the peace not just in your head ... the quietness ... but the peace that comes from having an open heart and the satisfaction of knowing you did your best, you helped another and another learned to help themselves. That's what you want to do. That's where the greatest amount of love comes in. You helped another and the other began to help themselves.

Our world is filled—and when I say filled, I mean filled—with people, beings, however you want to say it ... filled in the unseen worlds with those who want to help, those who are waiting. They hear the cries for help. But those who are really willing to take it ... really willing ... they keep asking, they keep wishing, they keep wanting and then something is produced for them. Something completely unexpected from someplace out of the blue, as they say, is given to them. It may not be in the exact way that they expected or wanted so they become disappointed or possibly even think they did not receive anything. Show gratitude. If someone offers you something, no matter if it's a thing or a sincere gesture, show gratitude by taking it. Even if what you receive is not what you expected, even if you don't want it, don't deprive another of the joy of giving. For what you don't want, you can give to someone else who may want it. No matter what you receive, with an open heart, have gratitude for receiving it.

I urge each and every one of you to find a way to sit quietly everyday just for a few minutes, just for a time for just you ... to be quiet, to listen, to be clear, to really hear what's being said, to really hear and feel the love of God in and around you. You can't think your way through it. It's not possible to think your way through it. We may understand things intellectually, but we must learn to feel, at a deep level, the love of God. A feeling of love so strong you feel as though your heart may burst.

So today, ladies and gentlemen, as we fly the friendly skies, we go in for a slow, smooth landing to give you an opportunity to just be still, to be quiet for a few more minutes. So much can be attained when the mind is quiet, when your heart is open and you are not filled with worry. So much can take place. We have to remember, so much can happen.

Until next time you take your journey with us, thank you for flying the friendly skies.

— *Captain Jim Petosa*

July 18, 2012

Elizabeth opens the session, as she always does, with a prayer of gratitude and blessings.

Elizabeth: Let's just do a little meditation until Jim comes into this reading a bit later. The less human emotion you feel about a situation, the greater expansion of your soul. That's because you're allowing the Holy Spirit to move through the soul body and clean it out so that you have a memory of what happened, but you don't have the memory of how it felt when the situation occurred. The Holy Spirit invokes a joyful feeling within the soul. It seems like there's a period of time coming up for you when you start to recognize, just as Jim has grown and has moved to higher levels, so have you.

We hear the words "Holy Spirit" as if it's something unattainable. Nothing could be further from the truth. The Holy Spirit is a loving energy that moves through each and every human being on the planet to uplift the soul. As it moves through your body, it's really phenomenal. There's a feeling of elation, expansion and joy that is complicated and requires contemplative thought to understand the explanation of it. In short, the Holy Spirit is the connective energy between the soul and God. Naturally we want more of anything that makes us feel so uplifted and ecstatic. When your soul fills with the Holy Spirit, it makes it easier for you to achieve interaction at a conscious level of understanding. You'll notice how easy it is to be aware of the spirit world as you allow the Holy Spirit to fill your soul more and more.

In other words, Jim is not coming back to this level, you're moving to it. One becomes vehemently aware of another's presence near them, around them, and it's not necessarily because they come and concern themselves so much with the physical world; it's because you start to concern yourself with what's non-physical.

So much has happened. Remember that the earthly situations of this time-frame we as humanity are in, have a lot to do with why Jim left at this time. Innately, his soul was explaining to him somehow, on some kind of level … a conscious, unconscious or subconscious level … there was a change coming, and this change had to do with the way his physical body felt. One of Jim's greatest lessons this lifetime was to understand—and he did, on a very deep level—that the body is really just an illusion, that human beings are so much more than their body. Your path of enlightenment this lifetime is very much in sync or in tune with Jim's path of enlightenment, and he decided he was going to leave his body behind and stay in his soul body to continue out this journey of enlightenment. You are reaching enlightenment while you still have a body.

There's a pattern of behavior for human beings who are going through a grieving process. There is always a time when anger starts to set in. The Angels know you're not an angry person; that isn't something that is typical of your behavior. So, please don't take it personally. What they're referring to is that as part of the "shedding" of the unconscious and the subconscious mind, anger is going to come out—anger at Jim for leaving you in this physical world while he has gone off to do whatever he wants, anger for being left behind, anger because everybody else is so happy and you're miserable. Anger of "why is this happening to me and not to someone else?"

Chris: I've felt that ... that he left me behind.

Elizabeth: All of these thoughts that are in the unconscious mind, where anger is stored, start to come up. It is typically the hardest emotion for people to work through. It's the hardest emotion because it's the one that people feel the most shameful about. And yet it's all just another emotion ... just like happiness, just like joy, just like any other emotion.

Anger is just like any other emotion. The difference is it feels uncomfortable in your body. Remember, a feeling is a sensation, not an emotion. Joy feels differently than anger does in your body. Anger feels heavy, sometimes hot, sometimes dense, especially over the heart.

Jim: I keep saying, "Fake it 'til you make it." That's one of the things that I had to concentrate on when I was going through the disease process. I was embarrassed to say that I was angry ... really angry, really pissed that I had this disease.

With all of my will, with all of my strength, with all the technology, with all the money, with everything that we had, I could not get better so that I could stay with you. I was very angry about it. We were so deeply connected and are still extremely connected and in tune. You may even feel anger that comes from me. If that happens, don't deny it's there. Instead, feel what it feels like to forgive.

The key to healing is feeling.

Returning to a state of peace is so helpful. You don't want to deny that you're angry about something, because what will that do? Suppressed anger gets stored in the unconscious, and until healed, that anger may show itself in ways that are uncharacteristic of your behavior.

I didn't ever believe that. I always thought that was nonsense. I always thought all you had to do was will what you wanted to happen. You will it. You put your mind on it, you put your focus on it and you put your intention into what you want. With all your will, with all your might, this is what's going to happen.

That wasn't always the case for me. I know now that just because you want it and you will it, it doesn't mean it's going to happen. There were times I wanted to be left alone from you. I didn't want you to know I was so angry that I was so sick and that this was happening to us. I had a lot of anger regarding this disease. It was never about you.

I'm telling you this now because I see it in you sometimes, like you want to hit something ... not hurt someone but just hit something or scream really loudly that I'm not there, and I know it's because you're mad.

Chris: It all comes out in crying. I almost can't separate the anger from the sadness.

Jim: I know that about you. Don't worry about it, Chris. There is a time and a place for everything. One of the deeper emotional issues that I have had to work through and address is being really angry about the fact that I had to leave you behind. That's what I'm working on these days in the afterlife. You asked me where I was and what I was doing. I haven't really wanted to leave you. It's not because I don't want to go to the Heaven worlds or that you can't do it on your own; I always believed that living life was something we were supposed to do together.

Therefore, all these conversations that I keep having with you and all this trying to communicate with you ... no matter what other people are saying, it really is me. I know communication really helps both of us.

Chris: Yes, I know it's you, and I also feel like our communication helps both of us.

Jim: I promised you I'd be there. Of course communicating with you helps us or we wouldn't be doing it. I promised you I wasn't going to leave right away. Remember, I promised that when the time was right, I would go. It's just not that time yet.

Chris: Are we close to that?

Jim: Not yet; it's going to be a little while. Remember, we talked before about you writing a book.

Chris: Yes, I still plan to write a book. At the moment I just don't have the energy.

Jim: I want to help you. I want you to talk about "will" ... the human will versus God's will ... the strength of God's will ... the power of it. You must learn to align yourself with God's will.

I wasn't going to ever let something stop me from getting in the way of what I wanted.

Elizabeth: He looks at me and smiles as he says this. He does, however, remind us that we don't tell God what to do.

Jim: *There's a price you pay when you push so hard for what you want and it's not something you're supposed to have all at once. I'm talking about flying. The process for me to be able to fly was so difficult. To go through the training, to go through the schooling, to come up with the money, the problems at home, the problems with family ... and the problems ... and the problems ... the constant roadblocks that I had to face until I finally got what I wanted.*

There is an energy that stays inside of you when you exercise your own will instead of God's will.

I've been doing a lot of contemplating since I left. I would sometimes sit in church and wonder if my will and determination was part of the reason I got sick. Those emotions must have done something to my body.

Chris: Do you wonder about that or you do think that's the case?

Jim: *I believe that the combination of my work environment and my intense feelings contributed to my problem. It was as if God was talking to me and telling me in very strange ways that maybe I wasn't supposed to fly for a career. With all the obstacles that were in my way, I still continued to pursue an aviation career. My mind kicked in and I was determined to fly.*

Originally I didn't believe that I had anything to do with the cause of the cancer, but now I'm not so sure.

Elizabeth: He is showing me that he read something (this might actually be in the spirit world) that has made him realize that his emotions could actually have contributed to the cancer. In the very beginning, he thought jet fuel was the major cause and that was really the end of it. But if we look at this in a deeper way, look at the roadblocks that were in his way for flying, you can see that his determination was a roadblock to help him to see that maybe he shouldn't be flying all the time.

Chris: As if God was trying to stop him and Jim forged ahead with his free will?

Elizabeth: Exactly.

God knows what's better for us than we do. That's always the case. Wisdom is the "knowing" that we have. That's part of the mystery of faith. So Jim says he had a strong ego, and I don't mean arrogance; his determination, perseverance, and to some degree his stubbornness contributed. It's seems that it's possible that energy in his body allowed for the attraction of this disease. He doesn't want that to happen to you. He reminds you that if you're pushing too hard for something to happen, let it go.

Jim: Chris, if you're trying so hard to make something happen and it doesn't, a lesson I have learned is to leave it alone.

Chris: What do you mean as far as I'm concerned?

Jim: I don't want you to do too much all at once in your life for so many other people, and forget about yourself. You've got to remember to do something for you and to not push others into something they don't want to do just because you want it.

Chris: (Crying.) I'm not sure what that is.

Jim: (Smiling.) You've always been like that—over the top when it comes to helping everyone. You've got to take time to sit and pray ... to contemplate, to let others do for themselves. The key is knowing when to help someone rather than trying to help someone who does not want it.

Chris: I do that. I do sit and contemplate. Do you see me do that?

Jim: Receiving Reiki and taking care of yourself—those things help.

Chris: You're talking about Michael and my mother?

Jim: Right. You've helped them so much. You've especially helped Michael get on his path and head in the right direction. You're putting forth a lot of effort to help Michael. He has to do some of this himself. Let people comfort you, too. I'm doing what I can to be there for you.

Chris: Just please comfort me.

Jim: I'm going to try to find new obvious ways to let you know that I'm around you.

Chris: Were you doing something with my phone this morning?

Jim: I was just getting you ready to come here. Not to feed my ego, or something like that. I just wanted to be able to talk to you so that you know the love that you have for somebody ... the love that I have for you ... hasn't just gone away. All the memories that we shared together ... . We had a good life.

Chris: (Crying.) Yes, we did. You remember everything? That doesn't go away from you either?

Jim: Those memories stay etched in my soul ... the joyful experiences, the love, the travel, vacations, staying at home, making love, all those things ... those memories have stayed with me for so long.
   Now that we've had the deep conversation ... thank you for singing "Happy Birthday" today.

Chris: At your gravesite?

Jim: Yes, you were singing "Happy Birthday" to me.

Elizabeth: He's laughing in a very sweet way.

Jim: Only you would sit there and sing "Happy Birthday" to me. I heard you. Thank you for that.

Chris: Did you see Roberta put the candles at your gravesite?

Jim: Yes. I really liked that. It was a thoughtful thing to do. It takes so long to realize how loved you are. I feel very fortunate to have had so many people love me when I was alive, when I was physical. People just accepted me for the way I was.
   That is what I tried to do for my father, too—accept him for the way he was. There was a period of time when I was really angry that my father behaved the way he did. I was angry about the way my life was when I was younger and that my mother had to be the one who took care of everyone and everything. I was angry about the ups and downs of the family and the struggle and the hardship. This

is the way life was for us. I was concerned that I would have the same problem my father did. Although I felt badly for my father, it was always in the back of my mind that one of my siblings or I might end up the way our father did.

Chris: Do you mean the odds that something like that would happen to you?

Jim: Yes. *I remember sitting in the barracks when I was in the Navy and thinking about home and my family—how homesick I was. Although I didn't like it, it didn't have to mean that I was going to fail. I could be homesick but still go through what I needed. I was sure of that. That's part of where the determination came from for me. I'll never forget Marianne for her strength and reminding me to be strong, to stay focused and to just accept things as they were and to be the best kind of person I could be. That focus was tremendously important to me throughout my whole life. When I met you, you were the other reason I wanted to be a good person.*

Chris: (Crying.) The reason I loved you is because you *were* a good person.

Jim: You allowed me to carry out what I really wanted in my life. You never complained about me being gone, the dangers of the career I chose, time away; I will never forget you for that. You were a good wife.

Chris: Thanks, Jim.

Jim: A really good wife.

Chris: You were the best husband.

Jim: When you're writing, to try to remember the details. Put them in order.

Chris: Of us?

Jim: Of us, but also the aspects of my recovery.

Chris: Well, you know I have it all in a binder! (Laughing.)

Elizabeth: He's showing me these notebooks and a big binder put together … stacks of them.

Jim: Jeesh, I'm telling you!

Elizabeth: He throws his hands up like this and says, "She's got every little detail all organized and put completely in order." Please remember, he thinks that his experience can help other people, and at this point that's what his goal is—to help other people through this process, this problem, and hopefully find a cure. He's very righteous.

Jim: We have the right to live in this world and be happy and healthy without others infringing on those rights ... without cancer in your body.
The fact that I had cancer—still haven't gotten over the anger of it. I did what I was supposed to do—exercise, no smoking, eating well, drinking well, all these factors—and still I got cancer. I get very frustrated that there wasn't a way to heal it.
I acquired the knowledge of flying, electronics and aviation—all things pertaining to science—during my physical lifetime with you. In the Heaven worlds, things take place in a different way. Technology, learning, discoveries—all of it takes place here in the Heavens. It's our job to find out as much as we can and how to cure these problems. Earthly technology is so primitive compared to what's available, which is why there is so much more to know.
Cancer doesn't exist in Heaven, but the knowledge of the cause does, Chris. That's exactly what my journey here in Heaven is about.
You asked me what I have been doing. I have been given access to the knowledge of how to find the cause of cancer and now my mission is to relay information learned, to people on Earth. I think that by you writing, by you listening to me, you can write it down and somehow we both can work together.

Chris: That's what I'm hoping.

Jim: When you get quiet, get your space all cleared out for meditation and writing, I'll be there.
I want you to talk about what it was like for me, not in a sense of an ego, but as a way of understanding so that others can do the same thing.
That is my mission now—to gain as much information, as much knowledge, as much insight as possible and then give it to you. I want you to give details of what it was like for me at different times as I found out that I just kept getting worse no matter what the treatment was. Tell about the treatments that helped and the ones that didn't.

The Heaven worlds and the information that's here ... it's all so extraordinary! I am amazed at the amount of knowledge, wisdom and understanding.

Chris: So if I meditate and get quiet, I'll be better able to write about the whole experience?

Elizabeth: Yes. Remember what the Angels said about having a space and a time to clean out that soul body. Grief can be like a sticky, heavy substance. It prevents us from getting past our own emotions and listening to the truth. Jim went through that process when he left his body.

Jim: You're going to go through the process of cleaning out your soul while you still have a body. It can be the hardest or the easiest thing you ever do. It all depends on how you choose to respond. In time to come, you'll be glad you made the effort. You'll be glad you took the time to get quiet. When you're quiet, it's easier to know when you're getting messages from beyond—the other side—however you want to say it. I'll be there every step of the way. It still takes energy for me to go to your world, so as you grow and progress, you'll move into this world.

I want you to know I've run into my pal, Mike.

Chris: Who's Mike?

Jim: And another pal named Bob.

Chris: Did I know of them when you were with me?

Jim: No.

Chris: Mike and Bob. What part of your life were they from?

Jim: People who were on the other side already—people with cancer. Friends that I knew before.

So much has happened in the short time I've been over here. The only reason that I know that time has gone by is because I watch you. There is no time here. It is just like I planned ... a lot of light, a lot of fun, a lot of learning.

Chris: Do you see me take a longer time to progress than you? Is that what you mean? That it's slower here than there?

Jim: *Chris, don't you get it? It's the opposite. With everything that you've had to deal with and have a body, your work is cut out for you. But you have a body to do it in. Remember, the body helps you feel the emotion and you take the initiative to heal it.*

Chris: (Crying.) Do you feel me being mad that you left me behind?

Jim: Sometimes.

Chris: I think it's more sadness than anything.

Jim: I'd be mad at you.

Chris: I know you would.

Jim: *I wouldn't expect this. We didn't expect this. I promised that I wasn't going to get stuck—stuck in between, like purgatory, almost. I realize that being "stuck in between" is where many, like me, work through any unfinished circumstances. It's actually in the afterlife that this happens. I know I can be of better help if I'm in Heaven than if I stayed stuck there in a body that didn't work anymore. I'm sorry that you had to see me all beat up.*

Chris: I loved taking care of you.

Jim: *It was hard for me to look in the mirror at myself. I just kept saying to myself, "I can't believe it."*

Chris: I know.

Jim: *I want you to know who you felt in the room the morning I died. There were friends that you knew who stayed with you. Some of my friends and family were calling me. There were so many Angels! It wasn't the Angels that made you sad, it was your own sadness that did that.*

There were Angels that came to be with you to comfort you. It was hard to feel the Angels, but they were there. The Angels came for me. I always wanted to see one and then there were so many. I couldn't believe my eyes—they really came! The Angels came for me!

Chris: All the stories we hear are true, then? Did you feel like you were going through the tunnel that we so often hear about?

Jim: Yes! It was just a blinding white light, and I went through this long passageway. It's where I saw all the people that I knew and loved. They were all standing in line waiting to greet me so I wouldn't be alone.

Chris: (Crying.) I love that thought!

Jim: I kept looking back to make sure you were okay. They kept telling me to come with them.

Chris: (Crying.) I was telling you to go, too.

Jim: When I saw them and I saw that tunnel, that's when I knew it was time. I knew you were exhausted.

Chris: (Crying.) I just didn't want you to suffer anymore.

Jim: I was so mad when I couldn't get my body to move.

Chris: Did you hear Woody, Roberta and me talk about how you could hardly talk or move and then when we tried to move you, you said in the clearest voice, "This isn't a good idea!"

Jim: I definitely remember.

Chris: We joke about that now, even. That helps. I have to resist the urge to ask God to take me early.

Jim: I don't want you to hurt yourself.

Chris: No, I don't mean that I would. Sometimes I just wish I could go early.

Jim: If God could expedite the process of this? (Laughing.)

Chris: Yes, exactly. Expedite the process. Let's get this thing moving. I would never hurt myself. I know better.

Jim: *(Laughing.) That's the way you always were. You wanted everything to be moving.*

Chris: I just want to be with you.

Jim: *They're showing me the door.*

Chris: Do you mean you have to go?

Jim: *I have to go. I have to go to a place that's kind of like school, but it's more like a temple where we go to gain knowledge.*

Chris: Do I have time to ask you a couple of questions?

Jim: *Yes.*

Chris: First, do you have anything I can tell Theresa from you for her birthday today?

Jim: *First of all, tell her happy birthday. Remind her ... she was born on "my" birthday, I wasn't born on hers!*

Elizabeth: He's laughing. He's really laughing.

Jim: *Tell her to have a good day—it's her day, too. There are a lot of people who are born on this day. One of them just happens to be my sister!*

Chris: Do you approve of, or like, the patio and the front steps?

Jim: *Good work! They did a good job.*

Chris: Oh, good. Did you help me pick out the stones, because I think you did.

Elizabeth: Again, Jim smiles.

Jim: *Well, we already talked about it before I left and it turned out exactly the way we wanted. It looks perfect.*

Chris: Did you have fun with us in Atlanta? Marianne and I laughed and laughed and laughed.

Jim: I was so glad to see you have so much fun. I was right there with you. You don't have to worry about me missing out on this. I would have gone if I were physical. It would have been great fun. I never got the opportunity to take care of a baby.

Chris: Everybody asked me to tell you happy birthday today, of course, but you know that already, right?

Elizabeth: It's like he's saluting with a glass of wine.

Jim: Thank you. We will all be together to celebrate.

Chris: Yes, we will. Will you be there at dinner today?

Jim: Of course. I want you to go buy yourself a present for my birthday. Something that you want—just for you. A new bracelet ... go buy yourself something for my birthday. Don't waste it on me. I don't have a body anymore to enjoy it. I really mean that.

Chris: (Crying.) I'll bet you do. I wore a whole bunch of your jewelry today. You always bought me things when all I needed was you.

Jim: I only have good memories.

Chris: Me, too.

Jim: Thank you for making my life so great. I know I've got to make my rounds today.

Chris: Your rounds?

Jim: With everyone, because it's my birthday and I would like to share it with family.

Elizabeth: He's going to go lie down and rest. (He's saying that for my benefit!)

253

Chris: You'll be at the party Saturday with all the family there, I'm sure.

Jim: Big celebration. I never missed a party!

Chris: No, you didn't, and you loved them. Both sides of the family will be there. Alright, Sweetie, go rest. I love you dearly. Happy birthday.

Jim: I'll be there to bother you on yours, too, since you're so much older than me and all! (Laughing.) You robbed the cradle!

Chris: Brat! Yes, I did. Thank you, Elizabeth.

Elizabeth: You're welcome. I'm sorry this is your life now. I really am. You deserve to have a really nice life and people around who love you.

Chris: I do still have a lot of them, just not number one. I do try not to ever, ever want to go earlier, or say to God, "Am I supposed to go earlier?"

Elizabeth: When we tell God we want to die, it's like saying we know more than God does and that's never true.

Chris: Of course, I really know it doesn't make any difference because what's going to happen is going to happen, and I know that I'm not supposed to want to go early and be with him.
  I do, though. I don't care if it's here or there; I just want to be with him. I just wish I could see him and be with him.

Elizabeth: You still have some things that you have to do here.

Chris: I know that, and I want to do them. I really do want to do them.

Elizabeth: Chris, it hasn't been very long and you guys were married how long?

Chris: In a month from when he died, it would have been seventeen years.

Elizabeth: And you were with him a while before you got married?

Chris: We were together a little over eighteen years. We got engaged eight and a half months after we started dating, so we moved along pretty quickly.

Elizabeth: Give it some time. It takes time.

Chris: I really do think I'm doing better.

Elizabeth: You're doing amazingly well compared to how most people in this situation do.

Chris: Well, it is because of God and all this work—the spirituality. That's what it is, I know. I know it is. I don't know what people do without their faith. I just can't imagine. It's hard enough even when I do have such a strong faith!

Chris's Reflections:

I had a major revelation as far as learning about my own grief—and many other people's as well, I'm sure—from this reading. I understand what it is to feel "guilty" when that physical gut-wrenching pain finally goes away. It feels so wonderful not to feel that physical pain, but emotionally it almost seems wrong to stop having that pain. I know myself well and I know how easily I can feel guilty about so many things. Without these readings and learning what God really intends for us, I would have felt guilty for a long time about starting to feel better. When I write that, it sounds so crazy—to feel guilty about feeling better—but it's true. It is so important that we know that God and our loved ones want us to feel good again, whole again, like ourselves again—not guilty because the pain is starting to leave our bodies.

Without this reading, I would not have realized that the light of the Holy Spirit flows through our soul so that we can "clean out" and feel better. We get help with that! What a difference it made in my healing when I learned that the Holy Spirit does its best work at helping us when we're sleeping, when we're meditating, when we're praying and when we're with groups of people who are very like-minded. The soul body expands and the spirit moves through the body.

Believe me, I wanted to feel better, so I began concentrating on ways to do that. I work on sleeping better, I meditate more often, I pray more than I did before and I've started to return to my active social life rather than choosing to stay home where I felt Jim was. Jim wasn't sitting at our house—he was out and about with me, with his family and with his friends. I know that.

It's so interesting that we can feel what our loved ones on the other side feel, and they can feel what we feel. That's why I believe it's so important that we do our best to stay in a good, positive frame of mind and pray for their ascension into the higher realms of Heaven. It's like a vicious cycle, but it's not "vicious"—it's a lovely cycle. We can help them feel better and go higher in the Heaven realms and they can help us get rid of our heavy, horrendous grief.

When Jim spoke in this reading about the possibility of the cancer partially being caused by his determination and perseverance to secure a pilot position, it blew my mind. I never thought I would hear that concept come from Jim. He certainly was persistent in his pursuit of an aviation career, and he met and overcame numerous obstacles along the way to his dream, but I know that when he was alive, he would never have considered this a part of the reason he had cancer.

This shows how much learning, investigation and contemplation goes on once a soul gets to Heaven *if* they choose the pursuit of learning and discovery. Keep in mind, Jim didn't say he would have changed his career path if he'd known this when he was physical; as a matter of fact, I'm quite sure he wouldn't have. It does, however, teach us information about human behavior and how it affects our health. It also gives us information about how God may try to help us change our paths in life, but we need to be listening and aware to realize that.

I so enjoy when Elizabeth mentions people who "pop in" to a reading to say hello or when Jim talks about people he has met up with. It was interesting that he mentioned the names of two people who had cancer and how they are now working together.

I also love when Jim talks about everyday things that go on in my life or our families' lives. It's amazing to sit with a medium and have a conversation with your loved ones and know that they are with us because they can prove it in every reading beyond a shadow of a doubt.

I was shocked to find out in this reading that Jim had harbored anger about family life being difficult growing up because his father was ill for many years. He did not voice those feelings to me while he was alive, and I now know that he didn't want it to appear as a weakness in him. It never would have to me, but that is the way he felt he would have appeared to other people. A lesson I've learned from this is that we all have issues in our family that can cause anger, hurt, fear, anxiety, poor self-esteem, et cetera, and if we don't address those feelings, they can have a major effect on our health.

My favorite part of this reading by far is the part where Jim describes the morning he died. That part itself is still very difficult for me, but to hear that Angels truly were in the room and that they helped him get to Heaven makes my heart so happy! I loved hearing about the "blinding white light" and the passageway that we hear about so often from people who have had near death experiences. To hear about all of the people that he knew and loved being lined up to greet him so he wouldn't be alone made my heart soar with happiness! There's nothing I want more than to know that when our loved ones cross to the other side that they are with souls who love them and that they're not afraid.

It was also so deeply comforting to me that Jim was looking back as he left because he didn't want to leave me. Of course he had to leave, and we knew that was going to be the result of this illness, but to be able to hear that your husband's last concern in his physical life was that I would be alright is a miracle, in my eyes. His last words to me were, "Chris, I love you so much." I am very blessed.

Jim's Reflections

The concept of life after death was always explained to me through priests and the lectures at church. Many of my family members and I believed we would go to a place beyond where we are now living and enjoy the paradise that would await us. Never were we told that what we did not complete in this lifetime, we would finish later in the afterlife before we entered into the glorious Heavens where I am now.

Everyone has a different view: Heaven is a "place," hell is a "place" and there is a "place" in between. The place in between, purgatory, was considered taboo by many, and even the church did away with the idea so long ago. Purgatory is the afterlife, and we have only the truth to tell here, that the afterlife is the place where we go to live out what we were unable to complete or to prepare for the next steps into higher and grander places.

Yes, Elizabeth, that's true. It is not a punishment; it's a "state" where we are introduced to all that is possible. We only consider this to be punishment if we are victims. The same is true for diseases like cancer. We are not victims. For everything there is a cause, and for everything an effect. That happens because of the cause. I cannot blame cancer for ending my life. I cannot attribute cancer as a means to cultivate gratitude on the Earth. Cancer was the reason I left my body.

Having cancer or not having cancer was not the reason I tried to be the best person that I possibly could be.

Cancer resulted in my physical death; however, my physical death propelled my soul to fly beyond what I could imagine in my physical body and mind.

From birth, we are taught to follow our dreams. Really, what would be best is to follow your heart. I often wonder if the truth is that I did not become a pilot as quickly as I wanted because doing so may contribute to my demise. That's the jet fuel, the carcinogens in the air and all the crappy drink and food. Nothing can change that now. Learn to fix the problem, not to depend on the cure.

It's certainly not anyone's fault what happened, nor was it anyone's responsibility but my own to change.

Ladies and gentlemen, it's just a short flight today. Thank you for flying the friendly skies. We hope to see you soon on your next journey.

— Captain Jim Petosa

Jim's Epilogue

*I*f you've read any or all parts of this book, I'd like to give you the exactitude of everything that happened just the way it happened. I can give you the memories. I can give you the things that I remember very deeply within my soul. I can give you how I felt, what I thought, what it was like, what it wasn't like; I can give you every exact detail that you could possibly ask. When I was physical I used to say, "It's good to be seen." What I meant by that was it was good to be recognized as a person, as if being physical was all there was. I remember it all just like it was yesterday. I remember every bit of my life as if I lived it just two seconds ago.

This epilogue is being written a little over three years after my death. I tell you this because the memory that exists in my soul, in my consciousness, in my "mind" as you might think, is not really in my mind at all. It's in the part of all of us that carries on forever and ever, the everlasting part of us ...the soul.

When I was physical, I thought that being physical was the greatest thing on the planet ... loving life, living life, going places, seeing the sights, going on vacation, making love with my wife, eating great food, doing all the things that I loved to do. But I realize that nothing compares to the feeling that I have now that I'm in this place. I say this "place" because most people believe that Heaven is a place, but really any "place" is just a state of existence. It is a place within each and every soul that exists, that allows you to feel the comfort of God, that allows you to feel the comfort of total and unconditional love that can never be felt elsewhere.

Our mothers love us, our brothers, our sisters, our friends, other family members, aunts and uncles ... you name it; they all do. Very rarely is it with contingency if there's truly love. In this space, in this place that I'm in, there is only love. There is never a moment without it. When I was reborn here, when I was brought to this world, so to speak, it was a place I'd never even dreamed of or imagined. It was a state of existence, my soul, that I never imagined could possibly happen. In this world it's good to be seen has a whole new meaning. It means it's good to see your light, your love. It validates your existence as a soul, not just a human.

As I said before, being physical was so fantastic. It was filled with so much fun. But being in my soul body, learning, growing, expanding, seeing the sights, seeing the people on Earth that I love from a totally different view ... nothing *compares to it! Not one thing on the Earth that I can think of compares to where I am now.*

I'd like to say that I still miss the Earth, that I miss the people that once were my friends, my partners in crime, so to speak, my siblings, everyone that I knew. I'd like to say that I miss them, but the fact is I'm never that far away. None of us who are here in this state of existence are. We're never that far away. When you call on us, when you speak our name ... when my wife calls on me, when she listens and she's quiet and she can hear me remind her where she puts things, where something doesn't belong, when she scratches my truck when she drives it, dents the license plate, makes a mess of things, when the dog chews on my belongings or hers, when all of the things that happen in everyday life do happen, I'm there, I'm watching.

Sometimes I'm a part of it and sometimes I'm not. Sometimes the dog goes crazy when I'm around; sometimes she's just content and quiet. It just depends on what kind of mood the dog's in; it has very little to do with what kind of mood I'm in, because I'm always in a good mood when I'm there.

Always, I feel love. I feel love for everyone and love from everyone that I'm around. Heaven is just different states of love. Just different states of love. It's not a love based on contingency. When you arrive here, you have to learn how to really detach ... not let go of the memories or the people, but from the feeling of what it's like to miss them. You still miss them but it's not in the same way. You might miss physically touching them or feeling them physically touch you, but you never really miss them because you're right there where all the action is. It just depends on what you want and what God wants for you.

This first book is just a short and easy read, an account of my life, how I felt about it, how my wife felt about it and how we felt about it together. There are more days of writing, more nights of writing, more days of listening, more days of writing when you hear and what you hear; there will be a lot more to come, as most is already recorded. It was a painstaking process putting together the notes, putting together the readings, recounting, reliving, going through the whole thing over and over again. Just to help people understand ... just to help people realize that once you leave your body a whole new world is in store for you.

You don't just leave your body and your body goes into the ground or is cremated or whatever happens. You go up—up above—and get a bird's eye view. Like flying, free as a bird. You can travel. You can visit. You can see things you've never seen before. When you choose, you can show up in pictures—little dots, little orbs of light, little streaks or streams of light—it just depends. It's amazing what one soul can do.

If we really, really put our heart into it, "we" can still be involved in everything that you do on the Earth. What we want you to do is be involved with everything that we are while we are here. We want you to listen. We want you to quiet yourselves. To find a place of peace and rest within you. To find a place where God exists. Because God does exist in each and every soul. That's something I learned and something I never want to forget. If I'm ever human again, and I expect to be someday, I never want to forget that thought, the feeling or what it's like to be where I am now. All the classes, all the things that I see my wife do, all the places she goes to and travels to, when she meditates, when she dreams, when she quiets herself and she listens ... that's what we're capable of here every moment, every second. That's what you, too, can be capable of wherever you are.

Contact happens in so many different ways. Sometimes it's through things that exist on the Earth like fortune cookie papers that blow away with no air touching them, or birds, or you hear a voice, or a song that will come on the radio or you ask for a sign ... we're there! Sometimes it's just the quiet mind and the open heart that allow you to hear us. But we are there—make no mistake! What we want is for you to be here with us. Not out of your body, but in your body while you're doing what you're doing. And feel that space, that place of blissful love that we all feel and experience while we're here.

We do not use words when we speak to one another like you may think. We don't use words like you all do on the Earth. We use the feeling in our hearts. We communicate through a telepathic means. We clean up our thoughts. Trust me, when you first realize that people know what you're thinking, you clean up your thoughts! Because you don't think about things in the physical way. You think about things from a soulful experience. There's a huge difference there.

So as you live out your life, as you see what it's really like to be alive, what it's like to be in the soul, as you walk through your days, as you sleep through your nights, as you spend time with your friends, your family, your loved ones ...love everyone the same. Because we are all the same here. And as you develop, as you grow on the Earth, you are all the same to us here. The ones that we are fortunate enough to connect with, like my wife, Chris, the love only grows stronger and deeper. It's not a romantic, sappy, chick-flick kind of love. It's a deep, deep love and understanding. An experience that very few people ever feel when they're alive, let alone still have after they leave the Earth. But it happens. It happens all the time. We just need to let it happen.

Many people forget how to let it happen. Many people don't want to know how it happens. Many people make the choice to stay angry, resentful and have regrets. Many people never budge for eons from their space of existence when they leave their physical body. Many people just wander and wonder and never look for life, never look for true, true life ... the light of the heart. Most people, when it's time, assume they're going into the ground and that's it. I never had that thought. I never had that belief.

We look at religion on the planet these days and say that religion is bad. That it's something that has put a hole in our lives or taught us things that were completely unreal. But the fact is religion—being Catholic, for example—taught me things I may never, ever have thought about. Perhaps they were not exactly as they were written, but you have to use your imagination. You have to view it with an open heart. You have to think of Jesus as not only just a man, but as something greater than a man. And you have to think of yourself, your mother, your sister, your brother, your friend in the same manner. You have to see them as people, but beyond each person that you see, there's a light in their eyes. A deep spark of light that is the soul that's within their heart. As you look to find this light, as you look to find this love, you'll find it without looking too hard, without trying too hard. You'll find it by just being still.

I urge each and every one of you who reads this ... be still. Open your heart to the unimaginable love that exists there. Do it while you're on the Earth. Love can conquer so many things: disease, hatred, sadness, pain. You name it, love fixes it. As corny, as silly, as crazy as it sounds, love does fix it. You have to find love. Not the love that's contingent, whether someone loves you back, but a love that you have for all things. All things living. Even things you don't believe are living have some sort of life, have some sort of story behind them. So treat your things respectfully. Share them with others. Give to others who may not have what you do, and allow others to give to you. Because they want to. Don't deny them the possibility of having the happiness of giving.

In the pages you've read, you witnessed the life that Chris and I led, the happiness that we shared and the joy that we knew just by being with one another. You read about the cancer, you read about how it went up and down, made a few twists and turns and turned our lives upside down. You read about the experience of me leaving the physical body. But what I hope you take most from this, what I know my wife, Chris, hopes to take and give to all of you is the idea that we never stop. That we go on forever and ever.

We take on new shapes, new forms and learn new lessons, but perhaps the biggest, most notable gift of this book is that you will finish what you start in one way or another. It may take eons, it may take days, it may take only moments just to realize that no matter what you do, you always have to finish what you start.

There's a beginning and an ending, for everything there is a cause and to that cause there is an effect. So be mindful of what you do, be watchful of your errors, change as you will and will yourself to change. Be the best that you can be and settle for nothing less.

It doesn't mean having the best, making the most money, having the greatest job; it means loving from the deepest place in your heart, loving all things as if those things will never, ever go away because they don't. And neither will you. In one way or another, you remain. You remain your self, your small self, for as long as you wish, until you choose to seek differently. I chose early in my progression. Many wait years and years and years in Earth time to make any kind of change at all. They get stuck. They stay stuck in the idea that they want only what they want.

The reality is you must expand yourself, you must grow, you must want what God wants for you ... and that is to achieve the highest level of love that you possibly can love. And then the next day you love a little more. It never stops. Never. Enjoy each moment of your life. Live as you will. Take care of yourself and each other. Let others care for you. But most important, above all else, listen. Listen with all of your heart to what is best for you. As you do, the best will come. The best you could ever imagine for you ... it will be there. With all your heart, just listen.

You'll make mistakes. They will show you your mistakes. They will show you the good that you've done. When I say "they," I mean those who wait for us as we arrive in this new state of existence. They show you how you lived your life. They remind you of things you could have done better. They expect from you only your best.

So start now and give only your best on the Earth. It will be good practice for when you arrive.

Make no mistake, we are all waiting. Each and every one of us wait for your arrival here. Some can't wait to return back to Earth, back to the body, to go back and enjoy earthly pleasures. You can have those same pleasures in the soul no matter where you are, whether you're physical or not physical. The one thing that truly remains is love.

I'd like to thank my wife, Chris, for her hard work, for her dedication, for her love, for her tears, for her laughter, for all that was put into this book, for the good memories and the bad. I'd like to thank her from every part of my being for doing this for mankind, for it is in service to mankind that we reach the greatest and simplest of hearts. That's what the hope is.

I'd like to thank Elizabeth. She just sits and waits, never complains and never worries because she knows beyond a shadow of a doubt that life never ends. It goes on forever and ever and ever, and that's a long, long time. No time is ever put on it.

If you ever have the opportunity to sit with a medium, take it. Take the opportunity for those who are true to their heart in service for God. Take the opportunity and do it. If you have any doubt, your doubts will disappear. If you have belief, your beliefs will be amplified. If you have a "knowing," you'll then be reassured. The most important factor here is to listen. You have the ability to listen and know. You don't have to go through a third party, but a third party can be helpful if that third party is true to their heart and willing to listen with you.

The first time I was able to sit with Elizabeth was an experience I'll never forget and one I hope each and every one of you have ... the ability to sit and listen to those who you've known, that you miss, and know they're no further away than just earshot.

With an open heart and the greatest of love, I thank both of you, Chris and Elizabeth, as well as all those who will read this and pass on the message that your soul will live forever and ever and ever. You can't even imagine the love that exists here, that exists there within you. If you're on a quest, search for the love within. It is within ... that's where you'll find it.

I hope you have enjoyed reading this book. Look for the rest to come. And look for the greatest experiences you'll ever know, as a soul, not just as a human. For what you think is good only gets better. What you think is great is unimaginably the greatest you can possibly be. Start today by being the greatest you can possibly be. Tomorrow it gets even better.

For now, this is Captain Jim Petosa signing off. All planes landed. We welcome you to this journey and many journeys to follow. There's no need to take your baggage that's stowed, for no baggage can be stowed or is stowed unless you leave it there unfinished for the next life.

Until then, thank you for flying the friendly skies.

— Captain Jim Petosa

PART THREE

Signs from Our Loved Ones

I believe wholeheartedly that people from the other worlds who have passed send signs to us here in our world to help us heal our grief. I look for them as I've always been a believer that those in the other world want us to know they're around.

I feel as though I am fortunate. I want my loved ones to show me they are around. When they do, it helps me to know I'm hearing from them. When I am alone and ask for reassurance, it's easy to see that Jim knows this and he makes signs happen. Usually it's something subtle that others might say is coincidence, but I have no doubt it's him.

It's normal and natural to want to feel our loved ones, especially immediately after they die. I had been going to a meditation class and never had this experience before. I felt Jim wrapped around me like a cocoon during meditation. This was about a month after he died. In a reading two days later, without me asking, he told me he was trying to comfort me during meditation class. I was completely shocked that without my even mentioning this during the reading that he would tell me about this.

Jim and I loved to go on nature walks. We were especially fascinated by geese and on our walks Jim would often stand for quite some time simply watching them. He was always amazed by anything that flew: birds, jets, flying squirrels —you name it, he loved watching the sky. We would go to a nearby nature center to see the geese flock and gather in the spring and fall, and we loved watching them fly in their V formation with what seemed like knowledge, intuition and teamwork. This might seem like something simple to the reader, but if you've ever watched geese fly, especially as much as we had, you can understand my point. As I was walking near our house one day a month or so after Jim died, I saw a flock of geese flying above me in their usual V formation when suddenly they started honking loudly and flew out of formation. They were in no formation whatsoever and their honking was unusually loud. After thirty to sixty seconds, they went back into formation and continued on their way. In my heart I knew it was Jim making them do that. Silly as it sounds, there is no doubt in my mind this is something he would do. This continues to happen three and a half years later. Some flocks fly above in perfect formation and I know Jim's not around. But when I see a flock fly totally out of their V formation and sound loud and bothered, I know Jim is making them do that for my awareness and to let me know he's nearby.

One of the greatest signs I had for a while after Jim died was the beeping of my cell phone while being charged. I can't tell you the exact day Jim started that but it was sometime in January 2012. I clearly remember the first time it happened. I plugged my phone in to charge the battery and I heard the usual beep. A short time later it beeped again. I thought it was the charging cable connection so I checked that, but the connection was fine. A little while later it beeped again. After a few of those I thought it might be Jim telling me hello. The beeping continued for at least seven months. Sometimes Jim would go days or weeks between beeps and sometimes he would beep me as many as ten to fifteen times during one charge. In one reading he told me to keep my phone charged. I loved that for so many reasons. He knew we had started the project and he realized I knew it was him. Eventually, he stopped beeping me and found other ways to connect with me. We even had a "conversation" once. I told Jim I was going to ask him some questions and to beep if the answer to my question was yes, but to stay silent if the answer was no. It really did feel like a conversation. Eventually Jim stopped the beeps on my phone but continued to communicate in other ways.

I was somewhat upset when Jim stopped beeping my phone. In my mind I thought that if he stopped beeping me it meant that he had forgotten about me and there was no more love between us. I knew the beeping would have to stop eventually, but I was still bothered by it. I had a Reiki session with Maryann at that time. During that Reiki session while I was in the "zone," Jim appeared to me as real as if he were physically alive. He spoke to me telepathically, telling me that I "knew" he loved me. We seemed to have a ceremony of some kind, as if we were married or our souls were joined. The following week I had a Reiki session with Elizabeth. I never said a word to her about my experience with Maryann the week before. As we were about to begin the session, Elizabeth told me Jim told her he had seen me during Reiki the previous week. I described to her what went on and she told me Jim said it wasn't a marriage; he was just letting me know that our souls were united forever.

My nephew lived with me for a while after Jim died. One day we heard what sounded like a smoke alarm beeping as if the battery was running out of juice. We checked all the alarms in the house even though it sounded like it was coming from the basement. It actually sounded like the beeping was coming from inside the wall. Joe, Jim's "practical joke" friend, stopped over and found it immediately. It was an old smoke alarm that wasn't even hooked up sitting way back in the drawer of a cabinet. When I asked Jim in a reading if he had anything to do with it, he said yes and was apparently laughing. Now and then Jim makes one of my smoke alarms beep a few times and then it stops.

Our wedding picture sat on Jim's bedroom dresser facing the same direction for over a year. I walked into the room one day and saw that picture facing a different direction than the way it had been. No one else goes into my bedroom … except Jim!

A Chinese fortune cookie paper moved from its spot on the top of the backsplash in the bathroom to sit underneath and perpendicular to Jim's funeral memorial card, which I also kept on the backsplash. I have a picture of it in its original position and in its final position, perpendicular to the picture. That was on July 21, 2013. The phrase on the paper is, "Trust your intuition."

On April 11, 2014, exactly two and a half years after Jim died, the same fortune cookie paper moved again, this time it was sitting under the edge of a container of dental floss at about a forty-five degree angle. The paper had been in the same position on the backsplash since July 21, 2013. I was the only one using that bathroom. There's no possible way the fortune cookie paper could have moved.

The Christmas after Jim passed, a dear friend gave me wind chimes. For the winter I hung them in the dining room, certainly not a place where there would be air movement. My nephew and I were relaxing in the living room when we both heard the sound of chimes in the dining room. I even went into the dining room to see what could have caused the sound. There was nothing moving, not even the chimes.

I was surprised and a little scared one day when I heard music start to play upstairs that I hadn't put on. A CD in the clock radio next to my bed started playing music at noon and it stopped at 1:00 p.m.. Every day thereafter, the music played at the same time. It just happens to have the song on it to which we walked down the aisle at our wedding as well as a song from when Jim appeared to me during a Reiki session. It has been happening every single day for about a year and a half so far.

Jim started turning streetlights on and off, sometimes flashing them, sometimes not, before Christmas 2013. He continues to do it with many lights on my street. He also often turns lights off and on when I am driving elsewhere, walking outside a restaurant … almost anywhere. This seems so unbelievable, yet I took a video of it happening and showed it at a family function. The reactions were varied, but most of the family believed it was Jim, knowing how he was with his practical jokes.

Jim's favorite holiday was Christmas. He loved having our house and tree decorated and was like a little kid with presents. We have a Santa Claus decoration that we have always placed in the foyer. It's a very smiley standing Santa. Two years ago I moved it to a table by the Christmas tree facing out toward the living room. I came home one day to find that it had moved from facing out toward the living room to facing the Christmas tree. I think Jim was telling me he still enjoys seeing the tree and house decorated for Christmas.

While on an annual vacation, I keep my laptop on the counter in the kitchen. During that vacation Jim changed my screensaver to a completely black screen with the words, "Add photos to the screen saver album to see them here."

I can tell when Jim messes with speakers to a radio or to the TV. Through a reading once, he told me he was the one playing with my radio and TV speakers. Often Elizabeth will use the phrase, "A glass of water is sometimes just a glass of water." I just assumed the speakers on the radio and TV was just that—a glass of water. I do try to go through my regular day without thinking everything is about Jim. If he hadn't told me this during a session, I would never have known it was Jim messing with my speakers.

Animals, at times, can sense what we cannot sense and see. My dog, Sunny, and the cats act very strange when I sit to work on the book or if they sense other souls in the house. It's a very distinct bark and behavior that Sunny displays. Sunny often hides under the furniture covers when Jim or other souls are in the room. Many times when Elizabeth and I are working, we will pray to St. Francis and ask him to keep Sunny quiet. It is obvious she can hear or see the souls as she's looking above, behind or around me when there is no one physically there. She does the same thing outside. At first, she used to see things outside and be so afraid that she would want to run home, but now she sees who I believe is Jim or other souls and her mannerisms change.

Jim was an animal lover and on many occasions we spoke of getting a dog. I can tell when Jim is teasing Sunny by the way she behaves. It is usually while I am sitting on the couch working on my laptop on this book. Sunny will suddenly come in front of me, look just behind me and bark like she is playing while wagging her tail.

One day in church I was standing next to a young boy about 8 years old. He was acting as 8-year-old boys typically would who don't want to be in church. In our church when it comes time to recite the "Our Father" we hold hands and sing it together as one family. This particular day I didn't try to hold his hand because I didn't think he would be receptive. I just held my hand up. The little boy took *my* hand and held it … lightly at first but then more securely. At the end of the prayer, he squeezed my hand before letting it go! We looked at each other, I said thank you and he said you're welcome. I felt like it was Jim standing next to me and that he was the reason the little boy did this. During a reading with Jim sometime after this incident, Jim mentioned the little boy in church without me having said one word to Elizabeth.

Jim puts orbs in pictures I take, often after I ask him to, but sometimes without me even asking. He puts orbs in pictures while I go on vacation. My niece and nephew attended a wedding in Hawaii in 2013 and while at the top of a volcano, my niece built a rock tower in Jim's honor. As she videotaped the horizon with the rock tower in it, a small dot left the rock tower, moved and jumped all around during the whole video. The spot came from where the heart area would be located in the tower of rocks.

Shortly after Jim's death, his brother, Paul, and wife, Leslie, had a daughter, Ava, her full name being Ava James. Lots of pictures were taken of little Ava James. Leslie, curious of what I might think, sent a picture of Ava. In the picture there is a stream of light around our niece. It looked as though it was Jim with his arm around Ava. Leslie said there was no window nearby that would have caused the stream of light in the picture.

After Jim was diagnosed with cancer people often said, "It's good to see you." Jim would respond, "It's good to be seen." I was at a party one day and I told my friend's stepfather it was good to see him. He answered, "It's good to be seen." When I asked my friend if he usually says that, she said she had never heard him say it before. She even asked him about it and he said he doesn't think he'd ever said it before and doesn't know why he did. It seems beyond coincidence that this would be said by this person when it was something that had been stated so often by Jim during his illness.

I was pushing my niece on a swing one day and she said, "777, as high as Heaven." (Seven is the Angel number for Heaven.) Then she said 727. (Airplane.) There was no reason for her to say those things and her father said he'd never heard her say anything like that before.

After Jim died, I kept his truck. Every so often I'll really miss Jim. It never fails. A song that I love or had meaning for us will come on the radio. Although this seems commonplace, a calm comes over me because I feel like Jim is around.

When I was little and bugging him like crazy, my father would ask me how much I would charge to haunt a house. I would always answer a nickel or a penny. Because they were bigger than a dime I thought they were worth more. My father was very generous with his money. After he died I would notice I found coins everywhere in the strangest of places. Sometimes I talk to my dad in my mind and ask him what he might do in a particular situation. Within minutes I'll have the answer and notice a coin in a weird place. Maybe it is a coincidence, or maybe it really is my dad.

Many mystical people say dragonflies show up when the departed are nearby. Dragonflies are known to live only near water. My sister, Kathy, was fishing and reading a book at the same time. A dragonfly landed on her book and sat there about three full minutes without moving. Kathy was certain it was our father. Dad also makes dragonflies show up for my siblings and me regularly, whether there's water in the area or not. For example when my mother's dog, Blackie, died, my brother was burying her. A dragonfly kept flying near Blackie in the grave. My brother was trying to fill the grave with dirt but didn't want to hurt the dragonfly so he kept shooing it away. The dragonfly was persistent, but Woody was finally able to fill Blackie's grave. In a reading shortly after this, my father confirmed that he did indeed make the dragonfly stay with Blackie during the burial.

My mother adored birds. She had numerous feeders around her yard so she could watch them. My mother seems to use birds for my siblings and me. She uses mourning doves and herons a great deal for me. My mother loved the cooing sound of mourning doves and the grace of the herons when they would fly. When Elizabeth and I were writing segments of the book speaking to my mother in the spirit world, a heron flew from out of nowhere directly over the spot where we were working. My sister, Kathy, and I have frequent conversations about birds that show up in the strangest of places. My father was especially fond of hummingbirds and he often sends them to my sister.

Before Jim's passing, he made sure I knew everything about how to care for the house. My memory at times is very poor and this often makes me very frustrated. When I get like this I often ask Jim where to find things when I have no idea where to look. I had to change the filter on our small shop vac and had no idea where Jim kept them. I looked and looked, but couldn't find one. Finally I asked Jim to show me where it was and I found myself going directly to a box in the basement where I never would have looked. There was the filter!

My brother, Woody, told me of two times he was in his kitchen when the coffeemaker turned on all by itself, without him even standing near it. He also told me the windows on his truck started going down without Woody being the one to open them. The horn on his truck also started beeping at different times and because Woody didn't have control over it, he had the horn disconnected. In a reading with Jim one day, I asked him if he was doing those things to my brother and he not only verified those actions, he told me he reminds Woody to take his medicine and teases their dogs so they'll bark at what seems like nothing.

From a vacation in Hawaii, I have numerous photos with orbs in them, particularly ones taken at sunrise at the top of a volcano, at a luau with cultural entertainment and on a whale watch. On our return trip, we visited Muir Woods in California and orbs appeared in many of those photos as well. On this vacation, the orbs weren't simple small orbs here and there. Many photos showed pink orbs in an intricate geometric pattern along with a fairly large green orb and a smaller yellow one.

My sister-in-law, Martha, and I have numerous glitches happen with our electronics. Martha's brother died about a year and a half ago and he was a technology wizard. Martha gets many unexplainable happenings with her electronics and she is quite sure it's her brother saying hello or teasing her.

Unknowingly, Martha and I both bought the exact camera to take on vacation. They have a 21x zoom capability. While on a whale watch, when I zoomed in on the whales, my zoom went to 42x instead of the maximum of 21x. Martha's went to 105x! Martha's brother, Mark, and Jim were playing games with us!

Often when souls of a higher vibration are with us we yawn, and the yawns can be very deep yawns. Almost every time I am at one of Jim's and my niece's or nephews' concerts or events, I will yawn nonstop. I always hope that no one notices, but if they do I'm sure they think I'm tired. What is really happening is that family members from the afterlife are gathered at the event also and the consciousness is raised, so I start yawning. The same thing happens at church and social events because Jim and other loved ones are enjoying those events with me/us.

Most mornings, I turn on my laptop first thing so I can check emails as I have my breakfast. In early March, 2015, I turned on my laptop and the screen was broken. I got absolutely no image on it at all. I had no idea how it could have broken. I needed my laptop in order to work on this book, so I quickly bought another and my friend and computer genius, Pete, went to work to transfer any information he could from the old on to the new one. When he had checked it all out, he told me that my email account had been hacked and it wasn't some small hack but a dangerous one involving international hackers. He said it was so bad that he couldn't safely transfer much from the old laptop to the new one. I later found out from Jim that HE is the one who broke my screen because he knew of the hacking. If I kept using that laptop, the hackers could have done much more damage.

In April 2014, I had learned a new form of divination. My intuition was strengthening. I knew this for sure and yet I was learning a new skill; one that while writing the book could be made useful. Divination can be used as a means to clarify what intuition already knows. It is always performed with the highest good in mind and heart. It is not to be taken lightly. The accuracy of this tool helped me when I would get "stuck" trying to answer a question about the book. It should be taught by someone who has been skilled in this area. In my case, Elizabeth had shown me the skill to help with the book project and my health conditions, not just to whimsically use it for random questions. People have used the art of divination for years. Even well-known farmers' magazines document the use of divination as a means to find water main lines and to drill for wells. On April 8, 2015, after at least three weeks of total frustration due to my TV not working correctly, I decided to see if I could use the tool of divination to solve my problem. My television showed a "snowy" screen and no matter what I did, I could not get a picture. By yes/no statements I was able to get the TV to work. I'm not electronically inclined so it took about twenty minutes. After pushing certain buttons, I was able to get a picture again on my TV. To some this might seem simple, yet I had already tried to figure it out myself over twenty times, to no avail.

The father of my friend, Lisa, shuts off her fireplace. After he had done it numerous times Jim told me in a reading that, indeed, it is Lisa's father shutting off her fireplace. Lisa also gets whiffs of cherry tobacco, a sign she assumes is from her grandfather. Lisa and her husband, Joey, both smell cigarette smoke from time to time although no one in their house smokes. It is a clear sign from Joey's father.

Some will say that these things could happen to anyone and are all in our minds. I'm not trying to prove the validity of these experiences to anyone; I simply want to let readers know that if you think you're getting signs from your loved one(s), you probably are. But we do have to be open to the possibility that they can happen. As I said earlier in this book, when someone dies, they simply shed their physical body ... simply a change of form of energy. We may not be able to see that energy but the souls can use their energy to do all of the actions you've read about in this section. Be aware, look for signs and you'll find them.

Caring for our Loved Ones

No one would deny that Jim went through an absolutely horrible ordeal from the time symptoms reared their ugly head through having to deal with every aspect of the cancer and treatments to the eventual experience of facing death head on. I did not have the cancer so I can only speak of what I know Jim went through from our conversations and what I witnessed. Nineteen months of knowing you have been given a death sentence in addition to the many months of symptoms before diagnosis is unimaginable to anyone unless you have lived it yourself.

Without a doubt, I can write about the caregiver's role in terminal illness. What I write in this space only pertains to myself. Every person is different and we all face fortune and adversity in our own way, so I do not intend for anything I write to infer that there is a "right" or a "wrong" way to handle the caregiver's role. I only tell my story.

My caregiver story is not only to do with Jim. As you will read in the next and last chapter of this book, my mother died on May 5, 2013, almost exactly a year and seven months after my husband. I feel fortunate that I was able to help the two people I loved so dearly through their death and dying processes. There were similarities but even more differences. A new caregiver could probably hear a hundred different stories from those who have lived that role and their own story would still be a foreign experience, unlike the stories heard.

Jim

Jim got sick quite often, as stated earlier in our story. He used to tell me he thought getting a haircut brought illness on. I don't mean "stay in bed and sleep" illnesses. He would get frequent sinus infections and bronchitis. Jim got infections so often that he really did wonder if getting a haircut somehow had to do with getting sick. I would laugh at him and tell him he was crazy.

During one reading with Elizabeth, Jim told me that since he died he has learned that the cancer had been growing for eight years before the diagnosis. Eight years. I couldn't believe it. That cancer had been growing for almost half of the time we'd been together. So I was laughing at him and joking when all the while he was getting sick because of infections developing, partly due to having a tumor in his esophagus. Guilt.

Jim's eating and exercise habits certainly weren't the best. He rarely ate breakfast and on some days didn't eat until dinner. If it was a day he flew to the West Coast, dinner time could be late at night and then he would go to sleep on a full stomach of (usually) very rich food and alcohol. How and when he chose to eat was certainly his responsibility. I always looked forward to Jim's arrival home from a trip. I wanted to treat him to meals he loved. Those meals included many foods that I wouldn't have planned if I'd known esophageal cancer was forming. So you might say my caregiver's guilt was retroactive to the time the cancer started. Was it logical for me to feel that way? No, but my feeling of responsibility certainly felt real.

I did go to the doctor with Jim in February when he was sent to the hospital for an MRI and a heart catheterization, but by that time he had already had numerous tests, mostly checking for a problem to do with his heart. It wasn't until March that I insisted more testing be done in the upper GI area. More guilt. When a large mass was seen on the upper GI test, all I could think of was that I should have been involved in Jim's doctor visits and done the insisting much sooner. More retroactive guilt. Was it my guilt to claim? It took me a long time to know it wasn't, but I did finally reach that truth.

Mix in the retroactive guilt with fear of losing my husband, fear of being left behind, fear of knowing what to do or not do, anger at Jim for not taking better care of his health, anger at the whole situation, anger at God, the feeling of responsibility to find the doctor, the hospital, the food or the medicine to cure him, anxiety about doing everything "right," even though I didn't know what "right" meant, and we had a big mess on our hands. I don't mean Jim, I mean me.

I was never a person to hide emotions well, at least when it came to crying. I did hide anger well, though. At some point several years ago and then again during Jim's illness, I realized that I didn't believe it was "okay" to get angry, be angry or act angry. There was very little anger shown in my house growing up so I believed that feeling or showing anger was unattractive and unacceptable. I thought I was a person who didn't have anger but I sure did know how to cry.

Jim was the person who saw all of my emotion. That meant he saw me cry at the slightest thing or knew I was on the edge. People often say we shouldn't hide our feelings and our emotion, but in the situation of Jim having terminal cancer I wish I could have hidden mine. I believe that Jim should have been able to spend his time and energy dealing with the cancer, not worrying about how I was feeling and whether or not I was going to cry the next time we talked about something serious. I am an extremely strong person but my emotion comes out in the form of tears. I know those tears made Jim worry about me more than he needed to. The reality is when terminal cancer occurs in a family, everyone is affected but each in their own way. It was understandable for Jim to be concerned about me but it was also understandable for me to shed tears.

The fact is a person can try to hide or bury their emotion but it will come out one way or another. Often it is in the physical body. When the patient needs the caregiver the most could be when the emotions turn into physical or emotional issues.

During the summer of 2010, I went to the emergency room due to severe abdominal pain. I didn't want Jim to go with me because of the possibility of picking up an infection or virus with his compromised immune system due to the cancer, but of course he did. I was diagnosed with diverticulitis of which one of the causes is stress. I had never had diverticulitis before this but had five attacks between that day and a year later when Jim died. This is a classic case of caregiver stress and repressed emotion coming out in physical form.

Jim and I always spent Christmas Eve with my family and Christmas day with his. We always made sure to have our own time to open presents from one another and share a Christmas dinner. The night before Christmas Eve 2010, we had our dinner and exchanged our presents. Although we didn't talk about it, we both knew this Christmas could be Jim's last. The presents exchanged were meaningful and that made the evening even more emotional.

I remember coming downstairs to the kitchen on Christmas Eve morning but that's the last thing I remember. Next, I remember seeing Jim standing near my hospital bed. I apparently didn't know or remember things that I should have that morning and Jim, afraid I was having a stroke, called 911. Apparently, for the next eight hours I did nothing but ask Jim the same five questions over and over. As I began to regain my memory, the first thing I remember is asking Jim a question and him practically yelling at me due to the frustration of answering that same question all day long.

As soon as I realized where we were and how long we had been there, I was upset because Jim had spent all day in the hospital, probably the worst place for him to be with his compromised immune system. The on-call doctor wanted to admit me but I fought it because I knew that meant Jim would stay at the hospital even longer and have more of a chance of picking up an infection or virus. My neurologist was kind enough to come see me on Christmas Eve and discharged me. He had seen this happen to people before. He called it an episode of Transient Global Amnesia (TGA), usually brought on by extreme stress and emotionality. Again, caregiver stress causing physical issues. Jim, the cancer patient, had to care for the caregiver.

Fear was the biggest battle I fought during the time Jim had cancer. My fears started during the symptoms stage and continued until long after Jim died. Waking up in the middle of the night to Jim sitting up so he could breathe was more than frightening. I was sure that could be the beginning of heart disease or a heart attack. To witness the cough that never went away and then realize how often the clearing of his throat was happening started to make me think of cancer, but I didn't allow myself to think of esophageal cancer. That would be too much to handle.

When the diagnosis of esophageal cancer (EC) was given, my fear level was off the charts. I didn't know the exact statistics of the chances of living through it at that point, but I did know of a couple of people who had died from it and I knew that by the time symptoms appeared, it was often stage IV. I was scared for Jim and what he would go through and I was scared for me losing him. I loved this man so much and I could not bear the slightest thought of him dying. I was scared.

Then my strength kicked in, or so I thought. Apparently it was just the presentation of strength and not always a good one at that. I asked all the questions, I did research; I did anything and everything I could think of to help keep Jim alive. I took the advice of a friend and joined an esophageal cancer online forum so I could hear from other people, not doctors, what they did, what medical centers they went to, how they coped, what they ate, how they dealt with every aspect of this disease.

I was grateful that Jim had doctors who appreciated someone who did their homework, unlike some stories I've heard of doctors who appear threatened by that. I would constantly go to Jim and tell him about a new treatment that was being done for EC, a new hospital or medical center we could visit for another opinion, foods that were helping others to sleep at night ... more and more and more ideas. When I think back to it all, I'm surprised Jim didn't just tell me to shut up about it and let him be. But he didn't, partly because that's the kind of person he was and partly because he wanted me to do the research and find something that would cure him. I often wonder if doing all that work wasn't just to help Jim but also to help me cope and be able to live my daily life without being a basket case every minute of every day.

Jim told me recently through Elizabeth that I didn't act strong all the time. I thought I did. I thought I hid my tears and my anguish. He told me I may have acted and seemed strong to others but he knew I was a mess most of the time. He knew I cried every day.

On top of the fear of my husband dying was the fear of being left behind. I was a part of the couple "Chris and Jim." I didn't want to be anything else. I had finished my career of teaching and Jim still loved his career. I wanted to take his place. I wanted Jim to be his old self, continue flying, being with family and all the other things he loved in life. I would have traded places with him in a heartbeat. I write this as if it were for him and I truly did feel that way, but it was also for me. I did not want to be left behind without him. I did not want to live in our house with our animals doing what we do, and live life without him. I was scared.

Then there was the fear of the practical, logistical part of life. Before dating Jim, I had been on my own for four years. I could do everything for myself. It became a joke with us way back then. Jim would offer to do something for me like change an outside light bulb and I would get the ladder out and say, "I can do that myself." I *could* do everything myself because I was used to that.

I was no longer used to that. Now I didn't think I could do anything myself. How would I know what to do if our basement flooded again? How would I change the filter on the refrigerator when it got stubborn and wouldn't fit right? How would I get the TV picture back when I pushed the wrong button and could only see a snowy picture? How would I clean out the gutters? My questions were endless. Yet I didn't want to face what could actually happen so we didn't even talk about those things until near the very end. I was so scared.

And I was angry. Angry at Jim for not eating breakfast and for drinking too much soda. Angry at God for letting this happen or worse yet, *making* this happen. I couldn't understand how such a good person could have this happen to him when there were so many "bad" people who didn't have anything wrong with them. I was angry at the situation that we were in and how our lives had drastically changed in a split second. And I was angry because I was going to be left behind.

Except for that short period of time when we thought Jim might be rid of the cancer, my stomach was in knots constantly. I used the term "gut-wrenching" too many times in our story because no other words come close to that feeling of physical pain in my stomach as I watched the one I loved most in this world go through nineteen months of torture and then die. Then I had to learn to live without him. That's gut-wrenching pain. It was literal pain in my stomach, not in my mind.

My stomach was in knots on the days Jim had to have chemotherapy because he so hated going that he would procrastinate in every way he could because he didn't want to go. In the infusion room my stomach was in knots as I watched the chemotherapy drugs—chemicals—flow through the tube to the port and into Jim's chest. My stomach was in knots on the few occasions Jim had some reaction and the nurses rushed to do what they do to get the patient back to normal. When Jim had to get the shot to keep his blood counts up and then ached for days after, my stomach was in knots.

My stomach was in knots when he had to wear the chemo pump in the fanny pack around his chest most days of those nineteen months, chemicals flowing into his body the whole time. Watching Jim rush into the house and into the bathroom to have dry heaves, trying to feed him something he might like when he had no appetite at all, seeing the chemo pump hang on the cabinet door while Jim took a shower and then listening to the noise it made during the night because he had to sleep with it attached to him … my stomach was in knots for all of it. This is the list that is endless: the list of reasons for a stomach to be in knots. And I felt I couldn't help Jim with any of this.

When would I use the word gut-wrenching? When we heard, "You have a large mass on your esophagus," and "You have esophageal cancer. You have a two to three percent chance to live. You have six months or less to live. Get your affairs in order." When we had to tell Jim's family and then mine that he had cancer. When we left the doctor's office after having heard the cancer was back. When we left the doctor's office having heard the cancer had spread to new organs and there was no more that could be done. When Jim no longer had the energy or desire to make love, eat, leave the house or have family and friends visit. Gut-wrenching.

When he had to go to the hospital for six days to get his pain under control. When, on the third day in the hospital, I arrived to see the yellow in Jim's eyes; the jaundice had begun. When he read the "Olivia" book to our little niece, Olivia, and didn't even sound like Jim. When he could barely move in bed. When, for the most part, he stopped communicating with us other than with his eyes.

When I could see him communicating and even waving to souls in the room who I knew were there to take him home. When his heart was beating so fast and he said, "Chris, help me! Please help me!" When he said, "Chris, I love you so much." When Jim died in my arms. Gut-wrenching.

As horrible as that gut-wrenching pain of Jim's death was, I also felt some relief. I felt relief because Jim no longer had to suffer. For a day or two or maybe even a few days, I felt that relief. I felt guilty about feeling the relief and then I felt selfish about wishing he was still with me. We knew this was coming yet I was totally unprepared. I couldn't go to bed at night until I knew I would fall asleep because all I could do was cry in our bed. Each morning I had to get out of bed immediately after I woke up because if I started thinking while lying in our bed, I would start the sobbing all over again. I wanted to die. I knew I couldn't and I knew I wouldn't, but I wanted to die.

I loved our house because Jim was everywhere in it but I hated it because he was no longer there with me, physically. Our kitties were the life in the house that kept me going. Family and friends were so good about calling and that lasted for a long time. My mother was 88 years old and I knew she needed more help than she let us know, so that gave me purpose. But as used to doing things on my own as I was because of Jim's job, suddenly I felt like he'd never been away. Of course, for the last nineteen months we were to-gether every day, so this feeling of him being away was new. At first it felt like he was just away on a trip, but then he didn't come home. I was left behind.

The part I have written is the agony of being a caregiver. Anyone who has been a caregiver for a dearly loved person knows how many more events I could have included.

For every agonizing event that I have mentioned, I know I can mention at least one great one. From the beginning, I was grateful that I was able to spend almost every day of Jim's nineteen month illness with him. After spend-ing years being apart during Jim's trips, I treasured every day that I was able to wake up next to him.

During those nineteen months, being able to accompany Jim to his medi-cal appointments as well as second, third and fourth opinions was invaluable to both of us. For a patient, the medical appointments can be overwhelming because of so much unfamiliar information being presented. In our case, Jim was able to focus all his attention and concentration on what the doctors told him as I took notes and kept all notes, test results, et cetera, in a binder. For me, the caregiver, accompanying Jim settled my fears of not knowing if all information was remembered by Jim who was continually trying to deal with the harsh realities of his cancer. As the chemotherapy treatments continued, the medicines affected his memory so my being at his appointments became even more important. With two of us at every appointment, we were sure to cover all questions necessary to be answered. Often it is impossible for a cancer patient to have the same person accompany him or her to all appointments, but it seemed extremely important to us that two people were at every appointment.

Although I've told you how seriously stress and emotions affected my health, I still believe I needed to hide my fear and crying from Jim as much as possible. Cancer patients need to retain strength for every single thing they do. Activities such as eating may seem simple and easy to someone else, but to the cancer patient, those simple activities often require monumental effort. I know it was necessary for me to act and stay strong even if I was pretending, not only for Jim but for myself. When I made myself act strong, I *felt* stronger. Even pretending made me feel stronger and that, in turn, reinforced knowing Jim could concentrate more on his health than my worry.

Throughout most of the months of the cancer, I kept up some semblance of a social life with friends. Clearly, I was not as active with friends as I typically would have been, but I knew it was important to continue my friendships and as many activities as was feasible. It was important for several reasons. First, my friendships were and are very important to me and I treasure them. Second, it gave me a chance to get some of that emotion out that I was hiding so poorly. Third, Jim needed his time alone. Even before he was sick Jim would often go downstairs to his "man cave." We all need our time alone but Jim seemed to need more than usual, so unless he was feeling terrible or it was near the end, I did get out on my own. The fourth reason I finally admitted to myself when we realized where the cancer was headed—I needed to keep some order and friends in my life because it wasn't going to be long before my husband was gone.

That was a difficult truth for me to face. I remember one evening I had plans to meet friends for dinner. I didn't really want to go; I just wanted to stay home with Jim because I wanted to spend as many days, hours, minutes and seconds with him as I possibly could. I went to Jim's man cave to say goodbye to him and as I tried, I decided I wouldn't go to dinner. I just wanted to stay home. Jim looked at me with such love in his eyes and said, "Chris, go to dinner. You made plans and you've got to do these things. I'll be here when you get back." Crying, I left for dinner. I knew he would be there; I was the one having the difficulty. But I did need to go. It was healthy for me and healthy for Jim.

Looking back, I wish I'd done even more of that. Not that I wanted to be out without Jim, but it would have been healthier for me to do more venting to friends. I always tried to wear the positive smile and attitude and only talk about Jim getting better and being in that two to three percent that lives through this monster of a disease. It was a rare time that I would talk about the what-ifs. Now I would say that if I vented the fear and anger, if I told others how scared I was, I may not have had the TGAs or five diverticulitis attacks in a year. Most important, Jim might really have been able to live with a stronger Chris and not worry so much about her and what she was going to do after he was gone. That is a change I would definitely make.

Another major change I would make knowing what I know now would be to start talking much earlier about the what-ifs with Jim. I realize it's easy to say now, but I truly know I would do that. I thought then that if you talked about the what-ifs, you were giving in to the cancer and saying, "I believe he's going to die." *That is not true.* If anything, it's being honest, looking cancer in the face and saying, "We'll prepare, but not because Jim's going to die. We'll prepare just because it's the smart thing to do."

In the late stages of Jim's cancer, I decided to start a notebook of instructions I would need for items around the house that only Jim dealt with, for example, how to turn the water off to our whole house. I would tear the name and model numbers from boxes of items like refrigerator filters or our shop vac and tape them into the notebook. I had finally realized I needed to face the music because Jim was probably not going to be in that two to three percent that made it through esophageal cancer. The trouble is I started too late. Only a couple of pages were used in that notebook.

It wasn't because Jim died before I could go further; it was because it became too hard to talk about those things so late in this disease. At the point I started doing what I needed to do to prepare myself for practical issues around the house, I could no longer listen to Jim give me instructions without sobbing. So the notebook barely got started. Take it from me, it might be hard to do the necessary undertakings early in the illness, but it's so much harder near the end. If you're faced with a terrible situation like this, start a notebook early. You don't have to put information in it every day or even every week, but once you've started it, you can jot things down when you can be strong about it. Maybe you'll be fortunate and not need that notebook even after it's filled up.

Jim was the greatest blessing in my life. By reading just a few examples out of so many, you know how heartbreaking it is to be a caregiver to a terminally ill loved one, but I will tell you I was and am so grateful that I was able to be Jim's primary caregiver while he had cancer. Remember all those stomach knots? Remember all the actions or conversations that caused that gut-wrenching pain in my stomach? I wouldn't trade them for anything. To be able to care for my husband when he needed me most was the greatest gift I could be given.

The most important piece that helped me through Jim's cancer was, unequivocally, prayer. I've written this before, but I'll say it again: I know God listens to me. I also know He gives us other divine beings to talk to through whom we can reach God.

I received the miracle I asked for—that Jim would live. We were told Jim could die within six months of his diagnosis and he lived for nineteen months. That is a miracle in itself. The bigger miracle is that his soul lives on forever and that I will see him again. The beauty is that I *know* that.

My Mother

My experience as the primary caregiver for my mother, Wanda, was so very different than my experience with Jim.

My mother had Lyme disease and possibly other tick-borne co-infections. This fact is important to compare the caregiver differences between my husband and my mother. Mom developed arthritis in her hand joints in her thirties, began losing her hearing in both ears in her forties, lost her sense of smell, and therefore taste, from a virus she contracted when she was in her fifties, and was diagnosed with macular degeneration and glaucoma when she was in her fifties. Clearly, those very serious losses occurred at young ages. She was first diagnosed with Lyme disease when she was in her seventies. My uncle, brother and I have also been diagnosed with Lyme disease as well as several of the family dogs. Two family dogs have died from tick-borne infections. You can see that in the area my family lives, disease-carrying ticks are prolific.

My mom was a strong, unflappable woman who was very loving and kind but did not show much verbal or physical affection. As you'll read in the last chapter of this book, she felt the facts in life were important rather than the way someone felt about a person, animal or thing (although she dearly loved birds and animals). Living a long life was in her lineage; my grandmother lived to be 96. If you had asked any of us, her children, we would have said Mom could live to be 100 even though all of her senses caused her difficulty.

Mom never complained about anything. Most people with her maladies would have complained incessantly but Mom just said, "That's the way things go sometimes." After Jim died I knew my mother would soon need some help due to the combination of all of her medical issues and aging. She was 88 when Jim died and I was then able to visit her more often and help if she needed my help. Mom was always quick to say she didn't need help when anyone asked. When each of us visited her, it became inevitable that we would find a pill on the floor, on the counter or the kitchen table because she had dropped it and couldn't find it. She always said, "Oh, I find them eventually; there's no problem."

In the late winter of 2013, however, Mom had become noticeably more tired and her vision and hearing were almost totally nonfunctional. We were finding more and more pills as well as other items out of order. We didn't feel she was getting the nutrition she needed. We celebrated Mom's 90th birthday on March 27 and all was well. It was a fun, happy celebration.

I went for a short visit with Mom on April 12, 2013, and never left. Although Mom napped quite a lot during the day, we still had great conversation, a glass of beer or wine before dinner and ate dinner together every day. I stayed with Mom mostly because her vision was so bad and my siblings and I were worried about whether or not she was taking her medicines as prescribed, not because I was worried about any of her medical conditions.

In the next week or so I began to notice a decline in my mom. She still dressed every day, but was asleep in her chair in the living room most of the time. She would wake up and we would chat a little but she soon went back to sleep. Her appetite quickly decreased and I had to try to get her to eat enough food to keep her strength up. She got up several times a night to use the only bathroom in the house which was downstairs, so she was coming down the stairs and climbing back up, as tired as she was. At that point, Mom was still sleeping upstairs in her bedroom and wouldn't hear of putting a bed downstairs when I suggested it.

Together, my siblings, uncle and I decided Mom should see her doctor to see if something specific was wrong. Mom was willing, so we went. After examining her, the doctor said there didn't appear to be anything wrong other than the Lyme disease, and Mom's fatigue certainly fit as a symptom of Lyme. The doctor asked us to stay in touch with her to keep her abreast of Mom's progress.

One night I came downstairs in the middle of the night to find my mother sitting in her chair in the living room, asleep. She woke up as I entered the room and when I asked what she was doing downstairs, she said she just didn't have the energy to go back upstairs. The next morning, she still would not consider sleeping in a bed downstairs. I had to call my brother to try to convince her. He had a way of saying the same exact thing I said but got Mom to agree when he said it. Woody suggested we put a bed downstairs and she began to consider it. I suggested that she never had to use it if she didn't want to but it would be there in case she was too tired to climb the stairs like the night before. Mom finally consented to the idea and from that night on Mom never slept upstairs again.

The next major decline happened a few days later when Mom said one morning that she didn't feel like getting dressed. She asked me if I thought it was okay if she stayed in her nightgown and bathrobe during the day. Of course I said yes. I don't think any of us had ever seen a day that Mom didn't get dressed, so this was a huge change. At first Mom still spent the days in her chair in the living room, but now I was bringing food into the living room for her to eat. Suddenly she didn't feel like eating solid food, but was willing to drink an instant nutritional drink with milk.

After a few days of sitting in her chair during the day, Mom asked if it would be alright if she lay down on the bed because she was so tired. Again, a major decline. From that day on, Mom never left the bed except to use the bathroom. She was very weak at this point, so she needed some assistance getting to the bathroom, but only so she didn't lose her balance and fall. Within days, Mom needed assistance while in the bathroom.

In the meantime, we let family members know what a drastic decline Mom had taken. It all happened so fast that Mom was already at a point where she didn't have the energy for visitors. Many of our family members didn't get to talk to Mom again because of her swift decline. Her brother, Charlie, drove two and a half hours twice to come see her and her other brother, John, lived right up the hill from her. They were positive Mom was going to snap out of this, she was just tired. But we, her children, knew better.

April 25, 2013, was the last day Mom got out of bed. For the next nine days Mom barely had the energy to move or lift her body when needed, let alone sit up or get out of bed. Mom was such a proud, private woman that I was afraid she would be embarrassed when I had to change and bathe her, but she didn't seem to be. If she was, it was only the first time and then everything was fine. Mom was the most compliant "patient" ever.

Mom went into the same semi-comatose state that Jim had been in. She showed awareness off and on but slept most of the time. Mom seemed a bit restless, so her doctor prescribed a medicine to help her relax. The doctor warned us that in about one percent of elderly patients, the medicine could have the opposite effect and cause a perturbed, maniacal behavior. We only planned to give it to Mom if she became quite agitated. That did happen and I gave her the prescribed dosage one evening so she could rest. Mom was in that one percent. Suddenly she was wide awake talking about nonsensical things. After a time, I called Woody to come to the house because, quite honestly, I was scared. I was afraid I caused something horrible to happen to my mother because I gave her the pill. Woody stayed a few hours and we spent that time listening to Mom. What began as nonsense became disjointed conversation that had bits and pieces of what we knew were from her younger days. It turned out to be a very interesting night with the last laughter my mother would laugh.

An important fact to know is that my mother had decided about thirty years prior that she was going to donate her body to a local medical college for the use of scientific investigation. My mom wanted to be a doctor as a profession, but in those days it never worked out for her. To my mom, this was a way she could contribute to scientific medical knowledge. Her brothers were totally against this happening now that we knew Mom was not going to live, but we siblings stuck together and made sure Mom's wishes were carried out.

I had been in touch with the medical college to make sure all paperwork was up to date and in order, and we needed to know the exact procedure we were to follow. We learned a valuable lesson just in time. We knew we were to call a specific funeral director as soon as possible after my mother died. We assumed that person would be the one to pronounce her death. On Friday, May 3, I called the college to make sure that we were correct in our assumption and was told no, that if my mother was not in the hospital or under Hospice care, we would have to call 911 when my mother passed and they would pronounce her death. We had no idea. That would mean rescue trucks, ambulance and more; not a very peaceful way to transition.

I quickly realized that we needed to get Hospice involved. Up to that point we were managing well and we didn't think Mom would want Hospice involved. Also, a friend told me the same medicines Jim had taken just before he died could help my mother relax and feel peaceful. I called Hospice and they were kind enough to make an appointment to come to the house the very next morning, a Saturday, to have an intake meeting and get my mom started with Hospice. Also on May 3, I called Elizabeth to see if she would connect with the Angels to see what my mom wanted us to do for her. I told Elizabeth how agitated Mom was. Elizabeth helps many people transition peacefully to the next life by hearing their needs and letting the family know of them. She rarely tells of a date that a person will leave their physical body. I begged her to give me an idea and she said it would be Sunday.

Mom kept asking why she couldn't "go." Some days she woke up and would ask me the time. If I told her 8:00, she would say, "At night?" I would have to tell her it was the morning, to which she would reply, "Oh no, I have to go through another day." Mom was ready.

We had our meeting with Hospice, but they said they wouldn't be able to get us the medicine Mom needed as soon as we wanted. Woody offered to drive *anywhere* to get it if that would help my mom. That is what we did. Mom's doctor prescribed the medicine, Woody picked it up and we were able to give it to Mom so she could relax. Hospice's diagnosis of my mother's medical problem was "failure to thrive." I suppose that's the diagnosis used when there seems to be no other problem and age is involved.

My sister, Kathy, had been very sick for much of the time Mom had declined. We all knew it wasn't safe for her to be in the house for fear she was contagious and would give her illness to Mom. Finally she was better and was able to come to the house. Kathy came to spend the night at Mom's house with me on the night of May 4.

I had been sleeping in a recliner next to Mom's bed from the time she started sleeping downstairs. This was the first night she was able to have the medicine to help her sleep. I set my alarm to be sure I gave her medicine on time. I was to give Mom her medicine about 1:00 a.m. but when I checked on her, her breathing was extremely slow and labored and I could hear a gurgling sound as she breathed. I called Woody and Uncle John to come right away, called Kathy who was upstairs and then sat with Mom and held her hand. I prayed there would be time for everyone to see her before she passed but as I held her hand, she took her last breath.

What a strange feeling I had on that Sunday morning, May 5, 2013. It felt horrible to lose my mother but I was happy for her because she was so ready to go. She was done with this life. It seemed impossible to believe that just three weeks earlier I had come to visit my mother and planned to go home after the weekend. Even when I did decide to stay, it was primarily because of her poor vision. And now, three weeks later, my mother was gone. It was probably the most peaceful three-week transition I could imagine. And she did die on Sunday as Elizabeth reported she would from the Angels.

My prayers for my mother were answered. She lived a great life and was a great influence on so many.

After my father died of a massive heart attack in July 2000, I constantly prayed that Mom be able to leave this world like Dad did because I thought that must be the best way for the person dying. But Dad didn't get to say or hear any good-byes, I love you's or what was in all of our hearts: "Dad, you meant the world to us."

So during the last couple of years before Mom died, I spoke with God further about that. I asked Him to let her leave this Earth the way she wanted. I asked that she be able to know beyond a shadow of a doubt how very loved she was and what that love meant to everyone around her. She meant the world to us, too, just like Dad. I believe she would say God answered my prayers.

Reflection

It's easy to tell from what you have read that Jim's and my mother's transitions to the other side couldn't have been more different. Jim wasn't ready to leave this Earth. He may have prepared himself but he didn't want to go. As far as we were concerned, Jim still had half of his life to live here on Earth. My mother, Wanda, was more than ready to go. She had reached that milestone age of 90, her body wasn't working anymore and her work here was done. As much as she loved her life on Earth, she was ready for the next adventure.

As a caregiver, Jim's death was clearly more difficult for me, not just because he was my husband but because we had both lived through a horrendous nineteen months. Even more important, even though I knew Jim was ready to leave, spiritually, I also knew beyond a shadow of a doubt that he did not want to leave his earthly life. My mother, on the other hand, asked me, "Why can't I go?" She asked me questions about my readings with Jim because she knew there was more. She knew she was going somewhere else and she was ready to go. That makes it so much easier on the caregiver. I love and miss my mother something fierce, but I'm ecstatic that she was able to leave the way she did.

I hope this chapter has helped you in some way. If you have been a caregiver for a terminally ill person, I hope it validates feelings you have or had. If you are just beginning your path as a caregiver, I hope you find some help through my words. If you have never been and are not a caregiver for a terminally ill person, I hope it brings possibilities to your awareness and enables you to help others if the calling comes to you.

Wanda

My name was Wanda Frank in this lifetime. I died a year and a half after my son-in-law, James Petosa, at age 90. Jim had a great respect for women, especially those who were older than he. I admired this about him so much.

I had four pregnancies and three births. My oldest son was nicknamed Woody, as his father's name was William. It could have created confusion to have two "children" with the same name! I miscarried during my second pregnancy which I now know would have been another son. My oldest daughter's name was Kathleen, or Kasie as we referred to her in Polish, and my youngest daughter was Christine, fondly known as Kiki. They used to laugh about who was my favorite, but they were all my favorites.

I loved being a mother, a daughter and a sister to my brothers, Charlie and John. We were raised with a strong sense of family. My husband, Bill, and I were married for more than fifty years. I give you this background as Kiki's Earth mother to tell you of my experience of leaving my physical body and entering into the world of light.

I believed in a Great God, one who never judged or complained about our foibles in life, rather one who forgives. In the human world I believed in a God who never wavered and was quick to forgive. It is our human self that holds onto the "bad" things we do, not God. I wanted to be like my father, a doctor, one who would help others without judgement, but rather through knowledge that was a part of everyday life. I tried very hard to live my life this way. The facts and only the facts.

Somehow I innately knew that being human was a great gift. How a person felt about someone or something meant very little compared to how much they knew, especially how much they knew how to help another. I innately knew having children was a great contribution to the world if we were able, as parents, to teach them well.

My son-in-law, Jim, who this book is about and my daughter, Kiki, shared a very special love. Jim left his body a year and a half earlier than I. The one reason among many that I adored him was that our experiences, although similar, were also very different. When Kiki would tell me stories about her experiences with the afterlife and Heaven that she learned by talking to her father and her husband through Elizabeth, I was intrigued and cared so much that she was finding happiness through her communication. As I was preparing to leave and go to Heaven, my experiences were very different from Jim's. Yet hearing what she had to say meant so much; it was soothing, comforting and informative.

There are some who would say that communication with those who have departed is wrong, yet for me during my process watching Kiki made all the difference in the world. My husband, Bill, would speak through Elizabeth along with Jim and many others who found their way to God. Each person's process was different and yet all seemed to end with the same result.

Many would ask why I would choose to stay on the Earth with a body that was in such bad shape. I couldn't hear, smell, taste or see—nothing a good head transplant couldn't fix! I knew it was God's will that I stay on the Earth. To be worried about my children who would be left behind, each with their own beliefs, and my brothers with their own pain way down deep inside was unnecessary because I knew that God was still with me and them.

No religion would tell me—no priest, no friend, no one—I just knew that the longer I stayed on the Earth and stayed objective, the easier it would be to help detach once I left. I found that to be true once I left my body. Only the facts mattered, not the way we prayed but the "knowing." Prayers certainly help; they always do. The real fact is there is a loving God that wants only what is best for each one of us. That is a fact. Religion or communication through someone who brings you closer to the same loving God is accepted by God.

Elizabeth, thank you for helping Kiki through the tough times. She will do the same for you always. That's how she was raised and what she knows to do.

She takes care of everyone. Remind her to tell readers that just believing isn't enough. It's knowing to believe that is important.

There is a source that is light that calls to us all. It shines within us. That source of light *is the fact*. The light will subside as we lose our loved ones, yet our truth will help make us whole as we are never separated, we are never without love and we are never that far away.

The new books to come after the publishing of this one will tell you beyond a shadow of a doubt that we are all one from the Almighty One. You're darn right—there is only one God. Stay on the Earth as long as you can. Be healthy, happy, strong, proud and most of all loving. No matter your circumstances, what you do not finish in this lifetime you will finish in another lifetime. Save yourself the time and the trouble ... love now.

Just the facts.

Readings with Wanda

Following, you will read segments from two separate readings with my mother, Wanda, through Elizabeth, after her death on May 5, 2013. These segments pertain to Wanda leaving her physical body and entering into the world of light.

Elizabeth: On May 3, I received a call from Chris who was at her mother's house in Delanson, New York. Part of my role with clients is to help the caregiver with the peaceful passing of loved ones to the other side. Knowing her mother was close to passing, I asked Chris to call and touch base to see how she and her family were doing at that time. Obliging my request, she called and asked if I had any advice about how to help her mother transition peacefully. We spoke about what to expect and because this was so close to her husband's passing, I wanted reassurance that she had the support that she needed.

The Angels informed us her mother would pass on Sunday, something I would not normally tell a client. Chris called early Sunday to say that her mother had passed. What you're about to read are two private sessions after her passing.

May 17, 2013

(Elizabeth greeted me and went through the usual opening blessings and prayers.)

Chris: Mom, can you see again?

Wanda: Very well. Not only can I see, smell and taste, but I am able to experience all kinds of things. What I missed most was being able to smell the flowers and enjoy the natural scents in nature that I so dearly loved. When I was physical, I couldn't smell anything at all, which meant I couldn't taste anything. I couldn't hear anything either. I knew I left my body when I started to hear a sound of music. I knew then that I was on my way up and out. I heard the music and am grateful for that.

Chris: Mom, did you hear the music when you stopped breathing or before that while in transition?

Wanda: Before that.

Chris: So you were still with us when you could hear the sound of music?

Wanda: Yes. It sounded like you were all in a tunnel and I kept going further and further away from you and went into a tunnel of light. I heard a different kind of music and kept moving toward it. I felt free like I was floating there. I felt so free!

Chris: Mom, did you go through the tunnel that Jim went through where you know everyone and then there is a party for you at the end?

Wanda: I never left until the night that you came back home from Woody's, were playing with the dog and letting the dog out. When everyone was tucked in and safe and sound—that's when I really left. I was invited to go and I wanted to go, but that's when I really took a leap and went into the other world. It didn't take long at all.

Chris: Did you know that I was sitting next to you when you took your last breath?

Wanda: Yes, I did know. I can't thank you enough. It's funny. I was there when you took your first breath and you were there when I took my last. That blessing was so important.

Chris: Mom, I cherished every second of those weeks with you.

Wanda: I loved having you there.

Chris: I miss calling you every day with things to say, but I know now that I can tell you just by thinking because I know you can hear me.

Wanda: I hear everything. But you can't expect me to listen too much during the day because I will be busy at work studying to be a scientist. It takes time, effort and energy. I have things to do! I want you to know I was approved by the Council.

Chris: That was one of my questions for you, Mom—about being judged.

Wanda: You're never judged, just noted for what you've done, what you learned and how you did so in accordance with God's will. You also learn what is to come. I'm excited! I got the seal of approval. In fact, I did fine. I'm thrilled about my opportunities and what life is going to be like for me here—full of learning and growing. They don't study like on Earth—the knowledge is simply absorbed into the soul.
    The colors are more vivid, the sounds are crisper and clearer and the smell of sweet nectar is everywhere. Everything is better here because of the joy that we feel—everything. I know I had to live a long time—not to suffer—really, it's the other way around. It's simply because I wanted to be there. I loved it there.

October 11, 2013

Chris: Mom, was it the Lyme disease that actually took you?

Wanda: No. I was old and I was ready. My body was ready. There was not one moment that I was ungrateful to have lived the life that I lived and have the life that I had.

Chris: Mom, what was your death process like?

Wanda: The deterioration of my body started so long ago that when I stopped feeling, smelling, hearing and tasting, it was a death in and of itself. Dying was a deepening of that feeling. Those feelings that were happening to me got more intense. I was never afraid—it was just that those feelings increased. I was never afraid.

Chris: No, I didn't think you were.

Wanda: *The feelings increased so it was as if I couldn't feel my feet, then I couldn't feel my lower legs and then I couldn't feel to my knees. It was like my body was numb. It didn't hurt, nor did it feel good. There was no feeling at all.*

Chris: Was that what was happening when you needed our help more?

Wanda: *Absolutely. I needed your help because I couldn't feel what my body was doing enough to be able to help myself. That's when I knew it was time for me to go. I was already prepared emotionally and mentally. I was prepared in every way possible. I had my peace with God, myself, with your father and with my children. It wasn't a question of that. I truly had no sensation in my body to be able to function appropriately.*

Chris: What did it feel like to leave your body? I remember you saying you heard birds singing.

Wanda: *I couldn't feel my body as much as I could feel myself going upward. I couldn't feel my body at all at a certain point. When you were all there and you were holding my hand, wiping my mouth, offering things to me and trying to talk to me ... it was as if you were getting further and further away. When I could stop feeling how badly you felt it was easy for me to let go.*

Chris: You mentioned once that you wished we gave you the medicine two weeks earlier. Do you still feel that way?

Wanda: *Yes, because dying was inevitable and it allowed me to have some control. I did not feel undignified; that was not the issue. I just didn't want to feel pain, I didn't want to not have my senses and I didn't want to not feel love for you all. The drugs kept me from feeling anything at all, and that was a good thing.*

Chris: Were you in pain?

Wanda: *There was no pain when I left.*

Chris: How about before you left?

Wanda: *Slight pain. The only way I can describe it is that it felt like when your leg falls asleep and then starts to wake up. It hurts but it doesn't hurt. It's just a different sensation, but there was no pain. The medicine helped with that.*

Chris: You've said that you weren't fearful. At the time of leaving your body, at the time when you knew your soul was going and your physical body was going to die, did you have any type of fear or other feelings you can tell me about?

Wanda: *I was happy. I was ready.*

Chris: So it wasn't scary?

Wanda: *It was not a feeling of being afraid; it was all peaceful. It was like when I was out with the birds. It was like when I would hear the kids laughing and the grandchildren playing. It was laughter, but it was a laughter that you can't hear ... it's a laughter that you feel inside, a satisfaction, a joy, a simple joy that made things so wonderful. I believed I was going home and the Lord was with me. Always.*

Chris: When your soul left your physical body, were you looking down at us? Could you see yourself?

Wanda: *I could see you crying. I could see you call Woody and John. I could see you get Kasie from upstairs. I could see that everyone came. I could see that you waited a little while. I could see you all crying and happy at the same time.*

Chris: Yes, we were.

Wanda: *I could see that you were worried about the animals. You knew what to do. I was grateful that you knew what to do, that you knew what I wanted and you knew what I didn't want.*

Chris: When your soul left your body, did you stay with us for a while or did you leave right away?

Wanda: *Initially, there was a bright light. A long light, like when the sun shines through the light in the window in the morning and it shines on something. It* *was this intense, bright white light in a long tube and I was floating upward. I went higher and higher and higher and as I got higher, I couldn't hear you. I could only see what was happening. The feeling of love got stronger as I went higher. But I could hear them all calling to me, saying it was time to come home.*

Chris: Who came to get you, Mom?

Wanda: *Mary, Auntie Jo, my mother, my father and my brother.*

Chris: You have a brother on the other side? Did Podzi have a miscarriage?

Wanda: *Yes. Before she was pregnant with me. There were so many souls, so many people who were waiting—friends, people I knew and those I didn't know. There were many, many, many I didn't know, but they were there to comfort and welcome me.*

Chris: Through the tunnel or on the other side?

Wanda: *Through the tunnel. Jesus was to the right on one side and all of this pure, pure, pure love ... indescribable ... everywhere. There was something like a throne there. The light was beyond what I can describe. Angels were everywhere, all singing, like in exaltation of a holy being ... God. It was a presence ... hard to tell if it was male or female energy ... more of a combination. It was an energy that engulfed me and swirled around my soul. There was crystal energy ... a pink that was not of the Earth, gold and blue ... all surrounding the white light as if I was going to the center of the sun and there was a presence there.*

I felt like the closer I got I was going to lose "Wanda" and become part of this stream. I was getting direction of what would take place but through my being, not my mind. Information was given to me through my soul body of the choices I had if I wanted them.

It was the first time I ever felt like I was completely one with everything ... not separate from God at all. It doesn't happen this way for everybody—not that I am better or worse than another—it was just my experience. I was passing one after another, after another and sometimes groups. It was like a long road that took a very short time.

Chris: Was it comforting to go through the tunnel?

Wanda: *Like a breeze on a warm day. And you forget. You don't remember what you're leaving. You only look ahead at what you are going to.*

Chris: Did Dad come to get you, too?

Wanda: *He was waiting with his hand out to welcome me. He already had people there with him. His mother and father, all of the Franks were there. They all stood in the line like a long procession to welcome me, smiling and laughing. Jim was the last one with his hand out and I took his arm and we walked. He was so happy to see me. He was so happy. Kiki, he looked so good! So happy and smiling, so fresh and handsome. And he was glorious! It was so good to see him ... to see him. It had been so long since I'd seen things so clearly. The first place that he wanted to go was to take me to where I could see all of you. That was the first place he wanted to go.*

And we were much younger than when we each left Earth. We remembered everything about being young. And you see the light. I recognized all of them. Auntie Jo, she couldn't wait. They were yelling, applauding, laughing and so happy. It was all so sweet. And I could see them!

Chris: And hear them?

Wanda: *And the smell was like flowers that you smell when you open the door in the summertime and the breeze would blow.*

Chris: What happened when you got to the other side?

Wanda: *I entered this place of light where I stayed for a short time and waited. That was a waiting area.*

Chris: Were you with other souls?

Wanda: *I was—people I didn't know. They gave me instructions. I asked if I could watch what happened to my body. I asked if I could watch what happened with all of you. I came to the service. I came with your father, Mary, Auntie Jo and Martha's parents. And Jim was there.*

Chris: Did you see our animals and especially Blackie soon after you got there?

Wanda: Blackie and Blackie and Blackie. We had three different dogs named Blackie and I've seen all of them. I have seen all of our animals including Ike, your horse. They were the first things I saw as I started through the tunnel.

Chris: Dad has mentioned Ike. Have you seen Chief, Stormy and Baby Jane, too?

Wanda: All of them. And the chickens.

Chris: The chickens from Easter?

Wanda:All three of them.

Chris: So all the dogs you've had throughout your life—you saw all of them?

Wanda: All of them.
We went to a garden and in the garden we sat. All of us. And we prayed. We prayed for all of you. We prayed for all of you ... that your pain would stop. They allowed us to stay in the garden—a place where we could view everyone.
We got to celebrate; it was like a party. A welcoming party. And little things happened, little things that we could talk about. I only stayed there a short time, maybe three weeks in your time. When I left, I was ready to go. I met with your father and thanked him for the life that we lived and the children. We could all talk to one another without talking. It was different.

Chris: Was that hard to get used to?

Wanda:Not at all.

 Chris: Mom, did any of the Saints or the Blessed Mother come and get you or have you met them?

Wanda: The first part of the reunion was all family and friends and people we knew, people I had forgotten about that did not forget about me and people from town, including the post man. There were people who were so much a part of our lives in the early days. And the music! We danced and we laughed and we played and we joked. Martha's parents were there. I thanked them for letting Martha come to our family.

We celebrated. We went to see the animals. We laughed, we joked and we regained our senses. We saw the funeral and we saw the burial. We were there for the whole thing.

There's so much freedom, but not freedom to do what you want, entirely. When I went in front of the Council, I asked that I would be able to study, that I would be a part of the team for the research that would be of improvement to mankind and they acknowledged that. The first time I ever remember not asking, but acknowledgment of my request. It was such a joy. It was so magical and so inspiring because they don't judge you by gender or race or by anything the way the human world does, the way the human world works. They don't do any of that. It doesn't work that way here.

We saw the Christ. You go to the feet of the Christ. I saw the Christ and the Blessed Mother. They were there at the door when I first left.

Chris: Did they assist you?

Wanda: They did.

Chris: Do you mean they came to get you along with our relatives?

Wanda: They guided me there. It's not because I didn't feel connected to myself; they reconnected to me. There's so much love it's indescribable. Everyone loves everyone here.

Chris: Do you have a job? Are you studying in classes?

Wanda: I'm studying in classes. I look young.

Chris: About how young?

Wanda: Thirty. I feel ... we feel through our feelings. It's telepathy—we communicate in this way. I can come to the house. I can come to where we lived. I can see all of you. But I pay attention to my study. I don't miss you because I don't feel separate from you. I don't miss you in the same way that Jim did or other people might. I accept that we're never disconnected. So only tears of joy. I don't miss or long for Earth.

You have a lot to write. You have a lot to say. You have a lot to give to others. There are many things you must do. There are many more that need to know.

Love that exists in this world is increasing rapidly. More and more people are causing less and less harm.

Chris: And you see all of this? Does everyone see all of this? Jim talks like this, too.

Wanda: Not everyone. Everyone is in a different place, just like on Earth. I'm looking for ways to help your Lyme disease and Woody's. I have a longing to improve humanity and I can do it from here.

Chris: Thank you.

Wanda: I'm hoping to study with the doctors. I'm trying to learn. I was one of the fortunate ones because I healed before I came. Some people come before they heal, and they have to do that here.

Chris: Like Jim did? He was resting for about a month before he was able to visit with any of us.

Wanda: Jim's biggest problem was how much he missed you. And his greatest desire to heal was to return to you.

I have to go now. I'm going to be back so we can talk again soon. Watch for the birds.

Chris: Okay, I will.

Wanda: Be kind to Sunny.

Chris: I get a little angry at her sometimes. I know … I saw the mourning dove come down one day when I was yelling at her. You were reminding me to be nice to her, weren't you? I think my anger is partly due to the Lyme disease. I think it's what they call that "Lyme rage" because it doesn't feel like me.

Wanda: I think you're right.

Bring some flowers every day. Have fresh flowers in your house. Warm up your life. You have people who love you everywhere. But it is time for me to go.

Chris: Okay. Bye, Mom. It was so wonderful to talk to you.

Wanda: *I love you very dearly.*

Chris: I love you and miss you. I miss calling you.

Wanda: *Call me any time.*

Elizabeth: There is a place for everyone, each and every soul. There is timing, although we may not like it, for all things to live or die. I knew in my heart how strong Chris was and is. No matter the circumstances, children learn to adapt to their surroundings. It was apparent that Chris was very well equipped with whatever was needed to adjust to the world around her. She was aware of my contact information and able to contact me.

Wanda: *The next part of the Project talks about how involved a person's passing can be. Although you were there most of the time due to less responsibility at home, Kiki, everyone in the family did their fair share of helping me during my process. I passed peacefully on Sunday at 1:20 a.m.*

Prayer of Saint Francis of Assisi

Lord, make me an instrument of your peace.
Where there is hatred, let me sow love;
Where there is injury, pardon;
Where there is doubt, faith;
Where there is despair, hope;
Where there is darkness, light;
Where there is sadness, joy.

O Divine Master,
grant that I may not so much seek to be consoled
As to console;
To be understood as to understand;
To be loved as to love.
For it is in giving that we receive;
It is in pardoning that we are pardoned;
And it is in dying that we are born to eternal life.
Amen

Acknowledgements

Christine Frank Petosa

It has been quite a journey from the time my husband, Jim, was diagnosed with terminal cancer until now as this book is published. I have had tremendous support from so many people who helped me through the grief process. However, when I began to have readings with Jim through professional medium Elizabeth Williams, only a portion of those supporters believed in what I was doing. You know who you are, and there are many more than I list below. My heartfelt thanks goes out to all of you who had an effect on this book in one way or another. I must specifically thank a small few.

Thanks to our cats, Ms. Crump and Thelma Lou, for the unconditional love they gave which helped Jim and me get through Jim's ordeal with cancer. Thanks to our dog, Sunny, who has added to that love and enabled me to manage the grief process. Thanks, also, to Uncle John, Heidi, Sue and Julie for taking care of our animals during the times I worked on the book away from home.

Thanks to the healers: the medical team who treated Jim, the priest who performed the healing masses from which Jim received so much love, KC and Carrie, who organized throngs of friends to attend the healing masses, Maryann and Elizabeth—Jim's Reiki practitioners—and all the prayer warriors who hoped for and believed in a cure.

Thanks to Elizabeth's children for the time required for Elizabeth to be away from home for the writing of this book.

Thanks to Lisa and Joey for being like-minded believers and for our inspirational discussions at breakfast after church.

Thanks to Fran, Carol, Jill, Schoony, Val, Joe and Rick (Jim's breakfast provider), as well as the Monday night Modern Mystics Group, my Fikawi dinner group and the Cape Cod '60' Bonaventure group for listening, talking and supporting, even when they weren't sure what they believed.

Thanks to David Schweighofer, a former colleague of Jim's, for contributing the pictures of Jim in the Prologue and on the front and back cover of this book.

Thanks to Judy and Dan for generously inviting me to enjoy their camp for the purposes of healing from losing Jim and to receive inspiration while writing this book.

Thanks to Judy for always listening, always "doing for," always being honest, always being there and always loving everyone.

Thanks to Liz Barrett, who helped edit our book.

Thanks to Laura Ponticello, our marketing expert, consultant and overall guide in the process of writing a first book. We couldn't have done it without you!

Thanks to Elizabeth Williams, a tremendously spiritual woman and friend as well as an amazingly accurate medium. Clearly, this story could not have been told without the benefit of her skills. This journey started out on a professional basis, but has developed into a forever friendship.

Thanks to Jim's family for tremendous love and support during and after Jim's illness … fun, laughter, great food, listening, talking, health and medical support of all kinds … the list goes on and on. I can't thank them enough.

Thanks to my family for more support than I could have imagined, especially since Jim's passing. Thank you for supporting my efforts in writing this book and for believing. It means more than you'll ever know.

Thanks to the Angels and all who guide me from beyond: family and friends who have left this physical world and entered the spirit world, especially my mom, dad and, mostly, Jim. Thank you, Jim, for continuing to love, guide and watch over me from the Heaven realms. The most beautiful part is that I know I'll be with you again.

Thanks to God for everything around me … our families, our friends, animals, all of nature … the list is endless. Thank you for teaching me unconditional love, kindness and respect for everything in this world. I am a work in progress.

Elizabeth Williams

First and foremost, I would like to give thanks to God for giving me this special gift in order to help guide and lead others. I would like to especially thank God for the gift of mediumship to help others heal grief in a special way.

I would like to thank the Angels and Saints for surrounding and loving me and for helping us find the words to put in this book.

I would like to thank my dear and very special friend, Christine Petosa, for her diligence, encouragement and persistence in helping humanity and sharing so graciously her story of Jim and their trials and tribulations. We are forever joined at the hip.

I would like to thank James Petosa, who I never had the opportunity to spend time with when he was physical, healthy and strong, but was given the privilege of helping with his illness and communicating with him from the light.

I would like to thank my parents for having me and handing down this gift.

I give special thanks to Lisa and Joey. Thanks to Lisa for her patience and kindness with my clients. Thanks to Joey for helping my son and for believing when he did not understand.

I give thanks to Betty and Kathy for making appointments and telling people to be patient because I was hard at work.

I thank Val for her gracious kindness and her husband for understanding how important the little things were that made the big things in life so much easier.

I would like to thank the Monday night Modern Mystics group for their willingness to heal and their interest in our project as well as their constant support and love.

I would like to thank those who stood in our way, the non-believers, the ones who laughed and joked behind our backs. They simply made us want to try harder to do what's best for humanity and be obedient to God.

I would like to thank my friends who I didn't name, too numerous to mention, who took an interest and supported the project in any way they could. There aren't enough words to express how gracious you all have been with your time, your love, your disappointment with wanting more time and your willingness to stay friends without the time that you wanted.

Most of all I would like to thank my children, my four favorite people in the world, for all their nights of eating macaroni and cheese and sitting home without a mom because I was so busy working. I will never forget what you did and what you gave up because I was your mother.

Chris and Elizabeth

We would like to express our gratitude and appreciation to those who were willing to take the time to read our public relations packet and/or our manuscript, provide commentary and give praise for *Jim's Flight: One Soul's Perspective from Heaven*:

Susan Hynds, Rick DePalma, Maria DiTullio, Julianne Cousineau, Doreen Miori-Merola, Laura Ponticello, Martha Frank, Fran Hudson, Grace Smith, Mark Brenneman, Kim Pontello, Susan Scharoun, Gloria Gold, Melina Carnicelli, Christina Michaelson, Beverly Ponticello, Mary Lia, Margaret Chao, Jessica Mazurowski, Jill Weston and Joan Cerio.

We have great gratitude and appreciation for you, Sabine Weeke, and the entire team at Findhorn Press for believing in our story.

About the Authors

CHRISTINE FRANK PETOSA (left) is an author and retired teacher of 33 years, familiar with all different walks of life. Christine received her B.S. in Elementary Education from St. Bonaventure University and her M.S. in Special Education from The College of St. Rose. She is an active member of New York State retiree teachers groups, and is involved with various alumni activities at St. Bonaventure University.

Christine was divinely inspired to pen this book with an inner knowing that this story may help another. As a caregiver, healer and educator she brings her very personal first-hand experience and perspective to her writing. Christine lives in Syracuse, NY.

For more information visit her website *chrisfrankpetosa.com* or connect through *facebook.com/christinefrankpetosaauthor*.

You can contact Christine at *cpetosa903@gmail.com*

ELIZABETH WILLIAMS (right) is a light worker and third generation Catholic Mystic, known in modern terms as a Modern Day Mystic. An ordained spiritualist minister, Reiki Master Teacher, certified hypnotherapist and licensed nurse, Elizabeth comes with an extensive background in mystical teachings, as well as psychology.

She is the founder of The Center of Truth and Light in Syracuse, New York. Her client base ranges globally across presidents of universities, celebrities, leadership authors and speakers, bestselling authors, CEOs, housewives, nurses, teachers, those in transition to the next dimension and caregivers. Elisabeth lives in Syracuse, NY.

For more information visit her website *elizabethwilliamsonline.com* or connect through *www.facebook.com/Elizabeth-Williams-The-Center-of-Truth-Light-647984221889508.*

You can contact Elizabeth at *elizabeth@elizabethwilliamsonline.com*

Reader Reflections

During our journey of writing Jim's Flight: One Soul's Perspective from Heaven, we kept notebooks with all readings and messages from Jim. Chris also kept a journal of all her experiences as a caregiver. Journaling is one way of allowing your feelings to be expressed without having to actually talk about them. If you are a caregiver it is also a way to document the path you are on. Plus, journaling can be extremely healing if you are assisting someone who is ill.

The following pages are purposely left blank. They are meant to serve as a space for you to write any thoughts or reflections that come to you as a result of reading this book; in essence, space for you to journal.

Also of interest from Findhorn Press

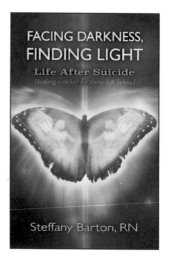

FACING DARKNESS, FINDING LIGHT
STEFFANY BARTON

IN THIS POWERFUL BOOK, Steffany Barton, RN, documents her decades long journey to understanding and embracing the valuable lessons offered in life after suicide. With personal passion and professional integrity, Steffany carefully listens to the voices of departed souls and compassionately speaks to those left behind, building a bridge of timeless love between heaven and earth. Those who commit suicide communicate clearly and lovingly from a place of unconditional Love where their souls dwell on the Other Side.

Facing Darkness, Finding Light provides insight into the afterlife of those who commit suicide, sheds the light on healing in life after suicide, and shares meaningful techniques for forging new bonds between the departed and those left behind. Though the journey begins in the darkness of death, there is hope, there is light. Find it in this truly exceptional book.

978-1-84409-688-6

Also of interest from Findhorn Press

HEAVEN THERAPY

ROSS BARTLETT

FOR ANYONE WHO HAS EVER WONDERED if there is something beyond our everyday existence, for every person who has felt the pain of someone close to them passing over, for any person who still grieves for that someone, this is likely to be the most emotionally raw, heart-felt, soothing, healing and ultimately uplifting book you will ever read.

Within these pages, Ross shares the intimate and extremely evidential messages that some of his most bereaved clients received from their loved ones who have passed over. Ross also offers his own reflections on the afterlife, mediumship and his research from his master studies into the efficacy of 'heaven therapy' for counselling the bereaved. His stories connect together and along the way demonstrate not just that our essence, our spirit and soul survive physical death, but that after we pass over we continue to be able to watch over, and visit with those we love and left behind here on Earth. These stories will show that yes, we all have eternal life and in fact, we cannot die for the life of us.

978-1-84409-697-8

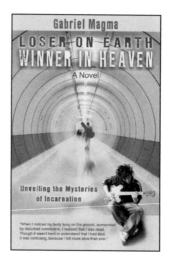

LOSER ON EARTH, WINNER IN HEAVEN

GABRIEL MAGMA

FAILED STREET MUSICIAN MATT sees himself as a complete loser until the day he is murdered in a Liverpool metro station. Then he meets his guardian angel and his soul who make him see that in fact he impacted many, many people extremely positively during his short time on Earth.

Loser on Earth, Winner in Heaven helps us to see our lives through the point of view of our soul and our guardian angel. The book reveals the hidden purpose of many of our thoughts and deeds. As a result, our interpretation of our lives changes drastically when we include elements such as pre-birth agreements, the perspective of our souls on matter, conscience and evolution and the subtle energies of orbs and egregores. Magma makes the abstract and difficult spiritual ideas accessible through a mysterious, captivating and suspenseful plot with surprises at every turn.

978-1-84409-695-4

FINDHORN PRESS

Life-Changing Books

Consult our catalogue online
(with secure order facility) on
www.findhornpress.com

For information on the Findhorn Foundation:
www.findhorn.org